THE ART OF
RECEIVING AND GIVING

The Art of
RECEIVING
and
GIVING

THE WHEEL OF CONSENT

Betty Martin, D.C.
with Robyn Dalzen

LUMINARE PRESS
WWW.LUMINAREPRESS.COM

Printed in the United States of America
Cover Design by Claire Flint Last

Luminare Press
442 Charnelton St.
Eugene, OR 97401
www.luminarepress.com

LCCN: 2020916914
ISBN: 978-1-64388-308-3

This book is dedicated to my students.

TABLE OF CONTENTS

PART 3: THE WHEEL OF CONSENT

PART 4: SOCIAL AND SPIRITUAL IMPLICATIONS

ACKNOWLEDGMENTS

Thank you to Robby Pellett for paying the rent for those first couple of years so I could write, for teaching me more of this than I was comfortable learning, and for loving me in spite of it. Rest in peace.

Thank you to Robyn Dalzen for many hours of reviewing, suggesting, and collaborating, for helping me put it all into an order that made sense and carrying me over the finish line. Thank you to Lola Houston for saving my you-know-what when I couldn't go on. This book would have taken a few more years without you. And for countless hours of listening, Mallory Austin, Lola Houston, Charla Hathaway, Avi Klepper, and Teri Ciacchi. And to my editors through various stages, Lola Houston, Robyn Dalzen, and Lori Stephens.

Thank you to my predecessors and colleagues in eros and sex, for teaching, guidance, inspiration, and healing. I stand on the shoulders of giants. Isa Magdalena, Joseph Kramer, Collin Brown, Carol Queen, Annie Sprinkle, Carol Leigh, Barbara Carrellas, Chester Mainerd, Alex Jade, Selah Martha, and Sequoia Lundy, and I'm sure there's more. And Alex, Selah, Sue and Carla. Thank you to Harry Faddis, for inventing the Three Minute Game and welcoming me into your circle just a few years ago.

Thank you to my teachers in the healing arts, notably Donald Epstein. Thank you to my predecessors in Cuddle Party, Marcia Baczynski, Reid Mihalko, and Len Daley. Thank you to my teachers of Co-counseling, notably Diane Balser and Charlie Kreiner.

Thank you to my students and clients, with whom I learned to clarify and hone the principles and practices, and who inspired me to no end. Thank you to my colleagues and partners in crime at the School of Consent, Robyn Dalzen, Carmen Leilani De Jesus, and Michael Dresser.

Finally, thank you to my kids, who also taught me more of this than I was comfortable learning and patiently kept asking me, "How's your book coming, Mom?" And to my grandkids, who bring me such joy. I hope this is helpful to your generation.

FOREWORD

I am deeply excited by the appearance of this long-awaited book. When I studied the Wheel of Consent with Betty Martin ten years ago, I immediately knew that the practices she taught, and the understandings she offered, were the key to unwinding the confusion that made my work as an intimacy educator—and my intimate world—so perilous. Wheel of Consent practices heal trauma by empowering choice and voice. They connect couples by offering a path of respectful relationship. They transform communities. They foster interactions based on generosity, integrity, gratitude, and willing sacrifice instead of survival and threat management.

Using these practices and understandings on a daily basis for a decade has only deepened my respect. They are transformative at every level. They have brought resourced, empowered, and enduring love into my work as a sacred intimate and educator as well as to my close relationships and community life. Betty's generous teaching, through her in-person workshops and online resources, has brought this deep level of healing and wellness to thousands of people around the world. With her focus on teaching teachers, she has brought the possibility of safe and wanted touch into the lives of all our students and their students. With her book, I imagine many more people and communities holding in their hands this key to a life of joy.

The practices in this book will guide you in understanding in an embodied way how we do not have choice—not without taking time to uncouple giving and receiving, doing and being done-to. We are trained in enduring unwanted touch. We live in intimacies, societies, and economies based on nonconsensual taking and overgiving. If we want to create safe-enough space to be brave and truly consensual in our relationships, we need to slow down and ask, "How do you want to be touched?" We need to take a sacred pause to inquire of ourselves and each other, "What can you give with a full heart?" We need to know, "Who is this for?" Having choice is a neurological and relational capacity that can only be built with practice. With all our deeply wired neural grooves, we will keep on going into habits of enduring. We won't know what we authentically want. We will be afraid to change our minds. We will act out cultural scripts and unconscious entitlements. A trustworthy guidance system within and between us needs to be cultivated with patient repetition, guided by the resourced understanding you will glean from this book.

Betty writes, "As we learn to notice what we want, to trust it, value it, and communicate it, the experience of receiving opens up into a rich, deep, gorgeous landscape." In this landscape, we will also enjoy the experience of giving fully and freely—no longer coerced by expectations and prerogatives but instead by knowing, communicating, and experiencing the pleasure of giving what we can authentically give with a full heart. This is a landscape of deepening self-trust, trust in trustworthy relationships, and trust in the web of life and death. Thanks to Betty's work, we are empowered to challenge "thousands of years of conditioning about how the world works" and create relationships and communities that are truly consensual. This is a gorgeous landscape of pleasure where we can feel and follow our inner "Hell, yes!" and have that wanted and welcomed. It is a sustainable landscape where vulnerabilities and limits are honored and courage and freedom can flourish.

In a mentor supervision session, Betty once guided me, "It is so easy to think we are being victimized when we are not. It is also so easy not to recognize that we are being victimized when we are." Lack of awareness and precision about consent, obfuscation of vectors of privilege and oppression, and a dearth of embodied experiences of respectful relationship all combine to create confusion. Blame, shame, dissociative compliance, ineffective complaints, and misplaced resentments all are signals of unsafety. But without methods to practice discernment, and choose effective actions for real change, we stay trapped in a fear-based world, hurting ourselves and each other. Wheel of Consent practices empower us to notice the difference between real dangers we must courageously face and potentially loving relationships we can carefully cultivate. This is an instruction manual for enduring love.

—Caffyn Jesse
Author of *Science for Sexual Happiness,*
Healers on the Edge, and *Elements of Intimacy*

INTRODUCTION

An Inquiry

Instructions for living a life:
Pay attention.
Be amazed.
Tell about it.
—Mary Oliver

This book is an inquiry into receiving and giving—what they are and what they are not, how they work, and how to fall in love with both of them, equally and completely. It teaches you a practice of taking turns with a partner or practice buddy based on using touch, but also possible without touch. In the end, it is not the ideas here that will change you. It's the practice. What many of us have learned from this practice has made receiving and giving clear, real, and liberating, and developed generosity and integrity. Further, it sheds light on the dynamics that underlie all relationships, whether sexual, social, business, or political, and that is what most inspires me about it. Welcome to the journey.

There is always a risk in increasing your awareness. You risk seeing things you might rather not notice. You risk feelings you might rather avoid. You risk having to change what you think and worse—having to change what you do. There are those of us who are willing to take that risk, who want to take that risk, because the freedom behind it calls to us. So it is with this practice. There will be moments of discomfort, and there will be "aha" moments, insights, and liberation. And fun. There will be things you learn here that are a big relief.

This book is for you who are willing to question what you know, in the service of uncovering the dynamics you create with others—the dynamics that don't serve you well and satisfy you even less, and those other dynamics that free you up, delight, and satisfy you because they are true and clear.

If you do the experiments in this book, some things are going to look different.

I have the best job in the world. It has been my joy and honor over the past number of years to coach people around sexuality and intimacy. People have come to me because they were losing the spark in their relationship, or they lacked confidence, or didn't know what they wanted, or felt stuck or lost, or confused, inadequate, or lonely. My work with them is experiential; that is, I guide them through experiences that help them learn. I teach them how to slow down to notice what they want or don't want, how to touch, how to communicate, and how to set things up so they feel safe enough to relax and enjoy themselves.

Along the way, I learned some things. One thing I learned was that even though most people thought their problem was about sex, it rarely was. More often it was a problem with knowing how to relax, how to attend to their sensation, or how to respect and accept their desires. They had trouble knowing how to be vulnerable, playful, or generous, or how to set limits. They had trouble receiving, or even knowing what it meant, and trouble giving and knowing what that meant. These things are much more fundamental, but because difficulty with them feels so normal, people often didn't notice them until sex was involved, so they thought it was about the sex. Far more often it was a challenge with these more basic skills.

This book is about what I learned about those basic skills through the lens of receiving and giving. The practice of taking turns gave rise to a model of receiving, giving, doing and being done-to, showing how they fit together and what that creates. The model is called the Wheel of Consent, and it is complete with quadrants, a circle, and even some arrows. The model grew out of experiences of touch, but the same dynamics play out in the world. For some, the sexual or touch aspects are of most interest, and for others, the social and political implications will take center stage.

This book is also about consent. The traditional meaning of consent means agreeing to something someone else wants: "I consent to X." In this meaning, you "give consent" or "get consent". I'd like to expand the definition and think of consent as being an agreement that two or more people come up with together. You don't give consent, you arrive at consent—together. That's how I use it in this book.

In this practice, you learn to tell the difference between receiving and giving. You learn why we need them and find how each of them feeds you in a different way. You learn about desire, consent, selfishness, generosity, boundaries, respect, and pleasure. The quality of your touch will vastly improve. Your receiving will become easy and nourishing, and your giving will become effective and satisfying. The skills you learn will help you access a full range of feelings, desires, and expressions and let you play with others in ways that are real, rich, and joyful.

The practice itself is simple, but the implications are broad. Touch turns out to be a window into our relationships. Learning to receive the gifts of others cracks our hearts open, and as we do that, we learn to be clear about what we actually want. This has implications far beyond touch. When we forget how to notice what we want, we lose our inner compass. This has a profound effect on society. We allow all manner of injustice, theft of our natural resources and our planet's future health—because it feels normal.

In an interview with Amy Goodman on Democracy Now!, environmental activist Derrick Jensen had this to say about the importance of knowing what we want: "So, I don't think that a lot of us think very clearly about what it is exactly we want. And, I mean, I do know what I want, which is I want to live in a world that has more wild salmon every year than the year before, and I want to live in a world that has less dioxin in every mother's breast milk every year than the year before, and a world that has more migratory songbirds every year than the year before...I'm not sure that a lot of us know what we want."

On the other hand, it is possible to know exactly what we want and reach for it with no regard for how it affects others. We live in a world in which many of us act as if some other person's body or labor belong to us, or as if some other nation's oil belongs to us, and we inflict pain on the people getting in our way. We act as if the future itself belongs to us, as we use up the slack in our planetary climate-generating systems, ocean fisheries, and the soil itself, upon which depend the food supply for our grandchildren.

When we learn to receive a gift in the most tangible way, through touch, something unexpected happens. We get very good at respecting other people's boundaries, and exploiting them becomes unthinkable. The world needs people who take responsibility for what they want and who respect the rights of other people so that we stop stealing land, labor, and resources and stop bombing villages on the other side of the world.

The world also needs connection. We are hungry to connect with others in ways that are real and satisfying, that feed our hearts and inspire us. We need to be with others in ways that help us to be who we really are, complex beings who need each other and bring joy to each other. We need to be able to receive and to give—and to tell the difference.

My friend tells me she's taking this to the nonprofit leadership development world. I'm not sure what that means, but it's why I wrote this book. The Wheel of Consent affects your touch and affection, your sex and your relationships, and that's wonderful. But what I care most about is how profoundly it shows up in every aspect of our lives. The way it changes how we see the world, how we take responsibility for our choices and what kind of freedom, compassion, and integrity then become possible.

WHAT THE PRACTICE LOOKS LIKE

The goal of the practice is to find out whatever you find out. The practice is simple but not always easy. In this practice, we take receiving and giving apart, that is, doing them only one at a time. This will challenge you. Long-held assumptions will crack open, and there will be insights that shake you up. There will be moments when it's awkward, vulnerable, or confusing. There will also be moments when it's pleasurable, funny, enlightening, or blissful. When the inner experience shifts, it teaches us something new is possible. When the body has a new experience, it allows the heart to have a new experience.

The thing people feel most here is relief: "Oh finally! I knew something was off, but I couldn't figure out what it was," or "Oh, I had forgotten that part of myself!" Relief and a certain kind of accountability: "What am I hungry for that I don't admit to, and what would happen if I asked for that?" and "Where else in my life have I been unclear?"

Exploring the quadrants of the Wheel of Consent is a lifelong journey. There will be some pauses, some ups and downs, and some favorites you come back to. You'll feel it in your skin, then you'll see the implications in your life. You will think you have it, and then the next week you'll find something deeper. Then the next year, deeper yet. Then five years down the road, you'll have an epiphany, and so it will go for the next few decades.

As a practice, it is something you return to again and again, each time with curiosity and something to notice. Over time, you develop new skills and new awareness, but it is not for some future reward. The reward of a practice is in the experience itself, and what makes any practice engaging is not the thing you do but the quality of attention you bring to it. With this practice, everything is an experiment. It helps to have some compassion for yourself. *I wonder what I will learn about myself here. I wonder what happens if...*

You could see this practice as a fun new way to play with each other. You could see it as a path of self-discovery, awareness, and healing. You could see it as a way to recover your ability to notice what you want and need and to set limits and respect yourself. You could see it as a study in power dynamics or a path to erotic maturity. You could see it as a spiritual journey toward clarity and integrity. You could see it as a way to find what makes your heart sing. It is all of those. Even with all that, no matter your inspiration, even if it's to save the world, what actually works is setting all that aside and bringing your attention to the microcosm of skin and sensation. In plainer words, do it because it feels good; the rest will follow naturally.

ABOUT THIS BOOK

Part 1 lays the groundwork. I'll tell the story of how I learned it, define receiving and giving, and introduce the quadrants. Part 2 shows you how to experience the quadrants. It includes three lessons and three labs. The first lesson, "Waking Up the Hands," changes the way you experience your hands. Everything else is built on this change. Then in the next two lessons, you find the quadrants; there is a moment when they "click." Then in the labs you get to dive as deeply as you like into them. I give you notes on each quadrant, where it takes you, how to find the ease and joy of it, and how to develop the art of it. Then Part 3 describes the model of the Wheel of Consent. That's where you get to see the lines, the circle, and the arrows. In Part 4, we take a look at the spiritual and social implications of the Wheel of Consent.

You may read the book in any order you like. Some people will want the theory first; others will start with the experiences. But each experience builds on the one before, so do the lessons and labs in order. If you skip the lessons and jump ahead, you are likely to wonder what I'm talking about. That's fine. Just go back to the first lesson, then the next two, give them time to click, and the rest of it will open up for you. Or if you start with the lessons, which take a few weeks, you may want to read ahead to understand more about what you're doing. That's great. Then when you come back to the experiences you'll go even deeper.

So read the book in any order you like, but do the experiences themselves *in order*.

Pronouns. In some places I use "he" and "she," because that is the way it happened, and in other places I use "they" in the singular. If you are not yet accustomed to "they" in the singular, know that it's proper grammar, and it will soon enough feel natural to you. (You already use "they" in the singular when you don't know someone's gender, as in when you say to your housemate, "Someone is calling you, and they didn't say their name.")

Examples. Some of the examples I use are actual people and happened that way; of course, I have changed the names and other details. Some of the examples are composites of several people.

My bias. I am a White, cisgender woman, elder, educated, nondisabled, middle-class, and mostly straight American. This predisposes me to think in certain ways and to assume that my way of seeing the world is both (because I am White) the normal way and applicable to everyone and (because I am a woman) automatically discounted. This book and the model it describes are based on my experiences and those of my students and clients, who have also been mostly White and cisgender though certainly not always. Some blind spots are going to show up. I want to acknowledge that.

Resources and extras. Footnotes and resources are on the book website: www.wheelofconsentbook.com/notes. Also on that webpage are nine extra chapters that did not fit into the book. The chapters include three more labs, a discussion of sexual touch and eros, and some Bonus Tracks!

PART 1

Two Offers

CHAPTER 1

Two Offers

What do you want to do to me?
What do you want me to do to you?
—Harry Faddis

I have the good fortune to have misspent my youth. Growing up in the hippie years offered some splendid adventures and burst any illusions I might have had about what was normal. I questioned everything, explored, and sat in many hot springs with other adventurers. For this, I am thankful.

Some years later, I learned chiropractic, which naturally got my hands on many, many people (even more people than my hippie years). My hands learned to take in a tremendous amount of information: which joints were moving, where they were stuck, muscle tone. Scientists and healers were starting to talk about the mind-body connection—that we could understand ourselves by becoming aware of our bodies, how we move and breathe, or as the case may be, how we don't move or breathe. I remember one time in a workshop being invited to lie backwards over a cushion so that my rib cage opened up in front. When I did so, I became aware of my heartache, both physical and emotional, and burst into tears. No narrative of what or why; just moving my body into a new position brought it up.

During those years, I learned co-counseling, which is pairing up with someone and taking turns listening to each other. I learned how to receive helpful attention from others and how to give it. For this I am thankful too. I learned that when it was my turn, it really was my turn, and when it was their turn, it really was their turn. I learned some fundamentals about human nature and where we so often get stuck, and I learned how to make good use of my turn.

In my midforties, I attended a women's workshop on sexuality. I remember this feeling at the end of the workshop: as if I had started out with a number of ideas, like sex, love, attraction, and arousal, all in some kind of relation to each other. During the workshop, all those words had been thrown into the air to resettle into some new configuration, and I had no idea what that would be. All I knew was that it would be different. And it was.

One thing that became clear was that my sexuality belonged to me. The realization was so sharp that it made me wonder what I had been thinking all those years before. As a woman of my generation, I had learned that my sexuality was always in response to someone else's—someone else's desire, someone else's idea of what was sexy. But now it belonged to me. I learned that we are each the source of our own eroticism, and we can bring it out to play if, when, how, and with whom we choose.

I got together with a few others who had attended, and we met regularly for some years. Eros became something of a spiritual path for me. *What is the nature of this force within me? What does it mean to have a body capable of this much pleasure?* And perhaps ironically, *Why is it that the more I attend to my body experience, the more spiritual it feels?* For that matter, what is "spiritual" anyway? Heck, what is "sex" anyway? We experimented with movement, play, touch, and massage, and we had much laughter and many tears. For this journey I am also thankful.

After some years of exploring, I became interested in offering some of this new insight to others. I left my chiropractic practice in a small town, moved to the city, and opened up a new practice. My brochure said something like "I guide you in experiences that help you learn about who you are sexually and heal the confusions and struggles you have with it. I keep you safe, support your exploring, and open new doors of possibility for you."

A little vague, yes, because essentially I didn't know what I was doing. I was good at listening, I was good at boundaries, I was good at supporting people in emotional states, and I was good with bodies in various states of undress and arousal. What I didn't know yet was what it would look like. What would we actually do in a session? And how would I have known? Nobody else I knew, other than a couple of those friends from my exploring days, had ever heard of such a thing. There were a few pioneers, and I am thankful for them, but mostly we were making it up as we went along. Eventually we did figure out what to do in our sessions, which I now frame as coaching, broadly defined. I began offering workshops too and these days train other practitioners in the Wheel of Consent.

At one of many workshops I attended during my exploring years, we learned the Three Minute Game, which was developed by Harry Faddis. It was a game of interaction based on two questions. We took turns asking those questions and then did whatever they led to that we had agreed on. I came to see each question as a kind of offer. A couple years later as I was starting to see clients, I dusted the game off and put it to work. I figured it would give me a sense of the client's level of comfort and skill with touch. It did show me that—and much more. The Three Minute Game became the foundation of my practice and led to the model of the Wheel of Consent and this book.

THE FIRST OFFER

The first offer of the Three Minute Game is this: "How do you want me to touch you?"

(The original game included "…for three minutes," and that's useful for a number of reasons, but for now, to simplify, I'm going to leave it off. We'll come back to it.)

HEARING THE OFFER

Ask a hundred people that question, which I have done, and here is what you will find: very few will know right away. Many will have no idea. Most will fidget a bit and get awkward. Some will say, "I don't know. No one has ever asked me that!" or "I don't know, I'm usually the giver," or "Wow, am I supposed to know that? Does anyone know that?" Some of them will have an extremely hard time, feeling ashamed, confused, or lost. A great many people, instead of telling you what they want, will tell you what they wouldn't mind terribly much: "Well, you could rub my shoulders, I guess." Some will ask what you would like: "Hmm, would you like to stroke my arm?"

I learned a lot by simply asking, including how tender and vulnerable it is to ask for what we want, how much fear and doubt we have about receiving it, and mainly how out of practice we are. The thing about working with clients is that whatever you see in your clients, you'll eventually (if you are honest) see in yourself. Once I saw this dynamic, I began to see where I was doing the same thing—where in my life I wasn't asking for what I wanted, where I was afraid or embarrassed or tenderhearted or didn't know.

Eventually, sometimes with much coaching, most clients were able to make a request. "Will you scratch my back?" or "Will you stroke my arms?" Then once the touch was happening, there was more to notice. Many people didn't know if it was okay to change their minds or make a refinement and ended up going along with something they didn't really want. This one turned out to be nearly universal.

At a workshop I was leading, Amy asked for her shoulders to be rubbed. Brent stood behind her and did so, both apparently comfortable and happy. After the three minutes were up, we talked. Amy said, "The first minute was wonderful. Then I spent the next two minutes wondering if it was okay to ask him to go lighter."

Not only do we go along with something, we often try to make ourselves like it more. Some years back, a colleague asked me, "I have a new girlfriend, and she likes to go down on me. It's okay but just doesn't do it for me. How can I become a better receiver?" Now, "a better receiver" can mean a lot of things, which is part of the problem, but he was thinking that because he was being done-to, his job was to like it. Essentially he was asking, *How do I get better at liking something I don't actually like?*

As I kept asking people this question, "How do you want me to touch you?" I was struck again and again by how strong our tendency is to go along with what we think we are supposed to want or like. Why on earth would we do that when it's our turn to have what we want?

One reason is that asking for what we want and receiving it are inherently vulnerable. It's just not that easy. Another reason is that we are confused about who it's really for. We act as if it's really for the benefit of the other person, the one who is "giving." They ask what we want, and we answer by saying what we don't mind too much. Then we go along with what we don't want and try to change ourselves. I have some ideas about why that is the case, which we'll explore in this book.

Another reason is that sometimes we don't know what it feels like to have something really be for us. It turned out that the key was finding exactly what we want.

In one session in my studio, as per his request, I was stroking Ken's hand.

Ken: Well, I know you said it's for me, but I'm not sure what that means. I guess I'm just used to whatever happens.
Me: Hmmm…yeah, so for right now, we're going to stop this, and you get to notice what it is that actually sounds good to you.
Ken: I have no idea. Would you do some different things and let me say if I like them?
Me: Sure! (pressing into his palms) How's this?
Ken: It's okay.
Me: Would you like more of it or something else?
Ken: Something else, please.
Me: (squeezing his fingers) How about this?
Ken: It's okay.
Me: I'm curious here, Ken. If I just kept going, what would you do?
Ken: Nothing. It's all okay with me.
Me: So let's find something that is not okay but is fabulous.
(We try a few more things.)
Me: And this?
Ken: Oohhh, yeah! That is really good.
(We do that a while, and he visibly sinks into it.)
Me: Okay, now, is this for me, or is this for you?
Ken: Oohhhh. I get it. This is for me, isn't it?
Me: Yes, it is.
He looked like he was holding back tears, and we sat quietly.

Yes, it can be hard to notice what we want and to ask for it. If these are not bad enough, there is what happens when we do finally, miraculously, receive the touch we want. We feel comfort and pleasure, and then that brings up more feelings of guilt, shame, and doubt. Sometimes the feelings are a little tug at our heart, and sometimes they are powerful. One person said, "There's something deep and primitive going on inside me, enjoying his touch, maybe needing—fear of needing? It's like an old warrior not wanting to admit they have needs, even deep needs like touch."

As I kept on making the offer and hearing these kinds of responses, I came to see that the crux of this kind of receiving was to distinguish between what we want and what we don't mind. In order to do that, we have to learn that there is in fact something we want and that it matters. As we learn to notice what we want, to trust it, value it and communicate it, the experience of receiving opens up into a rich, deep, gorgeous landscape. Not because we get better at going along but because we get better at requesting exactly what we want. This taught me that receiving is inherently wonderful. If it's not wonderful, it's not because you're not a "good receiver." It's because it's not the thing you want.

As we learn to make that distinction, receiving the touch we want brings us joy, pleasure, and gratitude. We come back to this theme throughout the practice and the book.

MAKING THE OFFER

What about the other side, the person who is making the offer: "How do you want me to touch you?"

The most common thing that happened when people made this offer was that they forgot they could set limits or say no. They sometimes assumed that they had to do whatever their partner asked of them. As someone said, "I'm not really comfortable with that, but I didn't know how to say no," or they forgot they could change their mind. "I thought this would be okay but it wasn't, but I kept going because I didn't know what else to do."

During a workshop, Kay was visibly tense when her partner asked her for something. She appeared to be weighing it in her mind. When I reminded her that there was a limit to what she was willing to do and that that is a good thing, she was relieved. She said, "Oh my gosh, you mean I don't have to do that? It never occurred to me that it didn't have to happen." When she thought about what she *was* willing to do, she relaxed and became delighted to do it.

I began to see that when we are worried about having to give too much, we become afraid to give anything at all. When we take full responsibility for our limits, we become relaxed and generous within those limits. It is backward from what we might think. The way to joy and generosity is not to push ourselves, but to own our limits.

I learned to take more notice of how the giver was setting it up. Did they find out what the receiver wanted, or did they get started anyway?

At a workshop:

Dane: How would you like me to touch your hands? (picks up his partner's hand to begin)

Me: Oops, I didn't hear him ask for what he wanted. Did you?

Dane: Oops, no, I guess I didn't.

Me: Then how do you know what he wants?

Dane: Oh, wow, I didn't even realize I did that. Do overs!

Dane: (to Mick) How would you like me to touch your hands?

Mick: I'd like you to massage them.

Dane: (picks one up and starts)

Me: Do you know what kind of massage, soft or firm or whatever?

Dane: Again? I did that again? (to Mick) Soft or firm or whatever?

Mick: Whatever is fine.

Dane: See? He doesn't care! (laughter)

Me: Then you get to hone your art of finding out. Don't let him off the hook. (more laughter)

Dane: Okay, how exactly? Our teacher is strict.

Mick: Hmmm. I don't know. Actually, you know I don't actually want massage. I think I'd rather have you sort of stroke it softly.

Dane: Front of your hand or back?

Mick: Wow, this is hard. (laughter again) Back.

Dane (to me): Do I start now?

Me: Do you have the information you need? And he asked you? And did you say yes?

Dane (to Mick): Yes. (to me) Yes.
Me: Okay then!

Sometimes the givers, in their enthusiasm, expanded on what was asked for, "giving" more. They thought—well, I'm not sure what they thought. Either that the receiver didn't actually know what they wanted, or that they, the giver, knew better, or that if they gave more, they would impress the receiver. Or sometimes the giver just didn't notice they were doing more.

Then there is this one: doing to get a response we want to see. This is so easy to do! I've done this, and I imagine you have too. We want to see the person relax, or moan and sigh, or be impressed with our skill, or have a mind-blowing breakthrough. This trap is especially common with sexual touch. I've found that mostly we don't know we're doing this until we don't get the response we want; then we say, "It didn't work." We blame ourselves for not having the right technique or blame the receiver for not being liberated enough or not being able to surrender. There are many problems with this, and we'll be looking at them.

This role, doing for the benefit of the receiver, taught me that we don't own their experience—they do. What we do is contribute to their experience in some way that is useful and meaningful to them, and that makes it meaningful to us. When we can do that, it becomes satisfying to us, no matter their response.

Like the other side, once I saw where my clients were getting lost, I noticed it more in myself. Where was I giving to get something back: appreciation, praise, feeling good about myself? Where was I giving what I thought they wanted, or thought they should want, without finding out what they actually wanted? Where was I giving more than I honestly felt I wanted to? I still ask myself those questions.

That's both sides of the first offer. Let's look at the second offer.

THE SECOND OFFER

The second offer is this: "How do you want to touch me?" This is where it really got interesting.

HEARING THE OFFER

I've always been a tactile person. Making mud pies as a kid, feeling the velvety leaves of plants or the warmth of a horse's neck. When my play buddy at the original workshop asked me this question, "How do you want to touch me?" I knew right away what it meant. It meant I could use my hands to feel them. *Hell yeah!* I could feel the shape of their arm, the contours of their hand. I could explore the dips and hollows of their clavicle. I could get a good grip on the muscles of their thigh. They graciously gave me this gift, and I drank it in.

When I used this question with clients (and a few willing friends), I found that it was rarely so clear. Maybe two or three understood right away that it was for their own enjoyment, and they would say, "Oh! I'd like to play with your hair!" or "May I explore your neck?"

Almost everyone else became confused. They most often responded by saying what they were willing to do *for me*. They would say, "Would you like a shoulder rub?" or "I'm fine with anything you want" (a generous offer but doesn't answer the question). It was as if the act of touching and the idea that they were giving were welded in their minds, and I came to see that for most people, they are.

I thought, *They just need a reminder to do what feels good to their hands. They just need a little permission.* It rarely worked that way. It turned out to be much more difficult for people. I tried everything I could think of to change the focus from touching for the other person to touching for themselves. I tried to get them to let their hands do what felt good to their hands. I coached them, reminding them to feel the shape and the texture. I reminded them that this was a gift they were receiving, not one they were giving.

I tried as many different ways to say it, coach it, and set it up as I could think of in order to get people to stop giving. I learned to use the word "feel" instead of "touch." To feel is to touch for the purpose of taking in information or pleasure. You feel the baby's bath water to make sure it's not too hot; you feel your partner's skin because it's pleasant to you.

I learned to have people say, "May I…" (feel your back, explore your hand, etc.). I noticed that "May I…" made it clearer that they were asking for a favor. It turned out to be a tender question and often an emotional one. Often just asking the question would bring up confusion, fear, or shame. I tried telling people they could be selfish. For some, that helped, but for others the word "selfish" was so offensive as to stop them completely.

For a few, the offer itself made no sense. At a workshop, Carrie had given her partner the shoulder rub he'd asked for, completely comfortable and generous. Then he asked, as per the instructions, "How would you like to touch me?" She looked to me for direction, and I went over to them.

Carrie: Huh? What are you talking about? I don't understand the question.
Me: He is inviting you to touch him in some way that you want.
Carrie: Okay, uh, why would I want to do that?
Me: I don't know. Maybe you don't, or maybe you are curious about the fuzzy sweater he's wearing, what it might feel like in your hands, or maybe you'd like to feel that soft spot in front of his ear (me trying to coach her).
Carrie (to him): Is that what you want?
Me: The previous question was about what he wanted. This question is about what *you* want.
Carrie: This is crazy. I have never done this before.

Sometimes people would say, "But giving you pleasure IS what gives me pleasure." This got me pondering two routes to pleasure, direct and indirect, which we'll come back to in Lesson 2.

Asking the question set the stage, and then there was the experience of it. I knew that *feeling* a person felt different than *giving* to them, and it was evident from the start that this was true for others. There was a definite aha moment when the difference clicked and the change was visible. For some people, all it took was to fiddle around a little. "Oh, yeah, this does feel good to me." For many, the experience of it was seriously elusive. Even with all the coaching, they couldn't find it. What was going on?

I had a client for whom touching for his own pleasure was particularly elusive. He was stroking my arm and could not stop trying to give no matter how I described it. I looked over to my shelf, saw a river stone with some interesting textures, and thought, *Ah! Let's see what he does when there is no one to give to!* I picked it up and put it in his hands, inviting him to feel it. I wanted to help him access the ability to take in sensation and feel it as pleasure. I naively expected him to say, "Oh, now

I get it!" but he didn't. He had trouble with that too. He couldn't take in the texture or anything about it; there was certainly no pleasure in it. I realized his challenge was not that he didn't know how to feel a person. He didn't know how to feel anything. He knew it was a stone, so he was taking in some basic information, but he was unable to attend to it or enjoy the sensation of it.

This was a big aha for me. I started using this exercise with everyone and found that though a few people were already "switched on" (very few), most people needed some time to take in the sensation (a few minutes to twenty minutes or more), and for some, it was extremely difficult.

It was clear we were onto something. When the sensation became pleasurable, when it clicked, it was often an emotional moment. Tenderness, relief, joy, shame, confusion. Something was going on in there!

Over the years, I've heard many responses to this exercise:

"This is weird…"

"I feel sad. I have no idea why."

"I didn't know I could feel this much!"

"I know what it is and I know what it is for, but I don't know what it *feels* like."

"I don't feel alone."

"Once you feel that avocado, you can never go back!"

"I have been using my hands in my work for years. I have a new dimension now."

This exercise turned out to be a foundation for everything else we'll be doing. I will be taking you through it in the lessons.

So yes, learning to feel someone for your own pleasure turns out to be challenging for almost everyone. I learned ways to make it more accessible. I learned that how we position our bodies makes a difference as does slowing down. I came to appreciate how tender it is for most people and how foreign. I learned to give it time. It often doesn't click the first time, and then when it does, it takes coming back to it again and again.

As people rediscover touching for their own pleasure, they often feel like they are recovering something that has been lost and is found again, which is exactly what happens. They recover the ability to touch another with no agenda, with no trying to get it right, to enjoy the sensation of their hands. It shows us that we are right to want to touch each other, and there is a sense of relief, freedom, and joy.

This experience made me reflect on what I meant by giving and receiving. It was obvious that the person "giving" the touch was not giving a gift—they were receiving one. This made me scratch my head.

MAKING THE OFFER

What about the other side, the person who is making the offer: "How do you want to touch me?"

When you make this offer, you are offering to be touched in the way the other person wants, not necessarily the way you want. What you are offering is access to yourself. People's feelings about hearing this offer, as we said, were consistently challenging, but their feelings about making this offer were all over the map. For some it was easy, natural, and a relief at having nothing to do. For some it was worrisome, disconcerting, even nearly debilitating. This turned out to be a major learning opportunity. Again, the biggest assumption people made was that they had to go along with whatever the other person wanted.

Sometimes you have an experience that makes it all crystal clear. Cal was in his sixties and struggling with his sexuality and confidence. He had had only a few dates and was seriously intimidated by women. Over several sessions, we explored the offers gently and slowly. It became his turn to ask me, "How do you want to touch me?" He looked worried, and I could tell he was trying very hard to trust me. As one does before jumping into a cold river, he leaned forward, then backed off, then leaned forward again, gathering courage. *Okay, ready? I think I can do that. Okay, ready, here we go!* He took a giant leap of faith and blurted out, "Do whatever you want!"

Me: Oh dear! Is that what you thought the question was?
Cal: Uh, that's not it?
Me: What's actually true is that though there might be something I would like to do, *you* get to decide if that is okay with you.
Cal (after a pause): I do?

Me: Yes, you do.

Cal: Oh.

It was clear at that moment that it had never occurred to him that he had any choice in the matter. So deep was this belief that he could not hear the question. The instructions were "How do you want to touch me?" He heard that as "Do whatever you want." Those are very different things.

I thought, *No wonder he is afraid of relationships! If you don't know that you get any choice about what happens, how can you get close to anyone? You can't risk being in the same room.* One has only a few options then. You can go along with everything and become a doormat, you can try to control everything, you can stay on the doing side of every inter-action, you can stay away from people altogether, or some combination. If you don't know and trust, bone deep, that you have a choice, you'll have to do one of those.

This and other experiences showed me that the one factor underlying whether we can enjoy being touched, in any way at all, is knowing that we have a choice in the matter. It turned out to be a direct correlation. If you know you can say no or stop, you relax. If you don't know you can say no or stop, you can't afford to make such an offer. You will be on guard, worried about what's coming next, because you have to be. I came to see that knowing it in our minds is not enough. We have to know it with our bodies—that is, we have to have a body experience of exercising that choice.

That day brought a big insight for me about how deep this goes, how invisible it is to us when we're in it, and how confusing and disempowering it is. Again, seeing it so clearly here let me see the same dynamic in myself. Where was I forgetting I had a choice?

This role of offering themselves to be touched for the other person's enjoyment was surprisingly rich. People noticed they had a choice and learned how to exercise that choice. They learned, perhaps for the first time, that someone could enjoy them. They learned that they were giving a gift even when it felt wonderful to them. Often the learning was that they did in fact have a limit to what they were willing to let someone do to them and that owning their limits leads to joy and freedom.

This dynamic too made me reflect on what I meant by giving and receiving. The person who was being touched was not receiving a gift; they were giving one. More head scratching.

It's been a long rich journey, one that I am still on. As I learned to take responsibility for my desires and my limits, everything became easier. I became more honest about requesting. I learned to appreciate the gifts I had been given. I still have my comfort limits for what I can ask for without shame, and I still have places I give away more than I want to. Of course I do. And I still have places where I am entitled and unaware of what others are giving up for me.

TWO OFFERS, FOUR QUADRANTS

Now we come to the part of the story where I notice that each of the two offers creates two roles and that the four roles are each a combination of who is doing and who it's for. This discovery turned out to be so compelling that I spent the next ten years pondering it, exploring it, and developing it.

I'll come back to this after the next chapter. First we have to understand about receiving and giving—where the head scratching led to.

THE THREE MINUTE GAME

This is a game for two (or more) people.

Two questions, each one an offer:

- How do you want me to touch you for three minutes?
- How do you want to touch me for three minutes?

Each person takes a turn asking each question and then you do what was agreed upon.

When your partner asks what you want, pause to notice what sounds wonderful. Ask for it as directly as you can.

When you ask your partner what they want and they tell you, pause again and notice, *Is this a gift I can give with a full heart?* Set limits as needed.

(Yes, you can change your mind in the middle, and yes, you can ask for more than three minutes, provided you both take an equal amount of time.)

Set a timer! Repeat for a few decades.

VARIATIONS

1) The original game:

This is the original Three Minute Game as developed by Harry Faddis. As you can see, the questions are more open ended.

- What do you want me to do to you for three minutes?
- What do you want to do to me for three minutes?

This is the game I started with and then changed to the "touch" version because it related more to what I was teaching.

2) The May I/Will You Game:

You can dispense with the two offers and start right off with the requests.

- May I...?

- Will you...?

Some people find this version with the two requests less confusing. I like hearing the offers, because hearing that my partner wants to know what I want makes it easier to ask. Either way is fine. The same dynamics are created.

3) Talking and Listening:

- What would you like to say for three minutes while I listen?

- What would you like to hear from me for three minutes?

It's recommended that you not use this time to complain about your partner.

4) Children:

Here's how to play the game with children: Keep the game focused on what the child wants and never what the adult wants. The adult asks the child, "What do you want me to do to you?" and/or "What do you want to do to me?" You are asking them what they want. They never ask you what you want. Later, when they're older, they will naturally begin to ask what you want. That's fine as long as they initiate it, not you. (And if it's a wrestling match—make sure the kid wins. *Never* physically overpower a child.)

5) Playing with three people:

The first question, "How do you want me to touch you?" becomes "How do you want *us* to touch you?" You can ask to have both people touching you or one person touching you and the other witness, sit aside, leave the room, or even cheer—it's up to you!

The second question, "How do you want to touch me?" becomes the two people asking, "How do you want to touch *us*?" Again, you can ask to feel both at the same time, alternate between both people, or ask to feel one while the other witnesses, sits aside, cheers, or leaves the room. Again, you get to decide.

CHAPTER 2

Defining Receiving and Giving

Lean on me when you're not strong
And I'll be your friend, I'll help you carry on
For it won't be long
'Til I'm gonna need somebody to lean on.
—Bill Withers

One day, a client was experimenting with touching for his own pleasure, and I described it as a gift he was receiving. "Oh!" he said, "You mean when I'm giving, I'm really receiving!" I said, "You mean when you're *doing*, you're receiving." He said, "Yeah, that's what I mean."

This showed me that what he meant by giving was not what I meant by giving. It made me ask, *Okay, if giving doesn't describe who is doing, what does it describe?*

Let's define receiving and giving. The dictionary lists a dozen meanings for each of them, but in this book, I use them in a particular way, and to understand them, we have to start with the difference between "Want-to" and "Willing-to."

WANT-TO AND WILLING-TO

There is a difference between what you want to do (or have done to you) and what you are willing to do (or have done to you).

Want-to. You want it for your own reasons because it brings you joy, and it may or may not involve anyone else: a walk in the woods, curling up with a good book, or reaching up your lover's shirt. You choose it because you want it. The question you ask yourself is, *What sounds wonderful? What do I prefer? What is my first choice?*

Willing-to. You would not otherwise choose it for yourself, but you are willing because someone else wants it, and it is okay with you: making them a cup of tea or scratching that spot on their back. You choose it because someone else wants it. The question you ask yourself is, *Is this okay with me? Is this something I genuinely don't mind?*

Your Willing-to list is longer than your Want-to list. There are a lot of things you might not choose for yourself but you don't mind for someone else. Both options occur in a range of intensity. Your Want-to can vary from a mild preference to a burning desire. Your Willing-to can vary from delighted to barely willing ("Only for you, baby!"), or you may be willing within certain limits, like for a short period of time.

We need both options fully functional. We need times to notice what we want and put that first and other times to set it aside and go with what someone else wants. Most important, we need to be able to tell the difference.

Based on that, we can look at receiving and giving.

TWO MEANINGS

"Receive" has many meanings, but two of them apply here.

The first use describes the fact that something is done to you or moves toward you and arrives. You receive a back rub, a compliment, a package in the mail, or a pass to the twenty-yard line. But what if it's something you don't want? You can also receive an insult or a punch in the jaw. This use of "receive" says it arrives but says nothing about whether or not you want it.

The second use of the word refers to a gift: that is, something you do want that someone else is willing to give you, but there's more to it. What if what you want is not to have something done for you but to be allowed to do something yourself? Maybe you want to borrow my truck, pick the plums in my yard, or put your hand up my shirt. Is this not also receiving a gift? Yes, it is. This use of the word says it's something you want (and someone is willing to give you) but not who does the action. They may be doing the action, or you may be doing the action.

So now we have two uses of the word "receive." The first describes who is doing but not who it's for. The second describes who it's for but not who is doing.

Sometimes the two meanings occur together, and sometimes they don't. Sometimes the receiver of the action is also the receiver of the gift, like that back rub they asked for, or a present in the mail. Sometimes the receiver of the action is not receiving a gift—they are actually giving a gift, like access to their truck or the plums in their yard. Said another way, sometimes the action and the gift move the same direction, and sometimes they move in opposite directions.

Because of these two uses, the word "receive" often gets conflated with being done to. The problem with conflating words is that we tend to conflate the experience. That's where the problem lies. When something is being done to us, we think "receive," and we assume it is for us or at least it should be. But if we are putting up with some touch we don't want, who is that for? Conflating done-to and receiving turns out to be at the root of a great many difficulties, which we'll see.

The same is true for "give." It can refer to something you do or deliver, or it can refer to a gift, and sometimes those occur together, and sometimes they do not. You can deliver a letter, a massage, or a punch in the jaw, though if the receiver doesn't want them, they are not a gift. Or you can give a gift, regardless of who takes action. You can give me the gift of your action, like helping me move my piano, or you can give me the gift of allowing me to take action, like putting my hand up your shirt. These two meanings are equally conflated. As with the example at the beginning, when you mean "do," you say "give."

So, "done-to" has become conflated with "receive," and "do" has become conflated with "give," and they can be difficult to separate. One thing that happens in this practice is that rather miraculously, they decouple. We'll be seeing what becomes possible when they do.

In the Three Minute Game, each question is an offer. The gift you offer with the first question is your doing: "How do you want me to touch you?" The gift you offer with the second question is access to you (within your limits): "How do you want to touch me?" Very different kinds of gifts.

THE GIFT

So then, "receive" and "give" don't refer to who is doing but refer to who it's for. Receiving a gift means it's for you; you bring your desires forward. You focus on your Want-to list. You ask someone to set aside what they want in order to go with what you want (and they say yes).

Giving a gift means it's for the other person; you set your desires aside. You move from your Want-to list to your Willing-to list in order to go with what the other person wants. It could be said that what really constitutes the gift is moving off your Want-to list.

For the gift to be real, there is another step. You must both respect the limits of the giver. As the receiver, you respect their limits so you don't pressure them. As the giver you respect your own limits and choose what you can give. "I can give you this but not this other thing."

So in receiving, you do two things at once: 1) bring your desires forward, and 2) respect the limits of your giver. You are doing both at once; neither one alone is enough. The aha may be that it is possible to do both at once.

In giving, you also do two things at once: 1) set aside what you might prefer, and 2) keep responsibility for your limits. Again, it's both at once. Going along with something because you don't know how not to doesn't constitute a gift.

The give-receive dynamic is based on what the receiver wants and what the giver is willing to give, not the other way around. The gift moves from the giver to the receiver, and it moves one direction. It's not always easy, though it is liberating. We talk about this in more depth in chapter 15.

In this book. When I say "receive" or "give," I mean the gift—that is, who it's for. When I want to describe what action happens, I will describe the action.

IN SUMMARY

- *Want-to* means you want it for your own reasons.
- *Willing-to* means you would not choose it for yourself, but you are willing to because someone else wants it.
- *Doing* means you are the one taking action.

- *Done-to* means you are the one being acted upon.
- *Receive* means it's what you want and it's for you (and the other person is willing to give you that). You may be the one who is doing, or you may not be.
- *Give* means it's what the other person wants and you are willing to do or allow it. It's for them. You may be the one who is doing, or you may not be.

WE NEED THEM BOTH

As adults, we need them both. We need to have some time in receiving and some time in giving. Neither can meet the need for the other. You cannot meet your need to receive by giving more, no matter how much you enjoy it.

TAKING THEM APART

In order to experience them, we have to separate them. We have to experience one of them at a time, undiluted by the other. Fortunately, this is wonderful. In the practice in this book, we take them apart, gently but surely. You find that each one nourishes you in a different way and brings its own kind of joy.

CHAPTER 3

The Quadrants

N ow that we've defined receiving and giving, we can have a look at the quadrants.

Each of the two offers creates two roles. In each role, you are either doing or being done to, and it's either for you or for the other person. Those two factors combine in four ways. Later when we draw the Wheel, you'll see they create four quadrants, and we'll talk about them in depth. For now, I want to introduce them.

The quadrants are: 1) you are doing and it's for the other person, 2) you are doing and it's for you, 3) you are being done to and it's for you, and 4) you are being done to and it's for the other person.

That part was obvious pretty quickly. What took time to notice was that each quadrant had something different to show me, which is where the adventure got interesting. I was working with clients at that time, so I got to see many people experience this. I imagine that had I been able to experience this with only a few people, I would not have noticed both the consistent themes and the rich variation. There were ways each quadrant was challenging, each brought a particular kind of freedom, and each one offered a particular kind of joy, and all this was created by the agreements.

People often started out not being able to tell the difference—until they could. For example, they were touching, and they couldn't tell if it was for them or for the other. Then there would be an aha moment including some emotional shift, and the distinctions became clear. There was a certain kind of relief or discovery.

This was exciting to me. I remember talking to people about it, assuming it would be easy and obvious once I pointed it out, but it rarely was. It took me some time to realize that for it to make sense, it usually had to be experienced. It is a felt sense; each quadrant *feels different*.

DOING AND GIVING: THE SERVING QUADRANT

This is touching for the other person's enjoyment. When you ask your partner, "How do you want me to touch you?" and they ask you to scratch their back and you say yes, you are in the Serving Quadrant.

This quadrant is the one most people think of as "Giving" and the one everyone seems to want to be better at. The Serving Quadrant combines doing and giving. The gift you are giving is your action. You are touching your partner the way they want you to. In order to do that, you first have to find out what they want, and that is the real art.

You'll learn a lot in Serving. You'll see where you are trying to get it right and how you can relax about that, where you are trying to get the right response, and how that distracts you. You'll be humbled by what happens when you get yourself out of the way.

DOING AND RECEIVING: THE TAKING QUADRANT

This is touching for your own enjoyment. When your partner asks, "How do you want to touch me?" and you answer, "May I touch your…" or "May I explore your…?" and they say yes, you are in the Taking Quadrant. Taking combines doing and receiving. The gift you are receiving is access to them, which is a real and significant gift. You use your hands to explore them, feel them, and enjoy them, and your hands become sensitive and perceptive.

This is challenging for almost everyone. It tends to feel odd, sometimes foreign, occasionally impossible, but when it clicks, there is often a feeling of relief and of recovering something you had lost.

The Taking Quadrant is profoundly liberating. You learn that you are welcome here, as you are, with your desire and curiosity. You learn to respect the other person's limits and begin to trust yourself, and that lets you play with more freedom and confidence. You learn that in order to touch someone, you don't need to give. What you do need is their permission. Learning Taking develops your ability to touch based on your own desire, curiosity, playfulness, authenticity, and, when wanted, eroticism. The Taking Quadrant is the key.

The word "taking" has some negative connotations, but the Taking Quadrant is not "taking-from." It is receiving a gift, freely given to you with a full heart.

BEING DONE-TO AND RECEIVING: THE ACCEPTING QUADRANT

This is being touched for your own enjoyment. Your partner has asked you, "How do you want me to touch you?" and you have answered with a request, asking to be touched the way you want, and they have said yes. It's for you; you get to choose exactly how you want to be touched. You focus on your Want-to list. This is often surprising. You may not know what it feels like to have your desire be the one that counts.

The Accepting Quadrant combines done-to and receiving. It's what most people think of as "Receiving," but Taking is also a form of receiving, so we needed a different word. In this quadrant, you are receiving the gift of your partner's action.

Accepting is likely to feel vulnerable, because it is. You will learn how to notice what you want, how to trust that, value it, and communicate it. You'll find that it feeds you in a way that nothing else can. You will bump up against your comfort limit for pleasure, and you'll find that there are many more things to ask for than you have thought of before now, and they run the full range of mood. Tender, playful, sensual, comforting, nurturing, silly, sexy or cozy—it's all here.

The word "accepting" also has some unfortunate connotations, but the Accepting Quadrant is never "going along with" something. It's getting exactly what you want.

BEING DONE-TO AND GIVING: THE ALLOWING QUADRANT

This is being touched for the other person's enjoyment. You have offered your partner, "How do you want to touch me?" They have asked, "May I ...?" and you have said yes. You are being touched, but it's not for you. The Allowing Quadrant combines being done-to and giving. The gift you are giving is access to yourself. In Allowing, you move from your Want-to list to your Willing-to list.

What you learn here is that you have limits around how you are willing to be touched, that your limits matter, and that you have a choice about what is done to you. You also learn that the more responsibility you take for your limits (what they are and how to communicate them), the more relaxed and generous you become.

In Allowing, your partner is touching you for their own pleasure, but that is not to say that it won't be pleasurable for you; it often is. Because they are not on a mission, the Taker's hands become relaxed and present. Sometimes the hardest part of Allowing is remembering that it's not about you. Other times the touch itself is not particularly pleasant, but there is satisfaction in giving the gift. This is the quadrant where surrender lives, and we'll talk about how to make that rich and delicious.

TWO DYNAMICS

In the Serve-Accept dynamic, one person touches another with the agreement that it's for the benefit of the one being touched. This is what most people consider normal or the right kind of touch, and it is common in many situations: massage, medical care, helping Grandma up the stairs, or holding a child to give them comfort.

In the Take-Allow dynamic, one person touches another with the agreement that it's for the enjoyment of the person doing the touching. This dynamic is rare and generally reserved for lovers, which is why it tends to feel intimate, even if it involves, for example, only the hands. It's also the dynamic that is needed between lovers but often missing. If there is no consent, that is, if the one being touched did not agree to it, this dynamic becomes groping and assault, which can make this dynamic confusing.

A student recently came up with this example: sitting at a restaurant table where someone brings your meal is Serve-Accept; walking through a buffet line is Take-Allow.

If you find yourself scratching your head trying to figure it out, don't worry. We're going to experience them first.

CHAPTER 4

About Pleasure

If you are capable of living deeply one moment of your life, you can learn to live the same way all the moments of your life.
—Thich Nhat Hanh

Like all mammals, we are built for pleasure. Pleasure is a biological guide to what is good for us: fresh air, clean water, food, rest, movement, touch, play. We have brain circuits that light up exactly for that purpose. It would seem odd that such creatures would have to remind ourselves that it's okay to experience it and would have to, as adults, learn it all over again. But so it is, and here we are.

There are as many kinds of pleasure as there are moments. The pleasure of good conversation, music (making it, hearing it, moving to it), a game of chess or volleyball, or as Richard Feynman, the physicist, describes, "the pleasure of finding things out." Of course there's sensory pleasure: touch, smell, taste, sound, and sight. In this book, I mostly talk about tactile pleasure, experiencing pleasure through the skin.

Some people think "pleasure" applies only in a sexual context. As one person said, "It's pleasant but it's not, you know, Pleeeeasure." The definition I am using for pleasure is general: it's whatever brings you joy and nourishment. It's definitely more than sexual.

Everything about pleasure is based on the fact that pleasure is a physiological process with changes in brain activity, blood chemistry, muscle engagement and more. The actual experience of pleasure is internal.

RELAXED PLEASURE AND EXCITED PLEASURE

You can experience pleasure in a relaxed state or in an excited state. In an excited state (this is an oversimplified description), your sympathetic nervous system is engaged. Certain functions are heightened, and most likely your body is moving faster. The sympathetic nervous system can engage for unpleasant reasons like fear or for pleasant reasons like going for a run or sexual arousal. Of course, excitement itself can be pleasurable. This is why we play with fear—scary movies, roller coasters, and some kinds of sexual play. It's what we call "thrill."

In a relaxed state, the parasympathetic nervous system engages, and certain other functions are heightened. The classic example of this is "resting and digesting." A relaxed state tends to be naturally pleasurable. In order to let ourselves relax, we have to feel safe enough (and many things influence that). You cannot force a relaxed state, but to some degree you do choose it. You set yourself up so it can happen, and then you learn how to feel it and how to deepen it. Unlike excited states, it doesn't make for good video; it's not dramatic enough.

A third branch of the autonomic nervous system, the social engagement system, enervates parts of the head, face, and chest and is specifically involved in detecting and creating engagement with others. This is key in creating a sense of connection and therefore safety, which is needed for experiencing both excited and relaxed states of pleasure. There is a constant interplay between the three systems; they are not as distinct as I make them sound.

We need access to both an excited state and a relaxed state. Some people are comfortable only in an excited state and have a hard time relaxing (it brings up fear). Other people like a relaxed state and are uncomfortable with excitement (it brings up fear).

Base Camp. It's the relaxed state that is the foundation for pleasure, a kind of base camp. It is from this base camp that you can reach out and explore and then come back. In the lessons, we start here. You are securing base camp.

To create a relaxed-state base camp, you need: 1) a sufficient sense of safety; you're not running from a tiger or worried about being ridiculed,

2) time to settle into your base camp; and the more you learn to access it, the less time it takes to open it, and 3) something pleasant to notice, in this case, your skin. Attending to sensation is a reliable way to get there. Once learned, dropping into base camp becomes easier and easier. Eventually it only takes changing your attention, and there it is.

Sexual arousal is often an excited state, and so is its close cousin, feeling anxious. Many people don't know how much anxiety they are feeling until they learn what a relaxed state feels like—not a few bits of pleasure peeking out from behind the tension and worry but a genuine, full-body relaxed state. When you can access this kind of relaxed state and then add sexual arousal to it, it's an entirely different kind of experience, where some of the most transcendent experiences happen. These are the bliss states.

A FEW THINGS TO KNOW ABOUT PLEASURE

It's good for you. No news here. Scientists have been saying this for a long time. There are changes in blood chemistry, nervous system, immune system, changes in feeling connected to people you experience it with, changes in perspective and resilience. Pleasure is good for you.

It's valuable in its own right. You don't need an excuse to experience pleasure. It doesn't have to be an accidental side effect of something else. It likewise doesn't like to be used for some other purpose, even self-improvement, and it doesn't like to be a strategy to get something, even sex.

You can't make it happen. You can't force pleasure, but you can contribute to the likelihood of it happening. In this practice, we show you how to set up the situation by getting clear on who it's for and what your desires and limits are and, to some extent, your physical posture. Then you can choose where you place your attention, and then the pleasure systems can engage.

You can learn how to access it. Accessing states of pleasure is not an accident you fall into—it is learned through a few simple steps, which are mostly setting yourself up for safety and learning how to attend to your sensation.

You can't give or receive pleasure. When you understand pleasure as physiology, you see that you can't give it or receive it. You access it within yourself. We can contribute to the likelihood that another will be able to access pleasure, but we can't actually give it. What we can give and receive is time and attention and sometimes, if requested, touch. Likewise, you may experience pleasure while receiving a gift or while giving a gift. The experience of pleasure does not mean you are receiving; it means you are experiencing pleasure.

Follow the pleasure. You can't tell pleasure where it should be. The fallacy is that if pleasure is not already happening (the way you think it is supposed to), you have to try harder or push yourself. This is backwards. Pushing yourself engages the defense response, and the pleasure response cannot engage. When you notice whatever pleasure is already there and follow it, the defense response calms down, and the pleasure response can engage. This is a major principle we'll come back to.

You can't predict where it will take you. When you follow your pleasure, you can't predict where it will take you: relief and comfort, playful exuberance, sexual turn-on, a mass of jelly, a heap of tears, fits of creative energy, joy, fear, surprise, sleep, and transcendent insights.

You have a pleasure ceiling. You have a ceiling on the amount of pleasure and the kind of pleasure with which you are emotionally comfortable. This is normal and universal. It may be a teaspoon, a bucket, or an ocean, but it's still there. In terms of pure sensory bliss, a two-hour, full-body, erotic massage is hard to beat, but the amount of fear, doubt, suspicion, shame and just general consternation would, for most people, cancel out any possible enjoyment. It's not usually the sensory enjoyment that is in question. It's the feelings we have about that enjoyment that is the limiting factor. It's self-protective in a sense—protecting yourself from feelings you don't know what to do with.

What raises your ceiling? Following the pleasure applies here. What is it that sounds appealing at the moment? You might want to back up a little so the feelings are less strong; you might want to stretch a little and feel more of the feelings. When you stop pushing yourself, the feelings gradually soften. That lets your ceiling rise, and then you can handle more pleasure. And then you hit another ceiling. So it goes for a few decades.

You are right to have mixed feelings about it. We crave pleasure and we fear it (because of the pleasure ceiling), and both are correct. We crave it because we need it. It awakens, calms, refreshes, nourishes, restores, and brings us relief and gratitude—and we fear it. It's going to bring us right up to our self-doubt and lead us to insight and change. We have an inner push-pull going on, which is normal and, as far as I can tell, unavoidable.

Here are some things that people have said when exploring their pleasure:

"Whenever I feel pleasure, I feel guilty."

"It's okay to experience a little pleasure, sure, if it happens by accident. You know, while I'm giving to someone else."

"It's not okay to feel this good myself, but it's okay to make my partner feel good, and that feels good to me too."

"Yeah, that's sort of pleasant, I guess, but I don't let myself really enjoy it very much."

"Wow! That feels phenomenal! I didn't know I could feel that! So why do I feel like crying?"

Pleasure is a powerful change agent. Pleasure lets you make friends with your body, and that changes your sense of who you are in the world, and your sense of self-worth, value, and compassion. Many fears and inner conflicts resolve. This is why it is often said that pleasure heals. Indeed, for many of us, as professionals, pleasure is our primary healing modality.

We're back to pleasure being a change in physiology. Change your physiology, and you change what you are able to perceive. Change what you can perceive, and you change what you are able to imagine. Change what you can imagine, and you change what you are able to choose in your life.

THE THREE COMPONENTS OF PLEASURE

Standing in your bedroom, you feel a caress down your neck to your collar bone. It's your lover. It feels wonderful. You get weak in the knees. The next day, you feel exactly that same touch, but now you're standing on a crowded bus and have no idea who is behind you. While the touch is the same, the experience is radically different.

Every experience of pleasure combines three factors: stimulus, attention, and meaning. Depending on the focus, it can create a very different experience.

Stimulus. This is the actual sensory data (in this case, touch): location, pressure, temperature, movement. It causes the neural sensors to fire in a particular pattern, which tells us how we are being touched. We have some degree of choice about how we are touched but not always.

Attention. Other factors being equal, more attention means more pleasure. While teaching couples erotic massage, I have seen some who are attentive to their experience and bring themselves and each other into rapture. I have seen others who, even though fabulous things were happening to their anatomy, were distracted and hardly noticed each other. The ability to choose where you bring your attention is developed. Eventually a very simple stimulus can become exquisitely enjoyable. Attention, too, is mostly a matter of choice.

Meaning. This is the context in which the stimulus is happening and the meaning you attach to it. This is the difference between your bedroom and the crowded bus. Meaning is the most complex factor and must be at least acceptable, or you won't engage the other two factors. For example, the meaning you attach to a hug determines whether you allow it to happen at all. Meaning is often a source of erotic charge and brings flavor to sensation. This is why it's said that the biggest sex organ is the brain.

Each quadrant is an agreed-upon meaning that sets the stage for the touch. Experiencing them shows you, among other things, how powerful meaning is. For example, your hand is stroked, and though the stimulus may be nearly identical, whether you are Accepting or Allowing will change your experience of it—likewise with Taking and Serving.

Mix and match. All three factors are always present, and the quality of your experience depends on their interplay. Change any one of them, and the whole experience changes. On the bus, the sensation is the same, but the meaning is different, and it gets your attention! A sumptuous massage with warmed oil can be boring, if your attention is elsewhere, or scary, if the meaning is not clear. If your attention is wandering, a change in stimulus can pull it sharply back: a playful bite, for example. When we create a temporary meaning, like in role-play, our attention goes up, and the simplest stimulus becomes exquisite. Then there are those long, intense, lustful gazes from across the room, with no touch at all, that can make you break out in a good sweat on the power of meaning alone.

You have a familiar combination that feels safe, whereas another combination will be a little edgy. I know some couples who love their connection (meaning) but don't get very fancy with the stimulus. Others can do the most outrageous things (stimulus) but hardly seem to notice it (attention). Many people are happy with mutual play, but changing the context by taking turns would be edgy for them. They would have a hard time with a massage. Others are happy taking turns but not comfortable with mutual play. Some people feel safe with warm affection, but a role-play in power dynamics would be scary. Other people are the opposite.

The activity (stimulus) matters, but the other two components determine the inner experience. The inner experience is what you are after and where the pleasure actually is.

In the practice, we play with all three. In Lesson 1, Waking Up the Hands, we set aside meaning, and that lets us play with attention. Later, we play very much with meaning, as the quadrants are all about meaning. The meaning we create sets you up to easily play with attention and stimulus. Any one of the three can change the other two.

CHAPTER 5

About Touch and Sex

What does the practice have to do with sex? Nothing, but it's a fair question. The practice isn't about sex; it's about experiencing the quadrants. As it happens, experiencing the quadrants develops awareness and skills that make for a vastly improved experience of (all varieties of) sex.

Defining sex. When you say the word "sex," chances are you have a movie that runs in your head about how it's supposed to progress from A to B to C, and chances are it includes some orifice or other. I'd like to invite you to throw that out so you can enlarge your idea of what sex actually is. By sex I mean *the presence of your own arousal and the decision to follow it.* If it involves another person, they are also following their arousal. If they are not equally engaged, it's not sex. For example, watching a hot babe cross the street may be arousing, but it's not sex. Likewise, doing something to someone who has not or cannot say yes is not sex—it's assault.

Sex is more than activity X, Y, or Z. Certainly it's more than intercourse; the genitals may not even be involved. It's possible to have sex without touching or even being in the same room. It's more accurate to say sexual activity or sexual play, which is what I use in this book, and it includes a wide range of ways to play, experiment, and enjoy yourselves.

What we want. I have worked with many people supporting them in their sexuality, and one thing that surprised me is the huge range of interests, feelings, and experiences. Still, with all that variety, what we seem to want is basically two things: 1) we want to express ourselves in ways that are real and meaningful to us, and 2) in the foggy maze of our mixed feelings, we want to find each other.

Expressing ourselves. The need for sex is not for sexual activity. The actual need is for sexual expression, to acknowledge who you are as a sexual being and express it in a way that is real and meaningful *to you.* Sexual expression means being yourself instead of someone else—how you express your gender, how you move, who you are attracted to and what you like to do with them, how you like to feel connected to your partner(s), what turns you on and has meaning for you.

Our culture has a pitifully narrow view of how to be sexual, with whom and under what circumstances it's allowed, and how it is supposed to look. This view cannot possibly fit the whole range of who we are, so we try to fit into a mold in which we can't fit, creating untold shame and heartache. What I and others want, and perhaps you, is to be able to access the full range of who we are and what is possible for us to feel. And we want to do that without feeling we are using someone or being used.

Finding each other. Along with self-expression, we want to find each other. All the assumptions, doubts, misconceptions, longings, and tensions about touch and sex are like a maze filled with fog. We fumble around wondering, *Where is that other person in here?* We want to see and be seen, to touch and be touched, in whatever different senses of these words we want.

There is a third thing too. We want a way to start where we are. We want a reasonable and accessible way to expand ease and confidence and free up our natural sensuality. We want a simple, direct, tangible way that does not require new deities. This practice is one way to do that.

TOUCH AND SEX

In our culture, we tend to conflate touch with sex. We think touch implies sex is somewhere close by or at least desired. We have forgotten how to touch in ways that are not about sex. One of the most powerful things you can do for better sex is to decouple these.

Touch. Our need for touch is lifelong. We are born with it and never outgrow it. The need is both physiological and emotional. Welcome touch engages the physiology of comfort and pleasure and can convey affirmation, connection, affection, nourishment, and support. It is well understood by science that these feelings are good for our immune system, hormonal system, and more. It's no longer a question.

Sex. Our need for sex is, as just said, not for sexual activity but for sexual expression. If we have touch and sex conflated, when we feel our need for touch, we interpret it as a need for sex. At best this is incomplete and at worst disastrous. For many people without sexual partners, this means not getting any touch at all, which is a terrible loss. For those with sexual partners, it often means if we aren't in the mood for sex, we don't risk touching at all. Also a terrible loss.

If touch is about getting to sex and sex is about getting to orgasm, then touch becomes strategic, designed to produce a result. Sometimes this works, but something is lost. If you can't experience touch without thinking it's sex, then your sex isn't really about sex either. It is trying to use sex to meet all those other needs—comfort, connection, affirmation, sensuality, affection, recreation—and touch.

In this practice, I encourage you to experiment with touch that is not about sex for several reasons. First, so you can tell the difference. So you can meet your need for touch with, well, touch. Second, you will open a whole new world of possibility about ways to touch that are more satisfying, in many ways, than sex. Third, because trying to learn the quadrants with sexual touch doesn't work; your habits are too strong. Finally, because the quality of your touch is a very big factor in the quality of your sexual activity. It's not the only factor, but it is a significant one, and to become very good at touch, you pretty much have to start with touch that is not about sex. When you do that, your touch gets better—and your sex also gets better.

A DIFFERENT APPROACH

Just when I thought I had it figured out—how to be good in bed— you come along with these damned two questions, and I see that what I've been doing is not at all what I thought I was doing, and now I'm questioning everything. I don't know whether to curse you or thank you!

—A student

There is a myth about sex: that good technique equals good sex. That there is some stroke or some body part that, if only you could find it, would open the gates of heaven. If only you could get it right, all would be fabulous, mystical, or smokin' hot. This is not true. In fact, *if you are relying on technique, you are missing the best part.* This myth is based on the idea that sex is something you do, so to do it better, learn fancier stuff to do. Much adult sex education is taught from this perspective, as you can see when you peruse the magazines in the checkout aisle.

You already know it is possible to do all manner of extraordinary things to interesting body parts and feel very little, even be bored. It's also possible to do very little and feel the ground give way under you. What makes the difference? To enjoy ourselves more, the thing to learn is not doing more stuff, it's learning how to feel. The different approach of this practice is in learning to notice yourself and each other, exquisitely. That journey is more challenging and much richer.

If it's not technique, what is the best part? Authentic sexual expression. Showing up and having the skill to notice and respond to the person right in front of you, exactly the way they are right now and exactly the way you are right now, and being able to keep responding as things change, moment by moment. That's where play and spontaneity become possible. That's where it gets good.

We need all four quadrants. For a full expression of our sexuality, we need access to all four quadrants. By access, I mean we need to be able to experience them, to find them within ourselves. Each one opens a different aspect of ourselves, each one teaches us specific skills, and each one challenges us and sheds light on where we are currently stuck or lost. And each one liberates us in a different way. This is the real treasure of the process. No matter what kind of sex you engage in, if it involves another person, this is the foundation.

For example, the ability to take action for your own pleasure, or to take action for your partner's pleasure, *and to tell the difference,* is more significant than it might appear at first and is fundamental to all relationships. With these skills comes the ability to express what is real for you, with confidence, responsiveness, creativity, and a vastly greater range of emotional tone. So yes, if you want the full potential of the gorgeous, messy, scary, promising, rich tapestry of who you are as a sexual being, you need access to all four quadrants.

The gears at the center. One way of thinking about this is like a big box of complex gears. If sex is less than easy, you may think the whole machine is broken. It's not—it's this little tiny gear that is rusty. It just happens to be the little gear right in the middle, so it affects everything, and in order to get anything happening, you have to make complicated adjustments and work-arounds. One could specialize in those work-arounds; many people do.

This practice goes to the heart of the gears, where it makes the most difference. You drop the smallest drop of oil, and the gear moves a tiny bit. Your skin wakes up. (That's one of the gears.) You start to notice what it is you want and notice that it's different than what you're okay with. (That's another one.) You start to trust that (more gears) and value it, and you learn when you communicate it, it works. You start to notice, trust, and value your limits (more gears), and you become more relaxed, generous, and playful. Sex, and many other things, stop being work.

If sex is less than easy, the problem is often not about sex. It's more about these gears at the center that teach you how to be vulnerable and spontaneous and let your body express itself. A student recently said, "The problem wasn't sex—the problem was the quadrant."

So, will it improve your sex life (however that looks for you)? Hell, yes! And perhaps not by the path you expect.

About sex and this practice. To have an inspiring sex life, the things that make the most difference are learned before you ever get your clothes off. It's likely that during this practice, you'll get turned on at some point, and that's fine, but during the lessons and labs in this book, we won't be including the option for genital touch. The reason is that if you do, you won't learn the quadrants. I've seen it many times. You learn the quadrants, and then genital touch is an option, and everything you've learned flies out the window, and you are right back to what you already know.

We do, however, have some notes for you, if you later want to include them, about how to do that with care and respect. The notes are included in the online resources along with a discussion about some other aspects of sex and sexuality (www.wheelofconsentbook.com/notes).

In Search of the Quadrants

CHAPTER 6

In Search of the Quadrants

The aim of any encounter is not to do the thing.
It's for consent to happen.
—Justin Hancock

I n Part 2, I show you how to find and explore the quadrants. It takes a little care and attention to find the quadrants—it's not necessarily obvious. For this reason, I give them to you carefully, and this happens in the lessons. The first lesson changes the way you experience your hands—they change from tools to a source of pleasure *to you*—and everything that follows is built on this change. Then in the next two lessons, you find the quadrants; they click. You'll come back to these lessons a dozen times or so each so the quadrants become natural and easy. Then once you have the quadrants, in the labs you get to explore them and dive in. For each quadrant, I give you notes on how to keep it, where it takes you, and how to develop the art of it.

It is possible to play the Three Minute Game and go from there. My experience though is that if you want to find the quadrants, quite often the game is not enough. Each quadrant is a distinct experience, and the habits we have around touch tend to blur the distinctions, but it's the distinctions that make each quadrant what it is, so it's natural to need a little coaching for that.

I was at a workshop recently that included a few yoga postures. Here we are, in a room of a dozen students, and I'm trying to get the posture right, but I couldn't figure out what I was supposed to be looking for. In short order I was in tears. When the teacher came over to help, he saw it right away. "Oh, I see, you're going too far here, and you need extra blocks over here." I asked him, "What am I looking for?" He answered, "You're not trying to stretch that part. You're trying to support this other part." Oh! I had thought the stretch was the thing! He changed some details, which got me into the right position, and I felt it! My lumbar spine was suddenly in communication with me, and I felt for the first time ever—supported. My heart cracked open in gratitude. Welcome home, lumbar spine.

That's a little like the journey of the quadrants (except for the yoga). First, if you haven't felt the quadrant before, you may be casting about for what it feels like. That's natural. Second, the connection is inherent in your body. All you need is to set yourself up the right way, and it clicks. And third, small changes make all the difference. In the lessons and labs, we set you up so it can click and let you know what to look for. Also like the yoga, instead of telling you to stretch this part, I'm going to show you how to support this other part.

WHAT IT TAKES TO FIND THE QUADRANTS

It takes someone to play with. You don't need to be lovers to play. It's fine to ask a friend to be your practice buddy. If your partner is not interested, see the online notes.

It takes a willingness to question what you know. This is going to challenge what you know and who you think you are as a lover and, quite possibly, as a person. The truth will set you free, but it usually shakes things up first.

It takes time. It takes time for the click—a few minutes, many minutes, a few weeks; it varies. Then it takes a few weeks or months for the quadrants to feel more natural and solid. It works best to set aside some time every few days, even if only twenty minutes. You are better off with five minutes a day than five hours twice a year. Here's how some people have set it up. Some parents take one night a week and hire a babysitter.

A retired couple spends twenty minutes every morning with a different quadrant each day. A professional couple sets aside one full Saturday every quarter. Some people form a local group that meets every couple weeks for an evening.

It takes following instructions. The instructions are extremely simple. Sometimes the hardest part is taking them seriously enough to do them. Most of the time I am teaching people in my studio, so I can see them as they try it. Since this is a book, I can't see what you're doing, but that's not a problem. The problem is that neither can you. For example, one instruction will say, "Lean back, flat against your chair or the wall," which means both shoulders equally in contact with what you are leaning against. It's amazing how many people will think they are doing that, and then when I have them look at themselves, they notice they are turned an inch to the side, and then we correct that, and they say, "Oh, this feels different!"

It's often easier to *see* what you are doing than it is to *feel* what you are doing, so it's best to read the instructions, give them a try, then pause and look, visually, at yourself, and see if you're actually doing them. I'll remind you when we get there.

SOME PRINCIPLES THAT WILL SHOW UP

Over the years, I have noticed a few principles as people go through the process. Here they are, and you'll see them highlighted throughout the book, like the one on the next page.

Let your skin do the work for you. When you bring your attention to your sensation, insights arise and questions resolve. You don't have to figure it out, just come back to your skin.

Inflow and outflow. When we change our focus from the "outflow" (what we are intending to give) and instead focus on the "inflow" (what we are taking in with our hands), it changes our experience.

Becoming trustworthy. There is a misconception that we should get better at trusting the other person, but the person we need to trust is ourselves, and we can do that only when we become trustworthy. Becoming trustworthy is based on specific skills in each quadrant.

Intensity. As any activity becomes more intense, we become more likely to revert to our default. The cure for intensity is to slow down.

Follow the pleasure. Don't tell the pleasure where you wish it was; follow it where it already is. This allows your brain's pleasure centers to engage.

Adapting ourselves. We will adapt ourselves unnecessarily to what is happening, and this feels so normal we don't notice it. In this practice, we reverse that. Instead of changing yourself to match what is happening, you will change what is happening to match yourself.

Two routes of pleasure. One route to pleasure is directly through sensation. Another route is the pleasure we experience when we create a response we want to see in another person.

The choosing is more important than the doing. The act of choosing has far more impact on your experience of touch than the actual touch. In this practice, we focus here.

The quadrants are not gendered. The quadrants are not gendered, but your gender conditioning is one factor in how difficult or easy it may be to find each quadrant.

PRINCIPLE:
LET YOUR SKIN DO THE WORK FOR YOU

When I started teaching this to others, sometimes people would start to feel a little lost and try to figure it out. "Wait, am I giving or receiving?" or "What is this feeling about?"

I noticed that when I had them bring their attention back to their skin, *to the sensation itself,* it all sorted itself out. They said things like, "Oh, I get it now, this is for me," or "Oh, I didn't know I felt this way," or "Oh, I'm afraid of taking anything for myself; I hadn't realized that," or "Oh, no wonder I'm always trying so hard to please."

You don't have to unravel the complexities of your psyche, heal your issues, figure out what boundaries are, or struggle to "get out of your head." Your skin will do that for you. First it will show you where you are lost or stuck, and then it will bring you insights that clear it up. Bring your attention back to your skin, and the insights will follow naturally, not the other way around. Let your skin do the work for you.

SENSATIONS AND FEELINGS

I often talk about the feelings that will arise as you explore, so let's define them.

Sensations. In this context, the sensation is the body signal. Sensation is the warmth in your chest, the tension in your gut, the tingling in your fingers, the butterflies in your belly.

Feelings and emotions. The feelings, or emotions, are the name you ascribe to what those sensations mean. You call them sadness, joy, confusion, shame, excitement, etc. Some people define feelings and emotions differently, but for our purposes here, I'm using them interchangeably. Essentially they are sensations whose purpose is to give you information about your current situation and the motivation and energy to change what you are doing.

The problem is not having feelings; it's what to do with them. *Aaaacckkk! Feelings!* What they need is only to be with them. Instead of trying so hard to not feel it, see if you can notice the sensation and be with it (for about ninety seconds). See if you can have compassion for yourself, and see it as useful information. In this practice, as you attend more to your sensation, feelings will arise. It cannot be otherwise. Some are feelings you would rather avoid, and some are feelings you like but that still surprise you, like delight and relief, and of course pleasure. Some, ironically, feel so good that it bumps up against your self-doubt (which is one reason we often avoid pleasure).

A CONTAINER

This was so freeing! We know it was an exercise, but all of a sudden it was safe to ask for whatever I wanted, because I trusted my partner to say yes or no.

—A student

In our regular sexual, sensual, and touch interactions, we have certain assumptions (which we mostly don't notice): who does what and why, what we are supposed to feel, and where we expect it to lead. We're not usually interested in a major upset of protocol. When exploring the quadrants, you will be finding dynamics that don't fit your norm, and this will bring up feelings. You will need a little extra safety.

A feeling of safety is a primary need. Nothing else can proceed until this is met. All senses will focus on getting safe or staying safe, with all manner of strategies. It helps to remember that there is no such thing as safety; you will be disappointed, annoyed, and offended at times. No one can promise that you won't. It is possible, however, to create a feeling of *relative* safety, because the safer you feel, the more interested you become in experimenting. Creating a container can provide that feeling. A container consists of your agreements, and sticking to your agreements makes a container strong. The stronger the container, the safer you feel, so you can experiment. With a container, you know where it's *not* going. That lets you experiment and dive into each quadrant. Another thing that helps you feel safe is knowing that when tender feelings arise, you will stay there and be with each other without trying to fix anything.

I recommend creating a container each time to do these experiments. You can think of your container as a learning lab, a sacred space, or an experiment. Outside the container, do what you usually do. Inside the container, you have a different set of agreements. For example, outside the container, you give spontaneously and get creative about it. Inside the container, give only what was asked for and nothing more. It's an experiment. Outside the container, you begin touching each other and let it go where it goes. Inside the container, stay in the quadrant you agreed to.

To create a container, you need some way to acknowledge that you are entering it so that you shift your context. It helps to make it both verbal and physical, as simple or as elaborate as you like. Light a candle, say a prayer, or read a poem. Or hang a "Do Not Disturb" sign on the door even though you live alone. Or stand on one foot facing the east and put a finger in your left ear while humming. It doesn't matter what it is. What matters is that you agree, verbally, that you are entering the container. Or stand up and look into each other's eyes and say, "Okay, honey, ready? Here we go."

Then once you are complete with the practice, you close the container and go back to your usual. Indeed, an important thing about a container is that you *do* close it. Use the same or different ritual to mark that. Blow out the candle, read a different poem, take the sign off the door, or say, "Okay, honey, let's leave the container now."

However you open your container, make certain both of you are choosing to be in it. One thing that does not work is one person thinking they are in the container and the other person expecting the usual dynamic. It's easy to hurt each other's feelings.

RESISTANCE AND A REASSURANCE

If you have read a book or watched a video that taught you a new stroke, or a new body part, and it was done on you but failed to inspire you, it's likely that the thought of another book about touch leaves you cold. As well it should. I can imagine you saying, *Oh great. Something else I'm supposed to like.* That's what I have said on occasion.

The reassurance is this. There are no strokes in this book and precious few body parts. I will not ask you to do more of what already doesn't inspire you. Who needs more practice at that? Not me, not you either. What I do teach you is how to slow down enough to notice what it is you do want. That is a very different question and a much more interesting one.

That may be a relief, or it may be a whole different kind of intimidating. It's meant to be reassuring. If you notice a sense of dread, ask yourself, *What is it that I think I am going to be expected to like?* Then throw that out. Then ask yourself, *What is it, instead of that, that sounds wonderful?* *That's* where we're going.

About resistance. Resistance has a bad reputation but is important to listen to. It is one of two things: 1) a no trying to get you to hear it, and any reason, or no reason, is good enough; or 2) it's a sign that there is something tender here that needs your attention, a sign that there are likely to be feelings arise that you're not sure you have enough resource for. Here is what I suggest: take your time; do what is described here only to the degree it sounds appealing, and let yourself enjoy that. Then see what's appealing next—not what you think you *should* do but what you actually *want* to do. If you're not up for it now, put the book down for a few months, mull it over, and pick it up again when you're inspired to.

PRINCIPLE:
THE CHOOSING IS MORE IMPORTANT THAN THE DOING

If you want to improve the quality of your experience of touch, the place to put your attention is not on the touch. It's on the choosing. I have seen many people, including myself, skate over the opportunity to choose, and then, if the touch is less than inspiring, try to like it more. Instead, if you attend to the process of noticing what you want and communicating it, the quality of your experience vastly improves.

First, it is empowering. You are choosing what happens instead of going along with whatever someone else is doing. Second, it tenderizes the heart. The process of choosing makes us notice our vulnerability and brings us right to the present moment. If it's for you, you are choosing what you want. If it's for the other person, you are choosing what you are genuinely okay with. If you are going along with whatever is happening, the exact same touch becomes dull, suspect, or worse, even if you are trying to like it. Be true to yourself, or there is no one home to play with.

There are four steps: noticing, trusting, valuing, and communicating. These same four steps apply to your desires (when receiving) or your limits (when giving). Sometimes the steps seem instantaneous; sometimes they come one at a time, but they're all there. Taking the time for this is not easy. But the degree to which you can slow yourself down so that you *can* notice, trust, value, and communicate is the degree to which you will stop trying to like what is done to you and instead have what you actually want. Then the touch you experience becomes deeply satisfying and liberating.

Let's look at each of those, for both desires and limits.

Desires. By desires, I mean whatever brings you joy, not just sexual desire. What opens the experience of receiving is first getting clear on what it is you actually want and not giving up on yourself before that becomes clear to you.

- **Notice:** It's not something you figure out; it's already there inside. If you give it time, it will eventually bubble up to consciousness. The question to ask yourself is not *Am I okay with this thing that is coming my way?* The question to ask yourself is *What is it that I actually want? What is it that sounds wonderful?* Then you commit to waiting until the answer is clear. Waiting can be awkward of course. That's why it's a commitment. Wait for the *Hell, yes, this is what I want!*

- **Trust:** Then trust that the information that arises is accurate. It may seem silly, trivial, too sexy, or not sexy enough, but you can trust it. It came from somewhere.

- **Value:** Then value it. What you want matters. You may, for various reasons, choose not to disclose it. That's fine, but know that it matters; it means something to you.

- **Communicate:** And then of course communicate your desire by asking "May I...?" or "Will you...?" Or if someone has offered you something, saying "Yes, please!"

Limits. By limits, I mean what you are willing to participate in and what you are not. What opens the experience of giving is getting clear on what your limits are for this interaction and owning them.

- **Notice:** Noticing your limits is like noticing your desires. You already know, at some level, what they are; give yourself time to let the knowing bubble up. The question to ask yourself is not *Why aren't I okay giving this?* The question to ask yourself is *What is the thing that I can give with a full heart?* Again, commit to waiting for your inner knowing.

- **Trust:** Trust that it's accurate. Don't try to second guess yourself or push yourself. A sign that you have noticed and owned your limits is that you breathe a sigh of relief because there is no more need to be on guard.

- **Value:** Know that your limits matter. Take them seriously, and don't discard them as trivial. Don't say to yourself, *I know what my limits are, but they don't matter. What they want is more important.*

- **Communicate:** Communicate your limits by responding yes or no, or "I'm willing to do this but not this other thing," or "Yes, only to here."

The hard part is not the doing but taking the time to notice what is already true. There can be a relief in telling the truth—both in speaking your desires and speaking your limits. Not just being allowed to tell the truth (having the truth welcomed and wanted) but being able to tell the truth (getting the words out of your mouth). In daily life, it can be hard to ask for what you want or to set a limit; sometimes you need superhuman determination. In the labs, we make it easier. The pauses are built in; you just have to follow the instructions.

Slow down and give it all the time it deserves. Finally the doing is a kind of happy bonus, a powerful and liberating bonus. Like everything here, this is learned gradually. First you commit to giving it the time it deserves, and it's probably awkward. Then it becomes natural. Then it becomes fun; you play with it. Then you take these same skills into your life, and that is where it's the most impactful.

Example: Not giving up

I once worked with a client who was struggling with knowing what she wanted. I could have made a suggestion, and she could probably have made the best of it—but she would have missed the opportunity to notice and, more importantly, to develop her ability to notice.

Me: How would you like me to touch you for a few minutes?

Kira (pausing, unsure. Moisture comes to her eyes as she looks into mine. She takes a slow, deep breath.): I have no idea.

Me: That's okay, we have plenty of time.

Kira: No one has ever asked me that before. It's hard. Why would it be so hard?

Me: I don't know. Maybe because no one has ever asked. (pause)

Kira: Well, what do you suggest?

Me: This is for you. You get to choose. Don't worry, it will come.

Kira: Well, I always like to have my head scratched.

Me: That's nice, but this is for right now. Is that what you would like right now?

Kira: Well, actually, no. I think I'd like to have my shoulders rubbed.

Me: Do you want to think about it a little longer?

Kira: No, that's what I want.

Me: Great. Would you like that firm or soft, or how?

Kira: Whatever you are okay with.

Me: I'm okay with anything. This turn is for you. You get to have it the way you want it.

Kira: My God, why is this so hard? (tears again) I just don't know! Am I supposed to know?

Me: Sometimes it takes a while. Your body knows what it wants. If you sit a while, it will tell you. (pause)

Kira: Okay. I have it. Will you rub my back and shoulders, deep like a massage?

Me: You bet. Would you like to sit up or lie down?

Kira: I'd like to lie down...God, I can't believe that was so hard... Are you sure this is okay with you? You don't mind doing this?

Me: No, I don't mind. I'm glad to do it. How's this pressure?

Kira: Perfect. It feels great. Thank you so much.

Me: You're welcome.

PRINCIPLE:
GENDER AND THE QUADRANTS

People sometimes ask if the quadrants are reflective of gender. The quadrants themselves are not gendered, but your belief about your gender can influence how you experience the quadrants, including making it more challenging to find any particular quadrant. But what is gender anyway? Gender is a social construct with a fluid definition. Ideas about it are evolving so rapidly that they are likely to change before this book goes to print. There is *much* more to say about gender than I do here. See the resources on the website.

Still, I'd like to define gender here as best I can at this time. In this book, I use the bi-modal model of gender in which gender is a spectrum with two main modes, men and women, and many people who fall somewhere else. This is different than what most people think of gender, which tends to be binary, that is, two opposite poles. We are talking about a spectrum. This is true both biologically and socially. As a biologist, I recognize that your reproductive system has a particular configuration relative to its role in perpetuating the species. This is usually thought of as what sex you are. Gender is different. Gender is constructed by humans to help us categorize each other—for useful reasons and less-than-useful reasons. This description doesn't include the fact that a great many people have reproductive organs that are ambiguous or in between. To be clear, this variation is a normal, natural aspect of biological diversity.

What do sex and gender have to do with each other? When we are born, the adults in the room have a look at our genitals and, based on what they see, make some decisions about us. If we have one configuration, we are raised with a certain set of expectations and permissions. Certain qualities are valued and others neglected or shamed. If we are born with another genital configuration, we are raised with a different set of expectations and permissions. Assertiveness, playfulness, nurturing abilities, intelligence, creativity, language and math abilities, and access to feelings of anger, fear, grief, and joy—all these and more are assigned to one group and punished in the other, and if we stray from these expectations, we may be punished or ostracized. Also on this list is how we are supposed to experience and express our sexuality, which includes what we are supposed to want or not want, and what we are supposed to do or not do, or have done to us or not have done to us—which is to say, how we are supposed to experience the quadrants.

There's more. When we were kids, they told us that everyone was either a boy or a girl, girls would grow up to be women, and boys would grow up to be men. For a great many people, that is not true. There are many people whose genes do not fit tidily into XX or XY or whose genital configuration does not fit easily into one category or the other. There are many people whose gender does not fit what they were assigned at birth and a great many people who don't fit the traditional ideas of what a man or woman is "supposed to be" and are more fluid between the two or combine the two. There are many people who, for good reason, skip the whole if-you're-a-man-you-are-this-way-and-if-you're-a-woman-you-are-that-way question and decline to side in either camp.

Both our genetic makeup and physical anatomy are far more variable than we have been told, and the spectrum of possibility for how we experience our gender is far more variable than we might have dreamed, and it's growing.

In common usage, we often conflate the words sex and gender. When someone asks what gender you are, they may mean, "Which configuration does your reproductive system conform to?" or they might mean, "Which particular set of assumptions, ways of thinking, moving, dressing, emoting, relating, working, and playing do you fit into (or have you been subjected to all your life)?" Most likely, they assume those two concepts mean the same thing. (While we're at it, who cares what configuration your reproductive system conforms to, and what business is it of theirs?) This is where the quadrants fit in. They have nothing to do with what reproductive organs you have *or* what gender you are.

Except this: the pressures you have been subjected to all your life (usually based on your genital configuration) have a large influence (but not the only influence) on what makes any given quadrant challenging. Your assumptions about how women or men are supposed to do or not do that quadrant can make it harder to find. It helps to know what those influences are, if for no other reason than to know you're not the only one having trouble with it. In the labs and in the Wheel section of the book, we'll look at how the gender conditioning you were subjected to may influence your experience in that quadrant.

Though the quadrants themselves are not gendered, they can be a good mirror for you. If you hear yourself say, "As a (man, woman, transgender person, genderqueer, etc.), I can't do this quadrant," this is not about the quadrant. It's about your beliefs about your gender. For example, people sometimes say the Taking Quadrant is the masculine one. This is not about the Taking Quadrant; it's a reflection of what you think "masculine" means. Why do you believe that?

There's another problem. As soon as you assign a gender to a quadrant (or to anything else), you have changed your relationship to it. It is now something you are supposed to do or not do, feel or not feel.

Then there is the concept of intersectionality, which refers to the fact that our gender intersects with our race, class, orientation, education, ablebodiedness, and more, so we have multiple factors and kinds of conditioning weighing on each of us. Again, see the online resources.

How I talk about gender in this book. There is nothing I can say about gender that would apply to everyone. When talking about the quadrants, I describe the themes for women and for men as I have seen them show up time and again, based on working mostly with cisgender people. (Cisgender refers to people who experience their gender as the one they were assigned at birth. It means not-transgender.) When working with gender fluid, nonbinary and transgender folks, I have seen fewer repeated themes. I imagine that is because their experiences vary widely depending on which gender they were raised and how, how they have had to adapt, and what their gender journey means to them. Trans and nonbinary folk, it's not that I don't see you. It's that I don't (as yet) see the strong repeating themes that I have seen in cisgender folks.

So start over. Every quadrant is inherent to every human, and every human needs access to all four quadrants. Many factors influence what is challenging, confusing, or liberating about each quadrant. One of those is how you experience your gender, and because it is a factor, I talk about it in each quadrant.

INTRODUCTION TO THE LESSONS

In the three lessons that follow, you "find" the quadrants. It's a little like feeling around inside yourself until you bump into them: *Oh, here it is!* It often starts out a bit odd, maybe awkward, and then something shifts. Come back to each one a dozen times or so. Each time you'll find something new, and the quadrants will get clearer. It's a gradual process that gets richer as you come back to it.

- Lesson 1 is Waking Up the Hands. This one changes how you experience your hands. It connects the neural circuits that the next two are built on. The click can take anywhere from a few minutes to a few weeks. It involves only you, so you can do it alone or together.

The next two build on that and introduce the dynamics:

- Lesson 2 opens up the Take-Allow dynamic.
- Lesson 3 opens up the Serve-Accept dynamic.

These two lessons (and all the labs) you do with a partner or practice buddy. The lessons involve touching each other's hands (and up to the elbow if you like).

You can do Take-Allow a few times and then switch to Serve-Accept, or you can alternate them, with Take-Allow one day and Serve-Accept the next time. Either way is fine. Just be sure you know which one you are doing, because the point is to be able to tell the difference between them.

Once you have found the quadrants and let them settle a bit, then in the labs you explore them as deeply as you like, and you can include more of the body than just the hands.

CHAPTER 7

Lesson 1:
Waking Up the Hands

Often the hands will solve a mystery that the intellect has struggled with in vain.
—Carl Jung

Your hands are made to take in information, and they are very good at it. You squeeze the avocado to see if it's ripe. You reach into your bag and feel around for the keys. My friend the motorcycle racer tells me he feels the texture of the road through the handlebars. We take in that information constantly. Wonderfully, we can enjoy that data as it comes in, so the sensation becomes pleasurable. We are born with this ability but tend to unlearn it as we grow up. This lesson reclaims it.

This lesson changes how you experience your hands. Your hands stop working and become a source of pleasure *to you*. This is pleasure that is not about anything or anyone, and this ability is the foundation for everything we're doing here. As we'll be seeing, it also turns out to be the foundation for sensuality, generosity, and integrity.

Finding the click takes time, from thirty seconds to thirty minutes to a few weeks. It doesn't matter how long it takes; give it all the time it needs. What we are waking up is the connection between the sensory nerves in the hands and the pleasure centers in the brain. This nerve cell starts talking to this brain cell. Something shifts, and it feels different. This connection is the highway we're going to be driving on, so we have to build it first. Later, you'll come back and drive on this highway when touching each other.

The lesson is extremely simple, and the hardest part may be taking it seriously enough to do it. There are a few small details that make it harder to find, so the instructions are exact and thorough. For some, it's fairly straightforward. For many, it's a little odd, and for some, it's difficult.

THE PARAMETERS

- Do this one alone or side by side with your partner/practice buddy. Either is fine.

- You will need twenty minutes or so, more if you can. It often takes a few times through it.

- One option is to play with it five minutes a day for three to six weeks. Some people take it up as a daily meditation.

THE STEPS

1) Lean back against your chair or the wall and get comfortable, with both shoulders equally in contact with whatever you are leaning against. Don't turn to the side, lean forward, or sit up straight. The idea is to disengage the muscles of the trunk and put yourself into the position you would be in if you were lounging about on the beach. Bring to your lap a pillow or whatever will let your arms rest.

2) Pick up whatever is next to you, rest it in your lap, and use your hands to feel it. This book, a couch cushion, leaf, shell, water bottle, a ballpoint pen. Inanimate only, no pets or people. The first thing that happens is immediate and automatic: you identify it. *Yep, it's a pen.* This is usually as far as we go.

3) Now stay there. Now that you know what it is, stay there and explore it. What do you notice about it? Feel for the weight, shape, and texture. The little bump in the corner, the ridges around the edge, the fuzzy surface.

Slow down. The slower you go, the more you notice. It's often easier to *see* what your hand is doing than it is to *feel* what your hand is doing, so I have people look at their hands and then slow them down by half.

Usually I have to say it again a couple minutes later because they have resumed their "normal" speed.

Let yourself be curious. *What does this thing feel like anyway?* Your mind will wander. Not a problem; that's its job. When it does, bring it back to your hands. Most people have to remind themselves a few times. Your eyes can be open or closed as you like.

4) Stay there longer, and a couple things begin to happen. First, your attention shifts. You started out focused on the object. Now you notice that what is more interesting is the sensation in your hands. The pen recedes; the sensations come forward.

Then you may notice that it is pleasant. Now you start to move your hands in ways that feel good. The pen is no longer a pen; it's something you use to please your hands. When that happens, there is an inner shift. Your body responds, your shoulders soften, and your breathing slows. *Aaahhhh.* You become quiet and absorbed. Your voice, if you speak at all, softens, slows, and deepens. The body response is visible to someone watching. Different people will have different things that feel pleasant to them. It may be quite different than what your partner likes.

This is the click. It is a change in your inner experience. Sensation comes forward, it feels pleasant, and your body responds. Time slows, there is nowhere to go, and the world "falls away." It can sometimes feel exquisitely pleasurable (which can make you wonder about yourself).

People often describe this as sinking into the experience. You can't make it happen; you let it happen. And it will happen if you slow down, hang out with it long enough, and let yourself be curious. The sensory data arriving in your brain is the same as it was; there are no new nerves in your hands. What changes is that as you attend to the sensation, new brain circuits light up, and it feels different. The signpost is that you have no interest in leaving. If you are eager to move on, you have not yet arrived.

Then, often, but not always, there will be an emotional response. It may be mild, vague, or acute. You may feel confused, confounded, self-conscious, guilty, delighted, playful, or full of wonder. Grief is fairly common, as is a big sense of relief or gratitude.

How long does this take? There is a wide range. I have taught this to over a thousand people, and the number for whom it was immediate and obvious was six. The number for whom it was extremely difficult, with challenging emotions or just elusive for a long time, was twenty or so. For everyone else: five, ten, twenty, or thirty minutes. Quite a few had to return to it several times before it clicked. Everyone found that returning to it, even a few minutes later, made it more clear and solid. If you find this particularly elusive or emotionally challenging, you are not alone. Some examples follow in a few pages.

5) Stay as long as you like. Hang out with your object as long as you like, or pick up a different object. In my workshops, I have my students feel three or four different objects, and they seem to fall in love with each of them. What do you notice about yourself?

A variation. Experiment with holding still. Sensation coming in from the hand activates one area of the brain, and the nerves that control the muscles of the hands arise from another area. When you activate both areas at the same time, sometimes the movement area will drown out the sensory area, so you can't feel much. It's fairly common. Moving more slowly helps, but sometimes it's not enough; sometimes you have to stop the hand movement altogether.

To do this, place one hand on the pillow on your lap, palm up. Look to see that it is relaxed. A relaxed hand will rest on the pillow, not hold itself in the air, and the fingers will be softly rounded, not straight out. With the other hand, pick up your object, and drag it across the "receiving" hand. Tickle, caress, scratch, poke, or whatever feels good.

6) Then come back to it. Return ten to twelve times over the next few weeks, or use the five-minutes-a-day option.

SOME REACTIONS

In chapter 1, in the river stone story, I gave a few examples of what people have said. Here are a few more.

"Oh my God, that feels great! And it's nothing. Nothing!"

"This feels great. So why do I feel so sad?"

"I have a whole new relationship with my water bottle!"

"The aha was resting my hand and not doing anything. All of it was magnified."

"I can feel it, I know what my hands are doing, and I know in my head that it feels good, but it feels like my hands are not really participating. They're just tools, like picking up a pair of pliers. In fact, I can generalize that to my whole body. It's a really deep sadness."

TROUBLESHOOTING

If the whole thing is a complete mystery, it feels like nothing is happening at all, and you can't figure out what the heck I am talking about, you are not alone. Neither are you broken. You're just out of practice. This is common and why I give you such detailed steps on how to find it. Those nerve cells have not talked to those brain cells in a long time, and they may not be comfortable doing so.

A few things will reliably block the reconnection: engaging the muscles required to lean forward or hold your item in the air (as opposed to sitting it on your lap) and engaging the hand muscles by moving too much or too fast. All of those are covered in the instructions. If it continues to be elusive after twenty minutes or so, go back, read the first step, and look at yourself, visually, to see if you are doing it. It's amazing how many people will say, "Yes, I'm comfortable." When I have them look, they notice they are turned or hunched over or holding their item a foot off their lap. When we correct that, they say, "Oh, this is different, isn't it?"

The biggest factor by far is slowing down. Look at your hands, and slow them down by half. Do that again twenty seconds later, because you will likely have sped up again. Lean back, feel the thing, move slowly, and give it some time. That's it. I have had many for whom it was elusive and a good number for whom it took some real support and coaching with the same things I give you in this lesson.

SOME COMMON QUESTIONS

"I don't feel anything." Yes, you do. If you know what the object is, sensory data is coming in. That is what you feel. That counts. What you might mean is "I don't feel much detail." This is not uncommon. You may be out of practice in noticing. Sometimes it helps to say what you notice, step by step: "I feel this bump over here. I feel this smooth place here. I notice the curve here."

Or you might mean, "I don't feel anything special." You may not feel anything earthshaking. This is an ordinary experience; you don't usually notice the sensations, and now you do. Even a small shift counts: "Oh yeah, that does feel kinda good now." Experiment until you find one thing that feels pleasant, even a little, and then hang out there and enjoy it. (See the example "Sharp Stick.")

"It's not that interesting." The key here is bringing your attention to your sensation. There is a wide range in ability to do this. Often people will say, "Yeah, it feels okay but not that interesting." When I have them bring their attention fully into their hands—all of it—it becomes compelling. "Oh, yeah, now I really feel it. Wow!"

"I can't make my mind stop chattering." It's a common idea that if we could somehow turn off our minds, we would be able to pay better attention to our skin. It's the other way around. You don't have to turn your mind to the *Off* setting; turn your skin to the *On* setting. Then the mind will settle itself. You bring your attention to your skin, your mind wanders, you bring your attention back to your skin, the mind wanders again, and you bring it back again. For most people, it takes quite a few reminders.

"When do we get to the good stuff?" This question is a sure sign that the click has not yet happened. When your hands find their pleasure, there is nowhere to go, because you are already there.

This question usually means, "When do we get to something sexy?" You are accessing a physiological state of relaxed pleasure. The ability to access that state is natural, though many of us have to relearn it. Until you learn it here, your ability to find it anywhere else is extremely limited. If you can't feel your hands now, what makes you think you will be able to feel them some other time?

Some reassurance may be in order. You are not likely to spend all your time feeling up objects around your house. (Then again, after this experiment, you might.) The shift you are finding here is the one that makes everything else possible: clearing up receiving and giving, the four quadrants, and all the rest.

Some encouragement: the harder it is to find, the deeper it goes and the more significant the changes for you—and quite often, the more tenderheartedness or sadness that will arise with it. There is no shame in taking time. It means that the neural circuit is out of practice, and there was a good reason for shutting it down in the first place. If it is extremely elusive, another possibility is neurological complications. If you have those, it's likely you already know.

THE FEELINGS THAT ARISE

A wide range of feelings arise as you wake up your hands, and these may be mild or acute. You may feel confused, self-conscious, guilty, ashamed, or vaguely uncomfortable. You may feel delighted, playful, or silly. Grief and a big sense of relief and gratitude are common. Not to worry. There is nothing wrong with you. Feelings arise because of the connections between the pleasure centers and the emotional centers in the brain. (We'll come back to this shortly.)

If having an emotional response is not acceptable to you, you will try to shut it off. You might stay in an analytical mode or fidget with your item instead of feel it. This can happen at the earliest glimpse that pleasure may be peeking over the horizon. *Uh oh, feelings are about to happen!* I have seen many people stop and sit with their hands still.

If having an emotional response is acceptable to you, you know how to let it be there. You don't worry what it means about you. We don't always know or need to know. You might have an insight about your relationship to pleasure; that's common. Feelings have something to tell us, and they pass. The important thing is that there is nothing to fix. Be kind to yourself. Never push yourself on this. Take a small taste, and when you feel like that's enough for now, stop and come back later. (See the example "Overwhelming.")

Your skin will do the work for you, as we talked about in chapter 6. You don't have to figure it out. You don't have to dissect your issues or resolve your past. All you need is to be curious and bring your attention to the sensation—then do that again and then again. All the rest of it happens by itself.

A FEW EXAMPLES

Stopping. I have seen many people stop moving their hands and perhaps put the object down—sometimes right away, sometimes after taking in the information but before it shifts into pleasure, and sometimes after registering a little pleasure but before sinking into it. They might say, "Oh, right, I get it. That's what you are talking about," and then put it down. One person said, "I hit this point where I felt like that should be enough. Like that's all the pleasure I get, and you know, I think I do that in the rest of my life too."

Deep tissue massage. Sheila was a massage therapist and sex educator. She picked up that couch cushion and attacked it as if performing deep tissue massage: kneading, pushing, and digging in. I had never seen anyone work it that hard. Many reminders to slow down helped, but in a few seconds, she'd be back at it again. It was not until she was able to stop her hand movement entirely that she could feel much of anything. What also helped her was having me stroke her palms while she remained non-active. There her hands learned to experience pleasure, and eventually she came back to the cushion and was able to slowly take in both information and pleasure while beginning to use her hands. The whole thing took over an hour. This is one of the sessions early on that showed me that the impulse to work can be so ingrained that the hands don't know how to do anything else. The only way around that was to stop the hand movement altogether.

A sharp stick. I met with Bryce for a one-time consult while visiting another city. We walked through the park to talk. When we started this lesson, he had an extremely hard time bringing his focus to his hands; it was just not going anywhere. At one point, I picked up a strong twig from the ground and offered it to him. We found that the only thing that registered was using the twig to press hard into his palms and feet, and I mean *hard*, and that felt great! Soft sensation was not going to do it for him, and I referred him to a colleague who could provide him intense sensations.

Intuitive. Kally was a body worker and intuitive healer. She picked up the object, and when I said, "See what information you can take in about the object," meaning feel it for its shape, she took her most familiar route and tried to intuit what she could. She began to say what came to mind about the energy and the history of it. I sent her back to the tangible, her skin. "Great, but set that aside for now. Just feel the actual tangible object. That's it." She settled into that and became melancholy. "Oh yeah, this is different. This is not easy."

Overwhelming. Mark was a gentle soul, kind and soft spoken. He and his wife of thirty years were trying to find their way back to enjoying sex. His feelings arose immediately and very tenderheartedly. He kept coming to tears, fighting them back, and trying it again. He expressed feeling sad, then scared, then overwhelmed, and more tears fell. I reminded him that we would stop when he wanted. He said he wanted to keep going a little more. After a few minutes, he said, "I think I've had enough for now. It's strange. I get afraid I am too selfish. It makes no sense. It's just a shell."

TOO ADVANCED FOR THIS

Because I work in the field of sexuality, I have had many people with extensive sexual experience, including professionals, assume that this exercise is too elementary. I have not found that to be the case. This experience is a different skill and not about sex at all. This skill is taking in tactile data and allowing yourself to experience that as pleasure that has nothing to do with anything. Surprisingly, this can be more challenging than the most complex sexual acts.

If you are eager to get to the "real stuff," it's because you are not showing up here, and if you are not showing up here, you are probably not showing up anywhere else. If you actually are "advanced," you are friendly with your skin and comfortable with pleasure in many forms. This lesson will be a welcome respite, and you will luxuriate in it as deeply as you have time for. If you are advanced, you are acquainted with your emotions and not afraid to uncover some surprises. Take this time to bliss out for no reason. Can you?

SIGNS YOU ARE READY TO GRADUATE

The cure for boredom is curiosity. There is no cure for curiosity.
—Dorothy Parker

You take in tactile data with your hands and enjoy it as it is without having to prop it up by attaching a meaning to it. Your hands like to feel things, and you let them; it feels natural and normal. You are not eager to move on. Occasionally you notice something in your hands, and you take a moment to enjoy it. Your hands have changed from implements to a source of pleasure. You are at least more comfortable with a state of relaxed pleasure; it's no longer weird or intimidating. This comfort will continue to deepen over a lifetime. For now, it's at least a little easier and feels more natural.

Once in a while, say in the shower, when sunshine hits your face, or you put your hands in hot dishwater, you notice it feels pleasant. You take a breath, bringing all your attention here for those few seconds, and then go on about your day.

THE KEY ELEMENTS

In pondering what made this work, I have come to see a few key elements without which it would not be what it is.

1) It's not *about* anything. It's impossible to separate the experience of touching another person from the meaning we attach to it. What the person means to you, how cute you think they are, what you want to convey, and on and on. In this lesson, there is no other person, so all that meaning is absent. Feeling your object is not about love or sex. It's not giving or receiving. No one is doing anything to you. There is nothing even to use the object for. There is no meaning at all—just you and your brain cells. This experience reveals your relationship to pleasure itself or, even more fundamentally, to sensation. Is it okay to feel it? Is it okay to enjoy it? What happens when you do?

2) You take action. First, *you* take the action as opposed to someone else. You can't use someone else's action as an excuse for how good it feels or doesn't. Second, you *take action*. It is your action that creates the pleasure, not your wishful thinking. It's not an accident or a lucky by-product of something else. It's not waiting for something pleasurable to drift your way. Third, you take action *toward pleasure* instead of away from pleasure.

3) Waiting for a change in body state. This is the click that I describe in the instructions (hands moving slowly, becoming quiet and absorbed, body softening and settling in). In chapter 4, I talked about the relaxed and excited states of pleasure and that a relaxed state of pleasure is like base camp. When I started playing with this exercise, I thought people needed a few seconds to remember what that state felt like, but not everyone remembered it. Many people had to relearn how to find it. I learned to watch for the signs of the body relaxing and not skip over it. I learned that if you can't access a state of relaxed pleasure here, it's not going to miraculously show up when things are more complex and happening faster.

Some people can access a state of relaxed pleasure easily, and others cannot. For some people, it's a matter of remembering, perhaps deepening. For many, it's elusive and takes some time and support. For some, it's extremely difficult and takes lots of time and support. It is very much worth it.

4) When your hands get it, you get it. I'm not sure why this is. I imagine it has to do with a couple of things. First, they contain so many nerve endings, more nerve endings per area than anywhere on the body other than the lips and genitals. Because of that, there is a large area of the brain dedicated to processing the incoming data and presumably many connections to other brain areas. Second, hands are symbolic. Imagine the gesture of holding your hands out, cupped in front of you, to receive a treasured gift. They seem to have a direct line to the heart, which is to say they are rich in connections to the emotional centers. We are more likely to have an emotional response with hands than a similar exercise with the elbows. Many people who love receiving a massage, even a hand massage, can have trouble finding this, and when they do, there are aha moments and moist eyes.

WHY SO MANY FEELINGS?

Sometimes people are surprised at the feelings that arise and wonder what the heck is going on. I want to offer some thoughts on why they show up. What's going on?

We are born with the innate capacity to enjoy sensation: the feel of velvet in our hands, sunshine on our skin, the sounds of birdsong, the smell of fresh earth, the rush of water when we dive naked into a river. This is part of being a mammal. However, we learn to shut that down for lots of reasons. It's unlikely you were ever punished for feeling up a shell or a pen; we're dealing with something more fundamental. Many of us live in a puritanical society in which pleasure is bad, sensation is bad, and it's basically suspect to have a body at all, much less to enjoy it. This varies by our situation, family, culture, etc., but we are all steeped in it to some degree, and that causes problems.

On the one hand, we have this innate drive to explore and enjoy, and on the other, this pressure to stuff it down, and they come into conflict. We create a mess of convoluted excuses that let us experience a little pleasure: *It's okay to have some pleasure if it's accidental, if it just sort of happens,* or *It's okay if it happens while I'm giving to someone else,* or *It's okay if it happens when someone else wants to give it to me.* It's okay if blah, blah, blah. In this lesson, there are no excuses. There is no one else involved, and you are taking action toward your own pleasure. This can be unsettling.

Still, attending to sensation and experiencing it as pleasurable is a fundamental neural circuit. It's one of the gears at the center of our human mechanism. When you activate it—get the gear turning—all the feelings that caused you to shut it down the first time come right back up—which is generally why you haven't gone there before now. The more pleasure you experience, the more shame arises with it.

If you feel confusion, self-doubt, sadness, shame, or guilt, and you think, *This makes no sense! What on earth would I feel guilty about,* this is what is happening. You are tapping into fundamental circuits that were built during early experiences. You are on the gear at the center of the whole thing.

You are not alone, and you are not broken. We all have this to some degree. There is no need to work at it. You get to choose how and when to experiment with your hands, and you get to choose when it's enough, when to set it aside for later, and when to pick it up again.

PRINCIPLE:
INFLOW AND OUTFLOW

Here is an image many people find helpful. When touching someone, we tend to think about what is flowing "out" our hands, which is usually our intention to give. If you think of it as a river, you can imagine it flows down your arms and out your hands.

Here you are learning to notice what flows "into" your hands. You take in information, which you might experience as pleasant. Again like a river, you can imagine that the information and the pleasure flow into your hands, up your arms, and into you. Later, in the Taking Quadrant, you take in (receive) a gift, and that, too, flows up the river and into you.

In the hands (and in life), effective outflow requires an inflow that is accurate. That is, you need accurate data. In order to hold your toothbrush, you have to feel it in your hand. If you are going to perform surgery, you need to know what is where. If you are going to make community decisions about poverty, you need accurate information about the current state of affairs. If you are going to caress your lover, you need to be able to feel their skin under your hands. What we will be finding is that the secret to improving the quality of your touch is not the outflow—it's opening the inflow.

CHAPTER 8

Lesson 2:
Finding the Take-Allow
Dynamic

This lesson opens the Take-Allow dynamic and lets you experience both the Taking and Allowing Quadrants. One of you will be in the Taking role and the other in the Allowing role, and then you'll switch. The Taking partner will be feeling the Allower's hands (if the Allower is willing), much like you felt the object in Waking Up the Hands.

The Taking Quadrant. When we touch another person without trying to give to them, an entirely new experience of touch becomes possible, including the awareness that instead of giving a gift, we are receiving one (the gift of access to them). Taking is the hardest quadrant to learn for most people. It's inherently vulnerable, tends to be unfamiliar, and can tap into our fears about selfishness. Taking is also the quadrant that opens up sensuality, confidence, and integrity.

In order for Taking to click, two conditions have to be in place: 1) hands—you have to be able to attend to the sensation in your hands and experience it, to some degree, as pleasurable. This is what happens in Waking Up the Hands, and without this pathway open, Taking cannot happen, and 2) permission—you must ask permission from the person whose hand you intend to feel. First, without permission, Take-Allow doesn't exist. Second, it reassures you that you are not stealing and lets you relax. This is verbal: you ask, "May I feel your hand?" and they say, "Yes, you may."

The Allowing Quadrant. While the Taking Quadrant is challenging for almost everyone, the Allowing Quadrant is all over the map. It can be easy and natural, a little odd, or seriously challenging. You may think the point of Allowing is to be okay with anything. It is not. The point of Allowing is to slow down enough to notice what you are in fact happy to give and to give only that. You have a choice about whether and how you are touched, and taking full responsibility for your limits—"This far and no farther"—is what allows you to enjoy Allowing.

I give you the instructions first, and then we'll come back and talk about each quadrant, Taking and Allowing.

It usually takes a few times through for the quadrants to click. In workshops, it is often the third or fourth time that people say, "Oh, I get it!"

THE PARAMETERS

- You'll need twenty minutes or more.
- You will be exploring each other's hands; it's okay to include up to the elbows but not beyond. (If you are not willing to allow your hand to be felt, you can offer your feet, arms, lower leg, or some other nonsexy body area.)
- Play with this a few times, and then read this chapter again. You'll see things you missed the first time through.
- Once it clicks, come back to it at least a dozen more times so that it becomes natural to you.

THE STEPS

 Create your container.

Agree on how much time you are going to spend, and divide it in half so you each get a turn. The first time or two, it's great if you can leave the turns open ended so you can play until it clicks and then switch roles. You can also play with shorter turns and go back and forth a few times.

 ## 2. Make an agreement.

The Taking partner:

1. Ask, "May I feel your hand?"
   - Use those exact words. Don't say, "Would you like me to touch your hand?" or "May I give you a hand massage?"
   - If you would like to include up to the elbows, ask for that as well. "May I include up to your elbows?"
2. Wait for their answer. Don't start until you hear their yes.

Why so particular about the words? The experience you are looking for is counterintuitive, so the words make a difference. The words we use not only reveal what we *are* thinking, they set us up for what we *can* think and therefore what we can experience. What you are asking for is permission to feel their hand. It is specific. If you use the words caress, massage, or even touch, which for most people means "give," you set yourself up to do those things, and it can be difficult to change gears and feel their hand instead.

The Allowing partner:

1. Pause and consider whether this is a gift you can give with a full heart.
   - Don't say yes on the outside until you hear it on the inside. If you hear an inner *Uh, yeah, I guess so,* that's not it. Wait for an inner resounding *Yes!* and then say, "Yes, you may."
   - Use those exact words. Don't say, "Yes, I would like that," or "Yes, please."
2. Set any limits you have: "I'm ticklish inside my arms; don't go there," or "Right hand only, not the left."

3. If it is not a gift you can give, say, "No, not today," and come back to it another day.

 ### 3. Sit side by side, lean back, and get comfortable.

First, the Taking partner:

1. Lean back as you did in Waking Up the Hands.
   - Have both shoulders equally in contact with whatever you are leaning against, not with one shoulder in contact and the other shoulder forward.
   - Do not turn toward your Allower.

2. Place a cushion on your lap, and bring the hand you are going to feel to the center of your lap, not toward the side.

3. Look at it visually to see that it's in the center.

Why so particular about the position? How you position your body is similar to using words. It reveals what you think you are doing, and it sets you up to have a certain experience. Set yourself up one way, and you experience yourself as working and giving. Set yourself up another way, and it opens up the experience of receiving. I have seen many Takers hold their Allower's hand over toward the side—but never once to the side away from the Allower, always on the side toward the Allower. They are subtly trying to accommodate their Allower. (See the example "Across the Room.")

The principle is: don't adapt yourself to your Allower. Let them adapt themselves to you. It can be hard to notice what you are doing, but if you were standing across the room watching yourself you'd see it. It's quite visible. It's easy to see when someone is facing forward and when they are turned a little to the side. Sometimes when I remind people to get comfortable, they will say, "Oh, I can make this work." Of course you can, but why would you? I tell them, "We're not going for workable; we're going for fabulous." Very often they suddenly get it.

Then the Allowing partner:

- Nothing special about your position; just get as comfy as you like. You may have to move around a bit.

- Sometimes I see Allowers holding their arm up, elbow stiff, as if trying to help. Ask yourself why you are doing that. Do you think your hand itself is not enough of a gift, that you have to be helpful too?

4. **Explore and experiment: feel your partner's hand.**

The Taking partner:

1. Respect any limits your partner has set, and then feel their hand. That's it.

    - Rest your hands in your lap instead of holding them up in the air.

    - Approach it with curiosity, just as you did when feeling the object. Locate the bones and joints. Fold it up, stretch it out, turn it over. Don't caress it, don't massage it, just feel the thing. Pretend you are a future hand surgeon and ask yourself, *How is this thing put together?*

    - Bring your attention to your hands—all of it. People often say, "Well, that's nice, and it's getting a little boring now." Invariably, when I tell them, "No worries; now bring ALL your attention to your hands, and see what happens," they say, "Oh yeah, that changes it. That is fantastic!"

2. Slow down by half. A minute later after you have sped up again, slow down by half again.

    - If your mind wanders, it's not a problem; that's its job. When it does, gently bring it back to your sensations. When it wanders again, bring it back again.

    - Remind yourself it's for you. Ask yourself a few times, *Who is this for?* Keep asking until it clicks that it's for you.

Sometimes I have the Taker hold the object on the pillow next to their Allower's hand. Feel the object so your hands remember what it's like to explore something without giving; take that idea with you and explore the hand, and go back and forth a few times between the object and their hand.

After some time, your hands will settle into their own enjoyment. The shift may be sudden or gradual—thirty seconds or thirty minutes, it doesn't matter. You'll have a similar melting into it as you did with Waking Up the Hands. Your body and breath soften, sensation takes center stage, the world melts away. It's likely your hands will change the way they are moving as well. They will slow down, become more sensual, maybe playful or tender.

At some point, you will notice that there is a gift being given, but it is not moving *from you to them*. It is moving *from them to you.* The gift you are receiving is being allowed to explore. To receive this gift, you have to stop giving. This is not partly for you, it is 100 percent for you.

That is the click: *This really is for me!* and you stop trying to give. When that shifts, you are likely to have some feelings arise. You may feel self-conscious, tenderhearted, relieved, or just odd. Moist eyes are common.

The Allowing partner:

- Your role is usually easy, and you have only one thing to do: take care of yourself.
- Change anything as needed. "Wait, I need to move over this way," or "I changed my mind. Please stay on my hand, not my forearm."
- Set aside what you prefer. The touch may feel great, or it may feel boring. It doesn't matter, as it's not about you.
- Stop if it feels awful. "This is uncomfortable, I need to stop," or "Ouch! Please don't move my hand that way."
- Enjoy it as much as you like.

The click for you is that you notice that the direction of the gift reverses. It is moving from you to the Taker, not from the Taker to you. It's clear you have a choice about it, and because you have a choice, you can relax.

5. Thank you/You're welcome.

Look each other in the eyes and say:

Taking partner (who received the gift):

- Say "Thank you." Nothing more.

Allowing partner (who gave the gift):
- Say "You're welcome." Nothing more. If it felt great, you may have the impulse to say, "Oh, but thank you." Don't. You gave the gift. Just say "You're welcome."

Why so strict? Saying thank you and you're welcome confirms what you just did. One or both partners may be a little confused about whether they gave or received. If you both say thank you, now you're more confused. It is sometimes at this point that the Taker realizes it was supposed to be for them. "Oh, that was for me, wasn't it?"

6. Switch roles.

7. Talk about what you noticed.

Talk about what you noticed *about yourself* (not about your partner). This might include sensations you felt or thoughts or emotions that arose. What was challenging? What was a relief?

8. Close your dedicated time.

This is where you can thank each other if you like.

9. Come back to it.

Return here ten to twenty times over the next few weeks.

NOTES ON THE TAKING QUADRANT

If the experience of the Taking Quadrant was easy and obvious, you wouldn't need this section. In fact, you wouldn't need this book. This quadrant takes a little playing around with it for it to land. It is the opposite of what most people think of as normal and is challenging for almost everyone. It can feel odd, uncomfortable, or seriously daunting. Still, it recovers a natural ability, so there is eventually a sense of relief and gratitude, a kind of "coming home."

The Taking Quadrant is receiving a gift, and to receive this gift you have to stop giving (temporarily). For most of us, when we start touching, we immediately give, or try to, but it is exactly this habit of trying to give that will throw you off track. The problem is that it feels so normal to try to give that it's difficult to experience it any other way—until you do.

What you find in Taking is that in order to touch someone, you don't need to give to them. What you do need is their permission, and regaining this option is liberating and profoundly satisfying. The instructions in this lesson set you up to experience that.

About the word. The word "taking" has some negative connotations. It could imply stealing or grabbing everything you can, but the Taking Quadrant is not that. It is receiving a gift freely given to you by the generosity of your partner or practice buddy. The gift is that you are allowed to touch them the way you want (within their limits). This is a real and significant gift.

This example might help. If I give you some pears from the tree in my yard, I can bring them to you in a nice basket, or I can let you come over and pick them. In Taking, you come over and pick them. The gift is here waiting for you; you take the action to collect it.

IF TAKING IS ELUSIVE

Look at how you are sitting. If you haven't felt at least some shift within twenty minutes, reread the steps, look at yourself, and see if you are doing each one before progressing to the next one. Look at your position, where your hands are, and how fast you're moving them.

Give it more time. Finding Taking needs time: thirty seconds, thirty minutes, or three weeks, it doesn't matter. What matters is that you give it the time it takes. Even when it clicks, you still need to come back to it a dozen times, or you can use the five-minutes-a-day option like you did for Waking Up the Hands.

For bodyworkers. Taking is often difficult to access. The experience of moving your hands is welded to the feeling of giving. There are lots of reasons for this, and you'll find some notes online.

No correlation with sexual experience. How easy it is to find Taking has no correlation to the amount of sexual experience you have. None. If you are timid, you can be sure this will be a key for you. But I have seen Taking strike fear into the hearts of the most experienced sexual explorers and teachers. Often those are the very people who, though good at technique, have trouble receiving a gift. For many of those folks, Taking is a revelation and not always an easy one.

SOME COMMON OBJECTIONS

"Well, okay…but…I want us both to enjoy it!" Of course you do. Who wouldn't? This sounds nice at first but reveals an assumption that you can control whether someone enjoys something or not. You cannot. Another assumption is that if you are touching for your pleasure, it won't be enjoyable to them, that the only thing they will or can enjoy is the correct stroke, carefully curated by you. That's a little arrogant. They enjoy many things you don't curate on their behalf, and they are capable of having their own experience, whatever it is. In this particular practice, you have one role, and they have the other. If you are touching for your own pleasure and abiding by any limits they have set, what makes you think it will not be enjoyable to them?

If you believe those assumptions, you must provide the correct stroke at all times and manage their experience. That's not much fun for you and not much respect for them. Come back to yourself, and feel their hand as they have given you permission to do. You are experimenting. Are you *able* to bring your attention to yourself, and what happens when you do?

"…but giving them pleasure IS what gives me pleasure!" This also sounds nice but is another way to avoid experiencing your own pleasure. This is also about two different routes of pleasure, which we talk about shortly.

"...but I like to give!" Of course you do. Everyone does. Giving is inherently satisfying and often enjoyable. It's interesting that this never comes up when it's your turn to give, only when it's your turn to receive.

"...but Taking is wrong, just wrong!" Taking can sometimes feel like stealing—until you understand how to create an agreement and receive a gift being given to you. One person said, "I was really struggling with Taking and couldn't figure out why it was so hard. Eventually I saw that I believed that anything I did for myself—anything—was automatically hurtful to someone else. No wonder it felt wrong!"

"...but when do we get to the good stuff?" This usually means, "When do we get to something sexy?" As it was in Waking Up the Hands, this is a sure sign Taking has not yet clicked. When Taking clicks, you have no need to get anywhere else, because you are already there. The gift of it lands in your heart. The sign you have arrived is that you have no interest in leaving.

"...but why not still give and receive at the same time and just bring some extra awareness to the receiving?" This person is trying awfully hard to keep one foot in the giving end of the equation! After you learn to receive, come back and ask me that question.

The reason behind these responses is that the Taking Quadrant (receiving a gift) is inherently vulnerable. It can be easier to handle the vulnerable feeling if you dilute it with trying to give at the same time, but when you do that, you won't find it. Stop giving and see what's left.

THE CLICK

At some point, you notice, *Oh, this really is for me, isn't it?* You stop trying to give, and the gift you have been given lands in your heart. It feels different. When that happens, your hands relax. They slow down, become curious and sensual, and take in a tremendous amount of information. The inflow is wide open. You begin to follow your hands. You stop thinking about what they are supposed to do and follow whatever they like to do.

Like Waking Up the Hands, the sensation engages you, your breath slows or deepens, and you settle into your seat. You stop talking. You are not glued to the face of your Allower to see if they are enjoying it. The direction the gift is going has reversed. That is, instead of the gift moving from you to your partner, it is moving from your partner to you. There will often be an emotional shift. Tenderheartedness, sometimes relief, shame, or sadness may arise.

Two factors intertwine here: one is the sensation, and the other is the fact of the gift. Sometimes attending to the sensation helps you notice that it's a gift for you, and sometimes realizing it's a gift for you allows you to attend to the sensation. Sometimes one will be foremost or will touch your heart the most, sometimes the other.

FEELINGS

It often happens that as Taking begins to open, there is an emotional response. This is understandable. We have an innate need to experience each other in a direct way, through touch. At the same time, there is a nearly universal taboo against it. Anytime you combine an inherent need with a taboo, there is going to be an emotional charge, from fear and confusion to relief and liberation. The feelings run the gamut: self-doubt, shame, and guilt to sensuality, pleasure, lust, freedom, playfulness, and gratitude.

There is a range of intensity as well, barely noticeable, all the way to tears. I have had a few people who felt overwhelmed. Whatever you feel is fine, and as before, there is nothing to fix. What the feelings need here is for you to be with them, to listen for what they have to tell you. If it is challenging, you get to decide how long to stay here, and you can stop any time you like. In chapter 20, The Taking Quadrant, we talk about why the feelings tend to be so deep.

TAKING EXAMPLES

Some things people have said about Taking:

"This is scary."
"This feels incredibly intimate, but it's just his hand. How can that be?"
"My mind got completely still, no chatter."
"I feel humbled."
"I didn't know I WAS giving until I stopped giving!"
"It feels so right!"
"This is a remembrance of what my hands have forgotten.
There's a sadness there."

Do you believe him?

I was working with a couple who had been together for years. Kari was touching Art's hand, but it had the look of a massage, with kneading and pressure, so I stepped in.

Me: To what degree is this for you?

Kari: Mostly, I think.

Me: Make it 100 percent for you. Zero thought about him.

Kari: Not sure I know how to do that.

Me: Go back to feel that shell again. (She picks it up and feels it for a bit) That's what 100 percent feels like. Nothing to give back.

Kari: But this is a person. How can I use him as an object?

Me: Only with his permission. Did he give you permission? Is this a gift he is willing to give you with a full heart?

Kari: Yes.

Me: How do you know?

Kari: I asked him, and he said so. It just doesn't feel right.

Me: You don't believe him?

Kari: Hmmm…not sure I do.

Me: Check in with yourself.

Kari (pauses): Yes, I believe him, I just don't believe the idea. I don't know *how*.

Me: Ask him again. Look right into his eyes, and ask him slowly and clearly, "May I feel your hand?" (She does that.)

Art: Yes, you may. (They linger in each other's eyes and hers become moist.)

Kari: Really?

Art: Yes.

Kari (with a few tears): I get it. It's a gift. I really love his hands. (She picks them up, tenderly exploring each shape, each finger, and every texture. At one point, she lifts his hand to her face, eyes still moist, and then brings it back down to her lap.)

Kari (after a few minutes): Thank you.

Art: You're welcome.

Across the room

Sometimes the way people position themselves is invisible to them. Mae was going to feel Rick's hand, and they were sitting side by side. Mae was turned slightly toward Rick, and when she took his hand, she held it slightly to the side, toward him. She was trying to make it easier for him. I was trying to get her to stop adapting to him and let him adapt to her instead. I asked her to lean flat back and take his hand into the center of her lap. She took his hand slightly more toward the center of her lap but not completely and didn't change her turning.

Mae: Like this?

Me: Well, not quite. See how you're turned to the side toward Rick?

(She wriggles in her seat but ends up still turned toward him.)

Me: Okay, let's back up a bit.

(I have him move back a few inches to give her more room. Still, she was turned slightly toward him. I tell Rick, "Go across the room, way over there.")

Me (to Mae): Now, sit as if you were going to feel the object.

(She adjusts her position, leaning flat against the chair.)

Mae: Oohhhh, this is different, isn't it? I couldn't feel it before.

(I have her take the object into her lap again, in the center, and look at where the center of her lap is.)

Me: This is where the center is, where you go when there is no one to accommodate. This is what I want you to do with Rick's hand when he comes back.

(I motion him to come back. He gives her his hand, and she holds it in the center of her lap.)

Mae: Ohhhh, this is different. Now I can feel that it's for me.

Too sexy

In a workshop, Dave was responding to the adventure with a sense that it was all very sexy. He was unable to do anything without emphasizing sexiness. His expressions, sounds, and body movements were exaggerated, almost as if he was doing an improv skit. Everything turned him on, but something was missing.

I had him return to feeling the coffee cup. I said, "Okay, Dave, stop the sexy thing for a minute. Just hold that cup, and slow way, way down. Describe to me each feature you feel there. The edge there, the handle, the rough spot." We continued this for about twenty minutes with various objects until I saw him relax. He got very quiet, looking like he was holding back tears.

Dave: I don't know how to do this.
Me: That's okay. Most people don't. Sometimes when we make everything sexual, it's because we are not comfortable with cozy and comforting. I don't know that about you, that's up to you, but that's what sometimes happens.
Dave: Shit, I think you're right. Sex, I know how. Comforting, I don't even know what that means.
Me: Now let's take what you found with that coffee cup, and see if you can feel your partner's hand with the same curiosity and attention to detail.

I reminded him that there's nothing to fix; he wasn't broken. He just needed to keep coming back to his skin. A truckload of comfort can be overwhelming, but a few tablespoons can be quite nice.

KEY ELEMENTS

The key elements of Taking start with same key elements as Waking Up the Hands: that it's not about anything, the experience of pleasure in your hands while they are moving, waiting for a change in body state, and when your hands get it, you get it. Now we've added two new elements that are the interpersonal dynamic: 1) consent (asking permission and believing it), and 2) receiving a gift from another. Sometimes those first elements work fine, but when the relational elements are added, it gets challenging all over again.

Two things at once. Earlier (chapter 2) we said that when receiving we do two things at once. Taking is a form of receiving, so that applies here. 1) Putting your desires and pleasure first, and 2) respecting the limits of your giver, in this case, the Allower. Sometimes the aha is that it is possible to do both at once.

Why the emphasis on the gift. On a couple of occasions, I had people object to the idea of a gift, but I have found it to be useful. First, when it comes to doing, there tends to be an automatic tendency to try to give. It doesn't work to try to stop giving so much. It requires completely reversing the direction of the gift, so it is no longer moving *from* you but is moving *toward* you. Second, the experience of receiving a gift touches the heart, which is to say it engages the emotional system. The degree and range of feelings it tends to bring up tells me we are onto something significant.

Inflow and outflow. In Taking, you close the outflow and open all the inflows—the inflow of information, pleasure, and receiving a gift.

Elusive for many reasons. The experience of Taking engages a host of inner dynamics, and difficulty with any one of them can slow you down. I have seen people challenged by this for many reasons.

- Their hands were not able to experience pleasure.
- They could experience pleasure when their hands were still but not when moving.
- They didn't know how to move their hands to create pleasure, so they could focus only on technique.
- They didn't believe or understand consent.
- They didn't know how to be curious.
- They had little or no experience touching anyone, so it was new territory in every sense.
- They had uncomfortable feelings about taking action toward pleasure.
- They had uncomfortable feelings about receiving a gift or didn't know *how* to receive a gift.
- They felt it was wrong to be "selfish" or were afraid of being perceived as selfish.
- They didn't trust the Allower to be honest.
- They felt that their experience of pleasure would automatically be unpleasant to the other.

Difficulty with any of these can slow you down.

PRINCIPLE:
TWO ROUTES OF PLEASURE

When I started playing with this dynamic, as I described in chapter 1, when most people were touching, they tried to "give." I tried to coach them in how to touch for their own pleasure (Taking), saying things like, "This is about touching for your pleasure; what do you want to do that feels good *to you*?" They often said, "Giving you pleasure IS what gives me pleasure!"

I found it interesting that I've never heard this when it's someone's turn to actually give, only when it's their turn to receive (Take). Still, enough people have said this that I began to understand it as two different routes, or access points, to pleasure.

The direct route. When you touch something or someone, the sensory receptors in your hand send impulses to your brain, which light up the pleasure centers. It's extremely simple—skin to pleasure. When you were feeling the object, you were using this route. The direct route is our foundation. It's how we took in information as an infant and made sense of the world. (It also works with the other senses: smell, taste, hearing, sight, and movement.)

The indirect route. You touch your partner, and they smile or sigh, and that lights up your pleasure centers. When you say, "Giving you pleasure is what gives me pleasure," you are talking about this route. The indirect route is like casting a fishing line, hoping to catch something. You do this thing *so that* this other thing happens. In the direct route, there is no *so that*. It is pleasurable as it is; no result is needed.

The indirect route sounds nicer; the direct route is often a little suspect. The direct route tends to tap into the primal nature of sensation, which, as you've seen, can surprise you. It may also sound selfish. Almost everyone has the direct route closed to some degree as a result of shame, guilt, social pressure, and many other reasons. For some people, it's rusted shut.

The problem is this. To the degree the direct route is closed, you have to use the indirect route, because that's all you have. You have to do whatever it takes to get that smile, sigh, or moan, or you have nothing. This is not giving to someone; this is using them. Now you are both in performance mode: you are trying to perform the right stroke, and they are trying to perform the right response. I have been on both sides of that, and I don't recommend it.

Real giving satisfies the heart, but that's not what we're talking about here. The indirect route is a vicarious route, a substitute. You don't know how to access pleasure directly, so you use your partner's pleasure instead. If this one thing is your only route to pleasure, you are probably avoiding something else. Indeed, opening the direct route is often accompanied by feelings of various kinds. Perhaps you remember this from Waking Up the Hands.

The Taking Quadrant. When I say, "Feel your partner's hand for your pleasure," I am talking about the direct route. Feel your partner's hand for the experience it creates in your skin. The Taking Quadrant requires the direct route. Without engaging the direct route, it's not the Taking Quadrant. Saying, "Giving you pleasure is what gives me pleasure," is not the Taking Quadrant.

Over the years, I have come to see how opening the direct route creates a fundamental change in how we experience ourselves. Imagine an extreme: what would it be like to experience no pleasure yourself and to only be allowed to contribute to the pleasure of others? Really. Sit down for a minute and imagine it. It's a sobering thought. Without the direct route, what would you replace it with?

Opening both routes. The direct route is primary. Once it is open and you can tell the difference between them, the indirect route becomes a secondary source of information and enjoyment, a kind of bonus. When both people interacting have access to the direct route and are also attuned to the experience of their partner, this is where the magic happens.

You have to start with the direct route, and that is what we are focusing on here. Once that opens, the rest will make sense.

NOTES ON THE ALLOWING QUADRANT

The experience of Allowing confirms something that people have sometimes felt but had no words for, and that is the feeling that being touched was for the benefit of the other person. Sadly, that has often happened without choice or clarity, but in Take-Allow, the choosing creates a refreshing clarity and allows for generosity.

When someone asks to touch you the way they want and you agree to it, you are in Allowing. You set aside how you might prefer to be touched and allow them to touch you the way they want (within your limits). The gift you are giving is you, or more precisely, the gift is access to you. The action is moving from them to you, but the gift is moving from you to them.

While the Taking Quadrant is challenging for almost everyone, the Allowing Quadrant is all over the map. It can be easy and natural, a little odd, or seriously challenging, so wherever you are is fine. The one thing that allows you to enjoy the experience of being touched is confidence you have a choice about it. I say "confidence" because it is a felt sense.

You probably know in your mind that you have a choice, but we must know it in our bodies. Without knowing you have a choice, there is no way to enjoy it even if you try. This is a direct correlation. If you feel relaxed, you already trust yourself to speak up as needed. If Allowing feels disconcerting or worrisome, you're not quite sure you have a choice (or how to exercise your choice). There is a full range in that knowing, and that is why the experience of Allowing varies so much.

Allowing teaches you that you do, in fact, have a choice about whether and how you are touched and that speaking up is your responsibility. Part of having a choice is being able to say no, and part of having a choice is being able to set a limit: "You can have this much but not this much." Part of having a choice is being able to change your mind. "Hmmm, that doesn't work for me, please stop now." Respecting your own limits is crucial. You can give a gift only to the degree that you own it, and the more responsibility you take for your limits, the more joy there is in giving the gift.

The touch that happens may or may not feel good to you, but often it does. I've had many people say this was the best touch they've ever felt. Your Taker's hands relax, and because of that, it feels better to you. Sometimes it feels so good that the hardest part is remembering that you are in fact giving. Sometimes people say, "Oh, I feel pleasure, so I must be receiving!" What is true is that you are experiencing pleasure. No one is giving it to you. It's a bonus. We talked about this in chapter 4.

FEELINGS

Allowing brings up a full range of feelings from relief, delight, and bliss to confusion and worry. This correlates with the degree to which the Allower knows they have a choice about what happens and how to exercise that choice. Most common is a certain relief. There's nothing to do and nothing to figure out! Sometimes people notice their own power to choose, maybe for the first time. Occasionally noticing you have a choice is so new it's disorienting.

ALLOWING EXAMPLES

Some things people have said about Allowing:

"I feel cherished."

"This is amazingly intimate."

"The reason I can relax is because I know it's not going anywhere else."

"Wow, this is the best touch I have ever had! How can that be? It isn't even for me!"

"I didn't know anyone could enjoy me like that."

Not for me

In one workshop, I had a couple playing with Take-Allow. He was feeling her hand, and the movements were gentle and slow, looking like a caress. She was very relaxed and enjoying it. I asked her if she could find the sense that she was giving the gift. She paused a moment and responded, "No, I actually can't. It really feels like it's for me." I asked if

I could try something, and she said sure. I took her hand, and instead of caressing motions, I lifted it up by the thumb, jiggled it a little, turned it over, bent the fingers back and forth, things I was pretty sure would not feel sensual to her. She said, "Oh, I get it. I can tell it's not for me. I get it now."

THE KEY ELEMENTS

The key elements are noticing you have a choice and exercising that choice. Without noticing you have a choice, you can't give a gift. All you can do is go along with, endure, or tolerate.

Two things at once. In chapter 2, we said that when giving we do two things at once. Allowing is a form of giving, so that applies here. 1) Setting aside what you prefer, and 2) keeping responsibility for your limits. Sometimes the aha is that it is possible to do both at once.

Inflow and outflow. The inflow of information and sensation is still open. It may be pleasurable too, but now there is the outflow of the gift. Sometimes people find it helpful (or enjoyable) to imagine a river of giving leaving their hand and going to their partner's hand.

ABOUT THE TAKE-ALLOW DYNAMIC

This dynamic is widely misunderstood and often difficult to find. Once reclaimed, it is profoundly liberating. When I defined receiving and giving, I said that "doing" is often conflated with "giving" and "done-to" is conflated with "receiving." The Take-Allow dynamic breaks the weld holding those pairs together. In Take-Allow, the person who is doing is not giving a gift; they are receiving one. The person who is being done to is not receiving a gift; they are giving one.

The other dynamic, Serve-Accept, is common in many situations like comforting a child or going to a massage therapist. Take-Allow, however, is permitted in only a few places. We allow small children to climb on us and stick their fingers in our ears, but other than that, it generally only happens with lovers, and with lovers, it is not just tolerated, it's needed. The fact that it feels intimate even when it is only hands is a recognition of this privileged mode of touch. When it's lacking, we often know something is missing but may not know what.

You could say the Take-Allow dynamic is opposite to the Serve-Accept dynamic. The direction the gift is going is reversed. It is the distinction between these two dynamics that makes them what they are and makes them rich and enjoyable. That is, the more you can distinguish between them, the more enjoyable they both are.

CHAPTER 9

Lesson 3:
Finding the Serve-Accept Dynamic

In this lesson, we open the Serve-Accept dynamic and experience the Serving and Accepting Quadrants. The Accepting partner will ask for the touch they want (still on the hands and forearms), and the Serving partner, if they are willing and able, will do that for them. Then you switch.

The Accepting Quadrant. In the previous lesson, you learned in Allowing that you have a choice about whether and how you are touched. In Accepting, you learn that it is possible to be touched exactly the way you want. For many people, this is a new experience and can feel vulnerable, challenging, natural, or like a big relief.

The Serving Quadrant. In the previous lesson, you learned in Taking to notice what you wanted to do and to ask permission to do it. In Serving, you set aside what you want, ask what the other person wants, and do that if you are willing.

The Serve-Accept dynamic is the one that feels more familiar to most people and everyone seems to want to get better at. It's not about techniques and strokes; it's about finding out what the Accepter wants.

I give you the instructions first, and then we'll come back and talk about each quadrant, Serving and Accepting.

THE PARAMETERS

- You'll need twenty minutes or more.

- Play with this a few times, and then read this chapter again. You'll see things you missed the first time through.

- If you want, you can alternate this lesson with the previous one, Take-Allow. Be sure you agree on which one you are doing. The point of it is to feel the difference between them.

- Once it clicks, come back to it at least a dozen more times, particularly if it's hard to ask for what you want, so it becomes natural to you.

THE STEPS

 ## Create your container.

Agree on how much time you are going to spend, and divide it in half so you each get a turn, or you can play with shorter turns (three to five minutes each), and go back and forth a few times.

 ## Make an agreement.

First the Serving partner:

1. Ask, "How would you like me to touch your hands?" (If you'd like to offer it, include the forearms.)

   - You may think your job is to guess correctly what your Accepter wants. It is not. It is to find out from them what they want. This is the most important step.

2. After you ask the question, wait for the answer.

Then the Accepting partner:

1. Pause. Take a few moments to notice what it is you'd like.

   - Don't settle for what sounds good enough. Wait for the inner *Oh yeah! That sounds wonderful!*

- You may not know right away. That is not a problem. It takes time—a few seconds, a few minutes, or many minutes.
- You might feel awkward waiting until you know—also not a problem and pretty common.

2. Request it. Don't tell them what they *can* do; tell them what you *want* them to do, and request it.

   - Use the words "Will you…"
     - Like this:
       "Will you…?" or "I would like…will you do that?"
     - Not this:
       "I usually like…"
       "You can…"
       "Whatever you want is fine with me"
       "Maybe…?"
     - For example:
       "Will you softly caress my palm with your fingertips?"
       "Will you tickle the back of my hand, light like a feather?"
       "I'd like scratches on my forearm. Will you do that?"
       "I want you to hold my hand. Will you do that?"
     - If you don't know how to describe it, demonstrate. "Will you do this, like this?"

Why so particular about the words? As we saw in Take-Allow, the words set you up for what you are able to experience. If you say "You can…," you are setting yourself up to Allow. Your Server has asked, "How would you like me to touch your hands?" but you heard it as, "How can I touch your hands in a way that you don't mind terribly much?" That is a very different question! Saying, "Will you…?" helps you notice that you are in fact asking for something you want.

Then the Serving partner again:

1. Ask anything you need to clarify. Do they mean soft, light, firm, slow, deep? Gently ask for the information you need so you can give them exactly what they want.

2. Pause and ask yourself: *Is this something I can give with a full*

heart? If it isn't, you may need to negotiate. If it is, and when you have the information you need, say, "Yes, I will."

- Respect your own limits. There may be something you are not comfortable doing.
- For example:

  "I'm not comfortable doing that, but I could do this."
  "Hmmm…I'm not sure what you mean. Can you tell me more please?"
  "Yes, I'd be happy to do that. Would you like it soft or firm?"
  "Yes, I can do that, but I'll need to turn around this way."

 ## Lean back and get comfortable.

First the Accepting partner:

As the receiver of the gift, you get comfortable first.

1. Lean back with your back flat against the chair, not turned toward your Server even a little, or you can lie down.

2. Put your hand where you want it and where it is relaxed (pillows help). You are on vacation.

3. Look at your hand. Are you holding it up? Are the fingers stiff? A hand that is holding itself up in the air is working.

Why so strict with the position? As we saw in the Take-Allow lesson, your position reveals what you *think* is happening and sets you up for what *can* happen. Set yourself up one way, and you will experience the touch as being for the benefit of the other person. Set yourself up another way, and you can experience it as being for you. I've heard people say, "Oh, this can work," or "This is okay." It may be true that you could make it work if you had to, but you don't have to, so why are you? Look at yourself and see whether you are adapting your position, trying to make it easier for the Server.

You can experiment with having the Server walk across the room and then have the Accepter get comfortable based on their *own* body. Then have the Server return and adjust themselves to the position of the Accepter. How does that change things?

Then the Serving partner:

1. Adjust yourself to the position of the receiver as needed to get reasonably comfortable and also be attentive.

   - You are not on vacation; you're on duty.

   - If your Accepting partner tries to adapt themselves to your comfort, don't let them. Encourage them to get comfortable first.

 Touch your partner's hand the way they asked you to.

Serving partner:

1. Do what has been asked as best you can and no more than was asked. Don't make up something new, no matter how cool you think it is.

   - Slow down. Almost always, slower is more pleasant.

2. Check in verbally. Checking in makes it easier for them to ask for changes. "Is this what you had in mind?" or "Anything you would like different?"

   - Let them have their own experience. Tenderness, excitement, bliss, sleep.

   - It's okay to enjoy it.

3. Watch the clock, and stick to the time you agreed to.

Accepting partner:

1. Change your mind any time and as many times as you like.

2. Don't try to like something you don't actually like. Instead, ask for changes.

   - A few examples:

     "Would you go deeper there?"
     "Lighter, please."

"Would you include my forearm now?"
"Let's see, slower please...Really slow...ahhh, yeah, that's it."
"Hmm, I thought that would be it, but that's not quite it.
 Will you try it like this instead, please?"
"Hmm, I need to move over this way."
"Oh yeah, perfect!"

When you receive exactly the touch you asked for, something lands in your heart. You notice, perhaps for the first time, that this really is for you. This is the click. There may be an aha moment of how different this feels than Allowing, and there is often relief and gratitude.

5. Thank you/You're welcome.

When the time is up, sit up and look each other in the eyes.

Accepting partner (who received the gift):

- Say "Thank you."

Serving partner (who gave the gift):

- Say "You're welcome" and nothing more. Don't thank the receiver, and don't deflect the appreciation; hear it and take it in.

6. Switch roles.

7. Talk about what you noticed.

Talk about what you noticed *about yourself* (not about your partner). This might include sensations you felt or thoughts or emotions that arose. What was challenging, a relief, or a surprise?

8. Close your dedicated time.

You can thank each other again if you like.

9. Come back to it.

Return here ten to twenty times over the next few weeks.

NOTES ON THE ACCEPTING QUADRANT

When you request to be touched the way you want and your partner does that for you, you are in the Accepting Quadrant. The gift you are receiving is your partner's action. In Allowing, you found you had a choice about whether and how you were touched. In Accepting, you find it is possible to be touched exactly the way you want. Then it becomes clear that those two are different things and the difference matters.

Being touched exactly the way you want can feel odd or awkward, like a big relief, or tenderhearted to the point of tears, but it is inherently wonderful. If it's anything less than wonderful, it's not because you are not a "good receiver;" it's because it's not the thing you want. The question to ask yourself is not *Why don't I like this?* The question to ask yourself is *What do I want? What sounds wonderful?*

It begs the question, *What if I don't know what I want?* We all have times when we don't know what we want. It's not a problem. Really, it's not. Somewhere in there, your body knows, and all you have to do is give it time for the knowing to bubble up to your conscious awareness—a few seconds, a few minutes, or many minutes. That can be awkward, but it is ultimately a luxury to have the time. It's not always the case that what we want matters, but here it does, and you get all the time you need to notice what that is. Really. It matters.

For many people, Accepting is an entirely new experience. It can be a new experience to be asked what we want, new to take the time to notice what that is, or new to receive it. Very often it's all three. One of the biggest tendencies in Accepting is to settle for crumbs. In Accepting, you have been invited to choose from your Want-to list. There will be the tendency to choose from your Willing-to list. This is what is happening when your partner asks how you would like to be touched, and you answer with how you are okay being touched. "Oh, you can..." or "Oh, this would be okay..." The challenge is often to notice the difference.

Why would we settle for crumbs? Because most of us are so accustomed to going along with whatever is done to us that we forget what it feels like to tend to what we want. This happens for a good reason, which we talk about in the labs. Because we tend to go along, you cannot learn Accepting by having someone else choose for you, no matter how "tuned in" they are. When someone else chooses (guesses), you are likely to go along and try to make the best of it. That is not the Accepting Quadrant. To learn Accepting, you must request the touch you want.

The irony is that when you were learning Taking, you were doing, and you thought it was for the other person. Now when you are being done to, it's for them again? What's going on? Your job in Accepting is not to try to like whatever is done to you. It's to notice what sounds wonderful to you, right now, and ask for that.

About the word. Like the word "take," the word "accept" has more than one meaning, and one of them is problematic. One use of the word means to come to terms with and settle for, as in "accepting" some touch you don't like. The other meaning is to receive a gift that delights you, and this is the meaning I am using. "Yes, I accept!" It's essentially a way to say, "Yes, please!"

IF ACCEPTING IS ELUSIVE

Are you worried about your giver? If so, what can you ask them to set your heart at ease? "Are you okay? You don't mind giving me this? Thanks." Once you have your concern answered, trust them to take care of their limits.

Stop talking. I've seen people talk about the weather and everything else. Stop. Bring your attention to your hands. If you like, experiment with closing your eyes.

Sometimes it takes time. Give yourself more than five minutes. It can take that long just to let your nervous system slow down.

Sometimes people don't like their hands being touched. If you don't want your hand touched, try the forearms, the back of the hand, the feet, or the shoulders. You can experiment with asking for deeper pressure, having the Server hold still, ask for a very short time like a few seconds, or ask them to use an object instead of their hands, like a feather or a hairbrush. There is *something* you like. Play around until you find it.

WHEN IT CLICKS

When it clicks, you notice, perhaps for the first time, that this really is for you, and the gift of it lands. Like Taking, two factors interweave here: one is the pleasure of the sensation, and the other is the awareness of your partner giving you a gift. Sometimes one will be more meaningful, sometimes the other, and either of them can open up the other. If you're unsure what's going on, come back to the sensation.

FEELINGS

A wide range of feelings may show up, and occasionally it's quite emotional. You may think, *Finally! It's for me!* You may feel surprised at how intimate it feels and how much pleasure is available in your hands. Ultimately, there is relief and gratitude. This is receiving a gift, so some themes are similar to what arose with Taking: feelings of guilt, fear, and sadness. Feelings of tenderness are common, knowing that your partner cares about you.

EXAMPLES

Some things people have said as they experience Accepting:

"I'm surprised that I'm so comfortable."

"This is a little weird. I'm not used to receiving."

"I could give myself over to this for an extended period of time!"

"What are you doing to me?!"

"I had no idea my hands could feel so much."

Fine with me

Mo and Tim had been partners for some years.

Tim: How would you like me to touch your hands?

Mo: However you like, love.

Tim: This is for you. It's about what you want.

Mo (to me): Oh, he usually does what he likes, and it's fine with me. I'm okay with it.

(There is an awkward pause.)

Tim: Wow. I don't do that. I always try to do what she wants.

(We are treading on tender ground.)

Me: Hmmm...and how do you figure out what she wants?

Tim: Well, I guess I don't know. When I ask her, she never says, so I guess I'm just guessing.

It took several more rounds before it landed for Mo that she actually got to choose. Both of them had felt like they were doing what the other one wanted, which may sound generous but is actually confusing.

Mostly guilty

In a session, when I offered to touch Ki's hand, they had a hard time believing it was okay to have something they wanted.

Ki: Well, we don't get to have everything we want!

Me: Of course not, but you do sometimes get to have what you want. How would you feel having some small thing, like a hand caress, exactly as you want it?

Ki: Relieved. And guilty. Mostly guilty.

Me (feeling a little playful): Let's see how guilty we can make you feel.

Ki (responding with playfulness): Oh no!

Me: Okay, so let's withdraw that offer. You don't get to have a hand caress. We'll just go on to some other exercise.

Ki: Wait! I do want it! I want to try it!

Me: Okay.

Ki: Will you stroke like this, right here?

Me: Yes, I will.

KEY ELEMENTS

The key element is that nothing happens unless and until you request it. This forces you to notice that you are the one choosing what happens next, not your partner. You ask, "Will you...?" and they say, "Yes."

Two things at once. Accepting is a form of receiving, so you are doing two things at once: 1) putting your desires and pleasure first, and 2) respecting the limits of your giver, in this case, the Server. Sometimes the aha moment is that it is possible to do both at once.

Inflow and outflow. In Accepting, all three inflows are open: the inflows of information and pleasure, and now you have added the inflow of receiving a gift. You close the outflow of trying to give something back.

NOTES ON THE SERVING QUADRANT

When your partner asks you to touch them the way they want, and you agree to do that and do it, you are in the Serving Quadrant. The gift you are giving is your action. This is the role most people call "giving," but Allowing is also a form of giving. To avoid confusion, I call this the Serving Quadrant.

What people often do is get started and hope it's the right thing. With a great deal of luck, it's fine. With less luck, it's uninspiring, and at worst, it's invasive. The problem is that your receiver will tend to go along anyway and try to make the best of it. To Serve, you must find out what they want *before* you start.

When you Serve, you might think it is your responsibility to give your partner pleasure. The truth is you do not cause their pleasure, you contribute to it. Understanding that their experience belongs to them (not to you) is profoundly liberating. The more you let go of how you think it should look or want it to look, the more of a gift it is and the more satisfying it is for both.

A mistake Servers often make is trying to get some response they'd like to see. You'd like to see them melt, get excited or turned on. It's easy to do, but this is not giving; it's using them to make yourself feel better. This is the indirect route we talked about earlier.

About the word. The word "serve" may hold some charge if it implies to you that it's a subservient role. Set that aside for now. As I'm using it here, the Serving Quadrant means to take action for the benefit of another. It is a true gift, which means you respect your own limits and give only what you can give with a full heart.

THE CLICK

There is not usually a dramatic shift like there is in Taking, but sometimes there is a gentle shift in clarity. You are not trying to make something happen, and you trust yourself to not give more than you are happy to give. You notice you don't have to produce a result, and there's a certain freedom in that.

FEELINGS

Serving tends to feel humbling, and there is often a satisfaction in knowing you are contributing. Sometimes there is gratitude; this doesn't mean your partner is giving to you (they are not setting aside what they want in order to go with what you want). It means you feel gratitude for the experience. Go ahead and feel gratitude, but don't thank them.

EXAMPLE

In a session with me, Bill asked his partner, Kay, to gently massage his hands. Kay did that, and he relaxed into it. After a bit, she began to include his wrist and then his forearm. Then she returned to his hand. Afterward, I asked them if they noticed that she had strayed beyond what he had asked. She hadn't noticed it, but he had. They had a laugh about that. When I asked her why she did that, she had no idea. She hadn't noticed it.

This is a small incident with big implications. When you stick to your agreement, your receiver can relax into their experience. When you go beyond it, they have to decide whether it's worth speaking up, which is distracting or worse.

This is also a great example of why the process is different inside the container than outside. Inside the container, you learn to be impeccable and develop trust so that outside the container, you can play more creatively.

KEY ELEMENTS

The key elements that make this Serving are: 1) asking what the receiver wants before doing anything, and 2) doing nothing except what was asked for.

The intention to give does not make it Serving. What makes it Serving is the agreement. They asked, "Will you...?" and you said, "Yes." It is possible (and common) to intend to Serve, even to feel like you are Serving, but if you have not found out what your intended receiver wants, it's not Serving.

Two things at once. Serving is a form of Giving, so you are doing two things at once: 1) setting aside what you might prefer to do, and 2) keeping responsibility for your limits. Sometimes the aha is that it is possible to do both at once.

Inflow and outflow. In Serving, the inflow of information, and possibly pleasure, remains open. Now you add to that the outflow of giving the gift.

ABOUT THE SERVE-ACCEPT DYNAMIC

The Serve-Accept dynamic is the one most people think of as Give-Receive, but as you have seen, receiving and giving also apply to Take-Allow, hence the terms Serve and Accept. In this dynamic, the action is going one direction, and the gift goes the same direction.

Serve-Accept fits many kinds of situations and relationships. It's the dynamic of a massage, physical therapy, surgery, or holding a child to give comfort. It's also the dynamic of helping your friend move his piano or having the fire department rescue your house.

Almost all teaching about touch, whether sexual or not, assumes this dynamic (such as massage techniques and strokes). As you are discovering, it's only half the picture.

SUMMARY OF THE LESSONS

So far, we have opened up the inflow in your hands for both information and pleasure, and that made it possible to open the inflow of receiving a gift (with your hands).

We found both dynamics and all four quadrants.

The Take-Allow dynamic. The action goes one direction, and the gift goes the other direction. With touch, this one is often an expression of affection or desire.

- Taking Quadrant: You touch for your own enjoyment, and the gift you receive is access to your partner.
- Allowing Quadrant: You allow yourself to be touched the way your partner wants (within your limits), and you are giving the gift of access.

The Serve-Accept dynamic. The action goes one direction, and the gift goes the same direction. This is the traditional idea of touch and is characterized by massage or helping someone.

- Serving Quadrant: You touch your partner the way they want (within your limits), and the gift you are giving is your action.
- Accepting Quadrant: You are touched the way you want, and you are receiving the gift of your partner's action.

You learned how to create each dynamic by asking for what you want.

"May I..." creates the Take-Allow dynamic.

"Will you..." creates the Serve-Accept dynamic.

Once you set up the dynamics, you learned to experience the difference between them. That is the point of the whole process, and now we're back to where we started with the Three Minute Game.

- How do you want to touch me? (You are offering to give by Allowing.)
- How do you want me to touch you? (You are offering to give by Serving.)

With those two questions, you now have what you need. You can toss the rest of the book out if you want. However, what I have found is that as we start to include more of the body, the stakes feel higher, and we tend to forget what we've learned. You start out in Taking, for example, doing for your own pleasure, and find that as you include more of the body, you get excited or speed up, and you revert back to your default, which is trying to Serve.

In the labs, we expand the options for body geography and extend the time as you like. The lessons showed you how to find the quadrants. The labs show you how to keep them.

CHAPTER 10

Introduction to the Labs

Who am I in this quadrant?
—Harry Faddis

Now that you found the quadrants, the labs are where you get to explore them. Here's the challenge: in order to explore the quadrant, you have to stay in it.

In the lessons, the parameters were already set. In the labs, they open up—which body areas are potentially available and how much time you spend there. That may be a big relief or a whole new kind of intimidating. Often it's both. Often it means that it becomes easier to slip out of the quadrant and back into whatever you were doing before. In the labs, the quadrants can be challenging all over again.

The instructions show you how to slow down so you can stay in the quadrant and explore it. You will find that it's better to go slowly and stay in the quadrant than it is to try fancier stuff (or fancier body parts) and fall out of it. It's also far more interesting to stay in it even with a more mundane body part. That's where the aha moments are.

Exploring the quadrants is a lifelong journey, so the instructions are designed to carry you from the beginning all the way to more complex experiences. They are detailed and include what will throw you off track, where the quadrant takes you, and how to develop the art of each of them.

HOW THE LABS WORK

The labs are based on the two offers. It's a kind of Three Minute Game with coaching.

- Lab 1 is Take-Allow ("How do you want to touch me?")
- Lab 2 is Serve-Accept ("How do you want me to touch you?")
- Lab 3 is Play. It's not about the quadrants per se; it takes what you've learned and opens up the play that is possible in the middle.

Labs 4, 5, and 6 are online. (www.wheelofconsentbook.com/notes)

- Labs 4 and 5: If you want the option to include the genitals in the labs, Labs 4 and 5 guide you in how to do that with the care and respect they deserve. These labs work best if you wait until the quadrants are solid, which usually means doing Labs 1 and 2 at least twenty times. Lab 6 offers some ideas to play with sexual arousal.
- Bonus Tracks! These include a few ways to play that are not so much about the quadrants. Add them in any time.

RECOMMENDED

- Do the lab a few times and then reread the instructions. You'll see things you didn't see the first time.
- Decide at the beginning how much time you are going to spend, and take equal turns. Use a clock. Your turns don't have to be on the same day; one person today and the other tomorrow is fine.
- Don't change your time agreement in the middle. If you want to add more time, close that turn as planned, and then take another pair of turns.
- You can alternate the labs if you want—Lab 1 today, Lab 2 tomorrow. As in the lessons, just be sure you know which one you're doing, because it's the difference between them that matters.
- It can help to start clothed or partially clothed. For most people, getting naked is too charged with meaning. Choose what is emotionally comfortable for you. Since your genitals are not on the menu, it's usually easier to relax if you keep them covered (undies on). It can also help to start outside the bedroom.

A LIFELONG JOURNEY

You will find a wide range of moods as you go: tender, silly, sexy, playful, contemplative, raucous, experimental, or comforting. You develop the skills that make you trustworthy, so you begin to trust yourself, and that lets you cut loose and play. You begin to ask for things you hadn't thought of before. You will have moments where you get lost and fall off the track. No problem. Just get back on.

A few examples:

You're ten minutes into Allowing. Your partner gets excited and starts moving faster. You get overwhelmed and start enduring. Thankfully the timer goes off and rescues you. You are mad at your partner for not noticing, and then realize you are mad at yourself for not speaking up. You back up a step, slow down, and find your voice the next time.

You go for weeks exploring Taking, months maybe, thinking you have it. It feels lovely, and then one day, something deeper lands. *Oh! This IS for me isn't it? I never got it before!*

You are twenty minutes into Accepting. It's been great, but you notice you are bored. You don't want to bother your Server or hurt their ego, so you spend the next five minutes pondering whether to say anything. You get a really good look at this pattern of yours. *Why on earth am I doing this?!* Your partner asks, "Is there anything you would like different?" You say, "Yes, actually there is." You swear to yourself you will never do that again. You do, but it takes less time to notice it.

You're in Taking. It starts innocently enough, but suddenly you are aware of deep, primal, lusty feelings. You want to hump and grind and bite, and you have no idea what to do with that. You shut down, wilt, and go back in your shell. Later you talk about it, and your partner says, "I really want to explore that! Let's keep going!"

You're in Serving. It's a nice long turn, your partner gets turned on, and you like seeing it, so you get more "creative" trying to amplify it. Afterward, you realize you were going for their response. You say so, and your partner says, "And I was trying to please you by responding." This is more truth than you have ever told each other about your sex life. You take a deep breath, and one of you asks, "Can we do that again? Let's see if we can find it just for five minutes."

One day while cuddling, you notice your hand lingering, feeling, not working, and you realize you are following it naturally and how rich it is.

Some months or years, you always ask for sexy things. Some other year you always ask for comforting things, and you fill a deep well you didn't know was there.

There will be at least one moment when you are being touched exactly as you have asked, and you notice it really is for you and what that feels like. You ask yourself, *What have I been doing all these years?*

ABOUT SEX AND THE LABS

I said earlier that our habits of touch tend to blur the distinctions that make the quadrants what they are. Nowhere are those habits more entrenched than in touching genitals. One reason is that we have strong feelings about them: attraction, aversion, intimidation, compulsion, and more. Another reason is all the sex tips you read that say, "Do this cool thing so that this other cool thing happens." Add to that that most of us tend to think our genitals' job is to get us somewhere, and so we do to them whatever it takes to get there.

If you do the lessons and then go straight for the genitals, I can pretty much guarantee that everything you have learned will evaporate, you will revert to getting the job done, and it's likely you won't notice because the habits are so strong. If the genitals are all you are interested in, that's a sad statement and a good indicator that the labs are exactly what you need to wake up the rest of you.

A caveat. You may find that when you explore the labs, you become sensually or sexually aroused. That's fine, but if every time you explore a lab you go right into sex, you've created a problem for yourself. You have set up an expectation that can backfire. When you ask your partner to play the game with you, they have to first decide whether they want to have sex. If they are not currently in the mood for sex, they can't afford to start the game, so you both lose out.

If you want the container of the lab, do the lab. If you want to express affection and let it go where it goes, do that, but don't use the lab as a way to get something else.

PRINCIPLE:
TRUST AND TRUSTWORTHINESS

In the Allowing Quadrant, I've had many people say, "Oh, I should trust my Taker more, shouldn't I?" I answer, "The person you need to trust is yourself, that you will speak up as needed." Then I realized there's more to it. Trusting yourself is nice, but it's pointless (and dangerous) unless you first become trustworthy. When you become trustworthy, you automatically begin to trust yourself, and then you relax. It happens in that order, not the other way around. Later, I learned that this applies in all four quadrants in different ways.

Becoming trustworthy depends on skills. These are the skills that allow you to be responsible for yourself, to respect your limits, and to respect your partner's limits. These are not doing skills; they are noticing skills. To notice yourself means to notice your inner signals—what you want and don't, where you are tense, what your gut is saying. To notice your partner means to notice their facial and body changes—where they relax, where they get tense or look worried or shut down. Further, this is noticing moment by moment. Noticing what once was is sometimes useful. Noticing what is so now is always useful. This is a matter of degree. You will be able to notice up to a certain level of intensity, and above that level, you revert to your default and forget your new skills. Then you develop your skills up to the next level of intensity and so on.

In the Allowing Quadrant, you gain the skill to notice your limits and speak up for them, even if they change. This makes you trustworthy. Then you trust yourself and breathe a sigh of relief, and giving becomes a joy.

In the Taking Quadrant, you gain the skill to ask what your Allower's limits are, abide by them even if you get excited, and notice if they become tense. This makes you trustworthy, and you begin to trust that you will not harm anyone. Then you relax and can receive the gift being given to you.

In the Accepting Quadrant, you gain the skill to notice what you would most like, trust and value it, communicate it with clarity, and respect the other person's limits so you don't assume more than is freely given. This makes you trustworthy. Then you trust yourself, and then you settle in and receive the gift being given to you.

In the Serving Quadrant, you gain the skill to find out what your receiver wants and to speak up for your limits. You don't give more than you care to give. This makes you trustworthy to yourself. Then you trust yourself. Then you relax, and your giving becomes a joy.

So skills make you trustworthy, then you trust yourself, and then you relax and enjoy receiving or giving your gift.

- *How does this quadrant nourish me or liberate me?*
- *How does it turn me on?*
- *What scares me in this quadrant?*
- *What sounds great about having this quadrant fully functioning and easy?*
- *What would be most helpful for me in developing this quadrant?*

CHAPTER 11

Lab 1:
Exploring the Take-Allow Dynamic

The challenge of exploring the Take and Allow Quadrants is that it is so easy to fall out of them, especially as the feelings become stronger, which we'll talk about shortly. The joy of exploring them is the quadrants themselves. There are so many discoveries to make here, not to mention the pleasure and fun of it.

In Taking, as you explore more of the body or get turned on, you'll tend to forget what you learned. This will show up in the words you use, the position you put yourself in, and the speed of your hands. You'll forget to lean back, forget to slow your hands down, and forget it's for you. Don't worry; we all do it. I'll remind you, and you'll have to remind yourself.

In Allowing, you might think it's your job to make yourself be okay with anything that is done to you. It's not. You will tend to forget to pause, consider your limits, and change your mind. We all do this too, and I'll be reminding you. As you slow down and gain the skills to speak up for yourself, Allowing become easier and more joyful.

In the lessons, we started with the Taker's request: "May I feel your hand?" In the lab, we start with an offer from the Allower: "How do you want to touch me for (three, five, ten, etc.) minutes?" This opens the door for the Taker to pause and consider what they want and ask for it. "May I feel your..?" or "May I explore your..?" or "May I play with your...?"

This lab is one question of the Three Minute Game with a couple of speed bumps added: 1) the Taker pauses to consider what they want, and 2) the Allower pauses to consider if they are willing to give that.

As before, I'll give you the steps, and then we'll look more closely at each quadrant.

THE PARAMETERS

- Start with short turns of three to five minutes. When you are ready, you will naturally start to ask for longer turns.
- Taker, start with using your hands to do the exploring, and explore body areas that feel fairly neutral to you. Later you will want to expand to using more of your own body like forearms, face, chest, or whole body. You'll be able to stay in your quadrant in gradually more intense and complex interactions.
- Do this lab for twenty or thirty sessions, then play with it for a lifetime.

THE STEPS

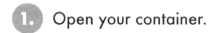 **1. Open your container.**

Decide how much time you are going to spend, and open with your dedication or ritual. Divide the time in half so you each get a turn. One person today and the other tomorrow is also fine.

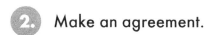 **2. Make an agreement.**

First the Allowing partner:

1. Ask, "How would you like to touch me for three minutes (or whatever time you have agreed to)?"

Then the Taking partner:

1. Take a twenty-second pause, or longer.

127

- If you think you know what you want, take the full twenty seconds anyway. Sometimes it changes.

2. Make a request.

- As in the lesson, use the words, "May I...?"
- There are two ways to do that:

   "May I...?"
   "I would like to...May I do that?"

- If you like, you can include a request about clothing.

   "May I explore your back? And would you mind taking your shirt off for that?"

- Do not:

   Make an offer: "Would you like...?"
   Make a statement and end it there: "I would like to..." or "I could..."
   Hint: "Such and such sounds nice."

- Some examples:

   "May I play with your hair?"
   "May I feel your back?"
   There are more examples in the notes on Taking.

Then the Allowing partner again:

1. Ask anything you need to clarify.

- Do they mean soft, light, deep? Ask.

2. Take a twenty-second pause.

- Ask yourself, *Is this something I can give with a full heart?*
- Wait for a resounding inner *Yes!* and include any limits. If you hesitate or hear an inner *Maybe,* that could mean:
  - You need more information. Ask for whatever you want to know. "I'm okay for the area, but what kind of touch are you thinking?"
  - You are a yes but with certain limits. "Yes, but only to here."
  - An inner no is trying to be heard.
  - If you wait a little longer, it will be clear which one it is.

3. Answer.

  - Some examples:

    "You bet!"
    "Yes, but only to here."
    "Yes, and would you like my shirt on or off for that?"
    "I'm not sure. What do you mean exactly?"
    "No, I'm not ready for that. What else might you like?"
    "No."

3. Lean back and get comfortable.

As in the lesson, the Taker does not adapt to the comfort of the Allower; the Allower adapts to the comfort of the Taker.

First the Taker:

1. Get comfortable first—*before you begin.* Same reasons as in the lesson. Lean your torso back, stretch out, put pillows where you want them.

2. Ask the Allower to drape over your lap, wrap around you, lean on you, or whatever gives you access to the area you want to explore.

Then the Allower:

  - Adjust your position to the Taker in some way that is reasonably comfortable for you too, again using cushions. You'll have to talk about it together and adjust accordingly.

4. Explore and experiment.

Both of you are responsible for your own comfort. Then stay in the role you have agreed to.

Taker:

  - Respect your Allower. Stay within the limits they have set.
  - Bring your attention to your hands. Close the outflow and open the inflow. Stop giving.

- If you want to change something or expand your territory, stop your hands and then ask. "Wow, this is great. May I include your arms too?"

Allower:

- You have only one responsibility: self-care. That means to communicate your limits and continue to do so as needed.
- If it happens that your Taker strays outside what they asked for, let them know: "That's not my arm" or "I didn't agree to my back."
- You are allowed to change your mind. For example:

    "I thought that would work, but it's not."
    "I need to move my legs...there, okay."

- You are allowed to enjoy it as much as you like.

5. Thank you/You're welcome

Sit up facing each other.

Taking partner:

- Say "Thank you."

Allowing partner:

- Say "You're welcome" and nothing more. No matter how much you enjoyed it, do not thank the Taker. (See Lesson 2.)

6. Switch roles.

If you have time, you can go back and forth a few times.

7. Talk about what you noticed.

Talk about what you noticed *about yourself*, not about your partner. Do not give a "review" of their performance (because it wasn't one). This might include sensations in your body or emotions or thoughts that arose. What was challenging? What was a relief?

As the Taker: *Did I stay within the limits of our agreement? Did I remember it was for me, or did I try to please my partner?*

As the Allower: *Did I endure anything unpleasant? If so, why?*

8. Close your dedicated time.

This is where you can thank each other if you like.

9. Come back to it.

Return twenty or thirty times—then for a few decades.

NOTES ON HUGGING AND KISSING

If you want to include hugging or kissing, it is possible to stay in Take-Allow, but it's not easy.

Hugging is usually (hopefully) a mutually engaged activity. In Take-Allow, though, you are active, and your Allower is not. In Taking, experiment with this: ask for wrapping your arms around your partner or, if you are lying down, draping yourself over them. Your partner is relatively stationary. How is that different from hugging? What can you discover there?

Likewise for kissing. Lips have even more sensory nerves than the hands. Like the hands, when the lips stop working, they are able to feel more. In Taking, if you ask to kiss your partner's mouth or body, notice that if you do a traditional kissing motion—puckering and smacking—you can't feel much. It has some meaning as a gesture but little sensation. Instead, change the focus of your attention from outflow (technique) to inflow (sensation). Soften your lips and use them to feel. Feel your partner's face, fingers, whatever you have asked for. Feel their lips, but don't do the kissing motion, and don't let them kiss you back. What do you find?

A HUNDRED THINGS TO TRY

Someone suggested I make a card deck of a hundred things to try, but you don't need a list. You need to recover your ability to have spontaneous impulses, notice what they are, trust them, and express them. As you recover that ability, there will be no end of things that pop into your mind that might be fun. Here are a few examples:

"May I feel your thighs, and is it okay to squeeze them?"
"May I use my face to feel your back?"
"I'd like to lie on top of you. Are you okay with that?"
"I'd like to explore your feet and toes. May I do that, and are you okay with them in my lap?"
"Will you lean back against me, and may I reach around you and feel your chest?"
"I'd like to drape you over my lap, and feel your back and butt. Is that okay with you?"

FEELINGS, EROS, AND TURN-ON

Play with this a few times, and you'll notice a wide range of moods and feelings. At times tenderhearted, at other times rowdy or raunchy, at other times trance-like bliss states, sometimes child-like, curious, silly, or hilarious, and at other times erotic. At some point, you are likely to get turned on.

Turn-on is a feeling and is not dependent on skin contact and certainly not dependent on genital contact. It is dependent on knowing how to access it in yourself. Part of erotic maturity is learning to take responsibility for your own arousal. You choose when to set it aside until later and when and how to let it come out to play.

The lab structure, in which there is no genital touch yet, does not at all mean no eros or no turn-on. In fact, it can make eros easier to play with, because knowing it's not leading to a different activity frees you up to explore and express it. *What does this arousal actually feel like? What is challenging here, and what is a relief?* Arousal likes to stretch, roll, reach, bite, hump, grind, growl, howl, and laugh. It may seem ironic that this can be easier with clothes on, but it often is. You are neither searching for orifices nor avoiding them, nor are you worried about fluids. This can create a tremendous amount of freedom.

You made your agreements for time, body areas, and what clothing may be on or off. Stick to those agreements no matter how turned on you get, and see where that lets you go that you may not have gone otherwise. When you stay in your agreements, it builds trust and safety, and the hotter it gets, the more you will need the safety. Stay in the container of your agreements.

EXPLORING TAKING

The Taking Quadrant is perhaps the heart of the practice. In this lab, you get to explore it and find the challenges, liberation, nourishment, and joy that live here. The important thing to know about Taking is that it is receiving a gift. The gift is access, which is a significant gift. In order to receive this gift, you have to stop giving. To be clear, you *care* about your Allower, but you are not doing for their benefit. You are receiving a gift—from them.

To review what you learned about Taking in the lessons, the experience requires the neural pathways you reconnected in Waking Up the Hands. Until you can attend to the sensation in your hands and experience it as enjoyable, the Taking Quadrant cannot click. You learned that in order to touch someone, you don't need to "give" to them. What you need is their permission, and you learned how to ask for that permission. You learned to lean back, slow down, and attend to the sensation in your hands, and that opened up the awareness that this touch was, indeed, for you. You learned to *feel* their hand instead of doing something to it. Now we are taking all those skills into this lab.

The two principles that show up most here are learning to trust that you will not harm your Allower and making room for the Intensity Factor.

It is impossible to enjoy Taking if you are worried you will harm or annoy your Allower. To enjoy Taking, you have to learn to trust yourself. As we talked about in chapter 10, in order to trust yourself, you first have to become trustworthy.

You become trustworthy by gaining consent skills. That means noticing what you want to do and asking for it in the most direct way possible by using the words "May I...?" Then it means waiting for the answer. When your partner says yes, you look them in the eyes and wait there until you believe them. When your partner says no or sets a limit, you believe them and abide by that. Part of consent skills is the ability to notice, keeping the inflow of information open. Are they holding their breath? Did their jaw tighten? If the inflow is open in your hands, you will notice changes in muscle tension, temperature, and moisture. You may not notice it consciously, but your nervous system registers it; your hands become intuitive. Noticing both yourself and the other person allows you to stay in consent. As you become trustworthy, you begin to trust yourself, and then you relax and explore and receive the gift you are being given. Feeling doubtful about Taking comes from many factors including your relationship to pleasure and desire. Becoming trustworthy is not the only factor in Taking, but for the joy of Taking, it is essential.

The other factor that shows up in Taking is the Intensity Factor. As you consider asking for more "exciting" body areas, for clothing to come off, or for longer times, you have more tension (fear) about it, and you start moving faster, which makes you lose Taking and revert to your habitual way to touch. When you can stay in Taking for five minutes, increase to eight or ten minutes. When you can stay in Taking with, say, their shirt on, expand to include asking for their shirt to be off. In this lab, we don't include genital touch, because it will increase the tension and almost certainly throw you out of Taking. It is more useful—and more interesting—to feel someone's kneecap and stay in Taking than to try sexier body parts and fall out of Taking.

Taking develops gradually. At first, you have to consciously remind yourself who it's for. Eventually it feels more natural. Then you increase the intensity, and you fall out. Then you are able to stay in it at that level, you increase it again, and fall out again. You are gradually able to remain trustworthy in exchanges that are longer or more erotically charged. You start asking for things that feel more vulnerable to ask for. Along the way, you notice new layers of Taking. In the lesson, you thought, *Okay, I* *get this.* In the lab, it clicks in a deeper way: *Oh, there's more here!* A few months or years later, it's deeper still.

THE ART OF TAKING: BECOMING THE GUARDIAN

It is possible to abide by your agreement but do so with a grumble: *Oh well, I guess so, if I have to.* Or to play brinksmanship: *How close can I get to the limit and not get caught?* There is another way. Taking becomes an art when you actively guard the agreement, plant your banner in the ground, and defend their limits with your honor. Images of knights come to mind.

The bare minimum for Taking is to not pressure your Allower. Becoming the guardian takes it a step further. You don't let your Allower pressure themselves. You don't give up the conversation until their limits are clear. If your Allower looks doubtful—the furrowed brow, the worried eyes, the words "Uh, yeah, I guess so"—stop right there. You don't want to do what they are barely okay with. You want to receive a gift, and a gift happens only with a full-hearted yes. When you care about this, it will become evident to them.

Allowing can be difficult. It can be next to impossible for the Allower to speak up and say, "Stop" or "I've changed my mind." Though you are not responsible, you can make it easier. As a guardian, the more you protect their limits, the more your Allower can relax. They don't have to be on guard against you. You may think that guarding the agreement is some balance between putting yourself first and putting them first. Not at all. Put your desires first—and—guard the agreement. Be clear in making your agreement, don't let them acquiesce, and tend yourself so you don't step over their limits. When done well, it's joyful and inspiring.

Being an excellent guardian helps you notice that the gift is for you, because you no longer worry about stealing, and you can receive the gift. And a Taker who is good guardian is very sexy. There is no one more fun to surrender to.

HOW TO STAY IN TAKING

Those are the main principles that show up in Taking: becoming trustworthy, the Intensity Factor, and guarding the agreement. Because

Taking tends to be slippery; here are some details that make a difference. They are the same factors we saw in the lesson about breaking the habits of giving, mainly in your words and your body. Let's look at those two: the agreement and the doing.

Making the agreement

In the instructions, there is the suggestion to pause. Let's look at that.

The agreement creates the dynamic. Without an agreement, there is no Taking Quadrant. The first step is recognizing that there is something you want to do—for you—and taking full responsibility for that. This is sometimes the hardest part, but once it becomes clear, the rest of it falls into place.

Listen to the question. You have just been asked, "How do you want to touch me?" It may be an unusual question, but it's an extremely simple one. It's a question about what you want. One challenge of Taking is that it's so foreign we have no idea where to start. Listen to the words, and wait for them to sink in. On the third day of a workshop in which Taking was not clicking for her, one person had an aha moment: "Oh, I was hearing the word *touch*, but I wasn't hearing the word *want*! How do I *want* to touch you—I get it now!"

Take your time. You might worry that waiting is a bother for your partner. It's not; this is part of their gift. Look at your partner, let your eyes wander, and see where you get curious or ask your hands what they are curious about.

It could be that you don't have much of a repertoire. In a recent workshop, people were playing with hair, exploring backs, and generally feeling each other up, and one person asked, "Will you lie face down? I'd like to roll around on you." The Allower did that. The Taker lay on them in perpendicular, waist at waist, and rolled across, up and down, using the Allower like a large pillow. Another person said, "Wow, that's an option? I never would have thought of that!" If you don't have much experience with nonsexual cuddling, contact improv, or rolling around like puppies, you probably don't know there are many ways to play with another person's body. Taking sex off the menu often opens up other ideas.

Then you make your request and respect the answer.

Words matter. We talked about this in the lesson. The words you use reveal what you *are* thinking and set you up for what you *can* think and therefore what you can experience. When you say, "May I feel your back?" your mind sets you up to have that experience, and you feel their back. If you don't have the vocabulary, or it feels impolite (or, more likely, you don't notice you are doing it), you will say, "Would you like me to touch your back?" or "Would you like a back massage?" or "May I massage your back?" If you use the word massage at all, your mind says *Oh I get it, we're giving a massage now!* and proceeds to do that. It is difficult to switch gears and feel their back instead.

Make a request that is explicit, direct, and as short as it takes to convey it while still giving the information about what you want. "May I touch your arm?" doesn't give much information. These say more: "May I feel your arm slowly?" or "May I explore the skin and the hairs on your arm?" or "May I play with your arm, moving it around in circles?"

Being explicit and direct can feel unnatural, even impossible. Something less direct may feel more familiar to you like, "Um, maybe you might like me to rub your back in such a way that I might also enjoy?" (someone actually said that). Saying, "May I feel your back?" helps you notice you are asking for a gift and sets you up to experience receiving one.

Wait for the answer. It may seem obvious to wait for the answer, but I have seen people get started before they hear a yes. If it's a no, respect that. Never pressure by saying, "Oh, come on now, are you sure?" It's more likely that you will hear a yes but won't entirely let it sink in. Look them in the eyes, and stay there until it sinks in. If necessary, ask again. With one person who was struggling with Taking, I had him look his partner in the eye and wait until he felt her yes. It took a few minutes. His eyes got moist, and he said, "I get it. She really is willing to give me this. I didn't get her yes before—now I do."

At first, waiting for the answer is simple. As your turns get longer and more body is involved, there may be some negotiation: "Yes for this but not that part." In that case, confirm the limits. "This is okay, and you want me to stay away from this, right?" This is part of the art of Taking.

Be strict inside the container; outside the container, you are welcome to communicate as you like.

The Doing

Now that you have permission and believe it, it's time to play! The instructions say, "Get comfortable." Let's look at that.

Muscle memory is the ability to reproduce a particular movement without conscious thought, built on repeated use of that movement. It also works in reverse. When you put yourself in a certain position or use a certain movement, you tend to create a certain inner experience. To access a different inner experience, put yourself into a different position. When you put yourself in the position in which you would normally be "giving" or "working" (holding yourself up and reaching forward), you experience yourself as giving or working. Your body is learning how to Take. It is your job to put it into the position in which it can.

Lean back. We did this in the lesson, but now that you have more options for what part you are feeling, it may take a little negotiating and fiddling around with it. You can experiment with leaning back with legs out, and drape your partner across your lap (this is especially great for backs, buttocks, legs, and arms), or lean back and have your legs open and ask your partner to lean back against you, facing away. This is a great way to reach around and explore the belly and chest. You can also lie down and have them drape an arm, leg, or torso over you.

Get out of symmetry. Symmetry means your right and left sides are mirror images. If you are going to give your partner a scalp massage, you likely have them lie in the middle and you sit at their crown, one hand on each side of their head. You are in symmetry. If you have asked for permission to play with their hair and you put them in this position, you automatically start giving them a massage. It's extremely difficult not to. In workshops I often say, "If it looks like a massage, it probably is."

Instead, lean back and extend your legs out in whatever way is comfortable. Place a pillow on your lap. Ask them to lie on their side with their head on your lap, their body stretched out to your side. Use one hand. Now explore and notice what is different. I have walked people through this many times, and they often say, "Ohhh, this feels different. I didn't know I had been giving, but I was!"

If you see someone else in these two positions (in symmetry and out of symmetry), it is immediately obvious who is working at it and who is there for the enjoyment of it. It's also likely that the position that is out of symmetry looks more intimate; it is clearly not a therapeutic setup.

For most people, the challenge is that they don't know how to touch without giving, so it all feels the same—until they change it in these ways.

Then the instructions say to explore and experiment.

Your hands. The other major factor in being able to stay in Taking is to slow down your hands by half—then slow them again. Start with feeling for the anatomy, and your hands will naturally shift toward feeling for their pleasure. It's often easier to *see* what your hands are doing than it is to *feel* what they are doing, so again, look. Hands that are curious are soft and tend to make full contact. They are not repetitive, predicable, or symmetrical. If your hands are feeling, they *will* move slowly, because if they don't, they can't feel much.

Here's something you can try. When you begin, hold your hands still. Rest them on the area you are feeling. Don't hold them up or push them down. Just rest their weight. Wait there until your Allower and you both soften. I've had people rest there for a full two or three minutes before seeing their hands relax. Time does not matter.

Open the inflow. If your hands are relaxed and the inflow is open, you will notice slight changes in your Allower's muscle tension and breath. This is part of what makes you trustworthy. If they tense up, stop what you are doing, make eye contact, and ask, "How are you doing?"

Your Allower. Of course you care about your Allower, but stop trying to please them. They get to have whatever experience they have. If you slip out of Taking, they can't be in Allowing, which is an experience in its own right. For the person who loves Allowing, sometimes the hardest part is finding someone who can stay in Taking long enough for them to dive in.

Who is this for? People are often focused on the experience of the Allower. Bring your attention back to your own experience and your own sensation. You'll probably have to remind yourself a few times. Ask yourself, *Who is this for?* Often people tell me, "Oh, I forgot until you asked me that."

The experience. Exploring Taking will surprise you. It is rich, varied, complex, nourishing, challenging, tender, liberating, surprising, sensual, playful, and potentially sexy. There will be times when it's awkward or odd and times when it is a welcome relief. There will be moments of exquisite tenderheartedness and gratitude, perhaps tears. You will be astounded at what you can feel. Desires will come to surface that you didn't know you had. You may feel self-conscious, embarrassed, or chagrined. You'll appreciate your partner's generosity. You learn to move your body to express what is inside—curiosity, delight, hunger, lust, tenderness, or gratitude. That may be a shock or a relief.

As you found in the lesson, a couple of threads intertwine: sensation and your awareness of the gift. Sometimes one will come to the forefront and sometimes the other. Sometimes the sensation will make you notice the gift. At other times, awareness of the gift will give you permission to attend to the sensation. Most fundamental is the sensation. If you're lost, go back to it again.

What to do with the feelings? You get to decide. Does it sound appealing to be held or listened to? Ask for that. Does it sound more appealing to keep going gently and let the tears fall or to slow down or take a break? You get to choose.

Too easy. If you think, *Oh man, this is a piece of cake,* it's one of two things. 1) It really is easy for you. This will be the case only if you were able to settle into a relaxed state of pleasure with Waking Up the Hands. If that is the case, lucky you! Now find the edge of your vulnerability. Where do you get tenderhearted? Usually it's when slowing down.

Or 2) you are going through the motions without taking it in. This is far more likely and fairly common among those with a lot of touch experience. It is not possible to be cavalier with Taking. It is a significant gift and touches your heart. When your partner says "Yes," stay there until you believe them. Move your hands even more slowly. When do your eyes become moist and your throat catch?

TAKING EXAMPLES

What some people have said

"I always ask for what I think the other person wants."

"Whatever you want…Oh, that's right. It's for me, isn't it?"

"I don't know how to touch someone's shoulders *without* giving a massage."

"This makes me nervous."

"Boy, my mind was going all over. I just had to keep bringing it back to my body."

"I've been touching women all my life and don't know any other way. Why—to give her pleasure. But I like touching. I didn't realize it!"

"This feels like a treat I have been denied."

"Heavenly, this feels so good!"

This is different

At a workshop for bodyworkers, we were learning Taking. Jen was sitting next to her practice buddy (who was lying down), running her hand along the back of their legs at a moderate speed. She looked bored or at least unimpressed.

Me: What are you noticing?

Jen: Well, yes, this is nice.

Me: What do you mean?

Jen: (She had the look of someone who was trying to do the right thing but not sure what it might be.) I think I get this. It feels okay.

Me: Experiment with this for a minute. Slow your hand waaaay down, and see what happens.

Jen: (She did so and right away tears came to her eyes. She was surprised and lifted her hand to her chest.) Oh my God, what is that, I have no idea. Even when I thought it was for me, it was still for him, and I didn't even know it. This is completely different. My God, how much have I been doing that in my life?

Back to the hands

Ben jumped in right away. They had a great sense of play and used their whole body. They lifted their partner up, held her, rolled across the floor, and rested their head on the small of her back, but their hands had not really felt anything. I had them back up and start with their hands. It took a few minutes, but when it clicked, they felt tender and vulnerable. Their eyes got moist. They said, "Oh, this is hard." Later, when they went back to playing with their whole body, they were more emotionally present.

More vulnerable

Adam was in a workshop for the second time. Last time, feeling the object was extremely confusing, and he could enjoy the candleholder only by playing with the idea that the candleholder was enjoying it too.

This time, for the Taking exercise, he wanted to have his Allower lie face down so he could lean forward and move his hands quickly over their body—poking and playing. It took some convincing to have him start over, lean back, and drape them over his lap. I said, "This is an experiment. I'm not sure what you'll find. If you don't find anything, you can go back to the poking." It still took some reminders to *feel* the person, and as he tried that, he became somber. He said, "Oh, this is different—it's a lot harder. It feels vulnerable. It's hard to stay here. I keep wanting to distract myself."

The most improved player award

James learned this process at a workshop by one of my students. He created a spreadsheet of the quadrants and how well he thought he was able to access each of them, where he felt stuck, even the feelings that arose in each one. He was right in his evaluation. For him, the Accepting Quadrant was tiny, the Allowing Quadrant was minuscule, and the Taking Quadrant was missing. Serving was huge.

We started with the object. It was difficult for him to take in any tactile sensation at all. He could focus by sheer force of will and so had the data, but he was unable to fall into pleasure. "I feel this bump over here. I feel this soft place right here." He took this exercise home, played with it five minutes a day for eight weeks, and came back for the next step. When feeling my hand, he was tentative, a little stiff, and used predictable strokes. His hands were performing. I asked, "Who is this for?" He said, "Well, you said I could explore, but I'm not sure I believe it, and I'm not sure I have permission to go into these feelings either. They're going to be big. This is hard stuff."

We explored all the quadrants in several sessions over a few months. Some things he noted about himself: "I have no idea what I want." "It's hard to say no." "I always start in Serving, because that's what I know how to do."

One day, he put the pieces together. "If you can't feel pleasure, of course you don't know what you want, because you don't know what feels good! And if you don't know what you want, you can't say no, so Allowing is terrifying! And then it's hard to trust others to say no either. You assume it's as hard for them as it is for you, so you have to second-guess everyone—that's exhausting! Once you can feel your skin, you can want something, because you have something to want something *with*!"

Until then, his erotic experience (which was considerable) had been vicarious. When you have so little neural basis for the experience of your own body, vicarious is all you have. He had said, "All I know how to do is make other people feel good, and I'm very good at that." James earned the Most Improved Player award. It was an inspiring journey to work with him.

PRINCIPLE:
THE INTENSITY FACTOR

As any activity becomes more intense, we become more likely to revert to doing what we have always done. This is called the Intensity Factor, and it happens in all four quadrants.

Here's something I noticed that puzzled me at first. I would guide someone through learning Taking by feeling their partner's hand. They would learn to lean back, explore slowly and attend to their sensation, and it would click. Then we would expand the options to include the rest of the body, and everything they had just learned would melt away. I'd have to remind them, and they would get it again. Then they would remove some piece of clothing, and it would happen again. They would forget what they had learned, I'd remind them, and then they would get it again. If we eventually progressed to sexual touch, it happened again—right back to their old habit of trying to get the job done. Eventually I saw that what was throwing people off track was the increase in intensity. By intensity, I mean:

1) Emotional charge, which can be feelings you like or feelings you don't like: fear, shame, joy, surprise, and sometimes pleasure.
2) Sexual charge, sometimes just the first glimmer of it.
3) Moving faster, either your body or their body. This one surprised me when I noticed it.

What constitutes intensity is subjective; what feels mild to one person feels intense to another, so an increase in intensity means in comparison to yourself. When the intensity goes up, we go backwards as it were, dropping out of our new learning mode and back into our previous default mode. This is not a character flaw—it's neurology. Of course, which situation brings up fear or joy varies from one person to the next.

Pleasure can be a factor too, because at some level of pleasure, we hit our self-doubt, shame, and guilt. It's not that the pleasure itself is too intense—it's the feelings that arise along with it, so we're back to emotional charge.

The Intensity Factor is guaranteed to happen; the only question is when. How much intensity and what kind does it take to throw you back to your previous habit? In the Doing Half, your default will most likely be trying to Serve, focusing on technique, holding your body in tension, moving your hands faster, or forgetting to attend to your sensation. In the Done-to Half, your default is likely to be going along with something you are less than inspired about.

Why the Intensity Factor is important. The point of the practice is to explore the quadrants. You can do that only to the degree you can stay *in* the quadrants, and as the intensity goes up, it will tend to throw you back to your default, which may not be the quadrant you are looking for. It's important to be aware of this tendency and to give yourself some slack for it.

The cure. The cure for the Intensity Factor is to slow down. This means take that pause to notice what you want and what you're okay with. It means starting with body areas that are relatively neutral to you and not being in a hurry to get to all the fancy parts. It means starting with turns of three to five minutes. For most people, it means starting clothed. It means moving your hands slowly—even slower. It can help to start somewhere other than the bedroom like the living room or a park bench.

Here's an example. Ken was in my studio learning the quadrants. He'd gotten Taking a few months before and had been playing with it with his partners in their sexual play and loving it. Now he was back for the next step. We returned to Taking with his hands on my back. I had him slow down, way down. He hit his tenderheartedness, becoming quiet with moist eyes. "Oh, I get it," he said. "This is something I was skipping right over. I should have been going much slower all along." "Tell me more," I said. "Well, not just my hands slower but also not taking it to sex, just staying in a regular body area. This is different. This is really receiving."

It grows. Get solid in your quadrant at the level of intensity at which you can easily stay in it, and it becomes more solid. Then your capacity to be with more intensity naturally increases. For example, starting in the Taking Quadrant, the experience is new. Today, if you move quickly or include sexual body areas, you'll slip into trying to Serve. Six months from now when you have explored Taking in less charged areas and stayed in it, you'll be able to include the same sexy body parts and enjoy the same level of turn-on and still stay in Taking.

In most of the experiences of the labs, the Intensity Factor will be subtle. It will tend to make the quadrants elusive again, but because that feels normal, you don't notice it. Then you do. Then you back up and slow down, and the quadrant reveals itself anew.

Overwhelm. A related idea is overwhelm. You have a letter in your mailbox—the old-fashioned kind, on paper with a stamp. It requires a thoughtful reply, so you ponder before answering. The next week, another one. This keeps up, and you notice that one letter a week is doable. One day, you find three. You manage to get them answered. Then you find ten. You begin to worry. The quality of your responses goes down. One day, a truck appears and drops off twenty bags of letters. You are overwhelmed. You slam the door and go hide under the bed.

"Overwhelm" means there is more coming in than your current capacity to process, much less respond to. Something is going to go unanswered. Your capacity may be one letter a day or ten, but whatever it is, there is a limit.

How much intensity it takes to reach overwhelm is different for everyone. For some, it's right away in the lessons. For others, it's not until things are moving quickly or erotically charged. It's different with different partners, on different days, with different activities. It's not a question of whether you have a point of overwhelm; it's a question of what particular situation and how much it takes. One person said, "When someone comes at me quickly or roughly, I push them away, no problem, but when someone comes at me slowly and sweetly, that's when I get overwhelmed and end up going along with something." For others, it will be the opposite.

It's helpful to acknowledge the existence of overwhelm, because it can help you notice when it's getting close without having to go over the cliff. If you do go over the cliff, you can forgive yourself.

EXPLORING ALLOWING

To review what you learned in the lessons, Allowing is a form of giving, so you set aside what you might prefer but stay responsible for your limits. You learned that the gift you are giving is access to you, and the more responsibility you take for your limits, the more you can enjoy giving the gift. Perhaps you also learned that when you take responsibility for your limits, you stop trying to make your Taker responsible for them. You stop hoping they will miraculously intuit them. Perhaps you also discovered how liberating that was!

The main principle that applies in Allowing is the principle of Adapting Ourselves which we talk about in a few pages. We so easily try to change how we feel so that whatever is happening can keep happening. You might expect me to say something like this: The secret to Allowing is to get over yourself, trust your Taker, and surrender. I am going to say the opposite. The secret to ease, generosity, and joy in Allowing is to stop trying to make yourself be okay with something. Instead, notice what you are in fact okay with and honor that. That is, own your limits. When you own your limits, you will automatically relax, you become generous within those limits, and Allowing becomes a joy. So it's limits first, then comes the joy. If it's not joyful, that's a sign there is some limit you have not yet noticed or spoken.

In workshops, we play with it like this. Imagine a giant circle around you that contains everything you may be asked to give. You can imagine writing things on pieces of paper and putting them inside the circle. Now bring the circle in closer so it contains only those things you are happy to give; the things that you are not happy to give are outside the circle. At some point, when you bring it in close enough, you breathe a sigh of relief. "Ah, yeah, this much I can easily give." The limits may seem small (the little finger for twenty seconds) or may seem large (your body for an hour), but the size of the circle does not matter. What matters is that you don't give up on yourself until you notice what that limit is. When you say, "Yes, you can play with my little finger for twenty seconds," you sigh with relief, because you know it won't go beyond that. The sigh of relief is the sign that you have brought the circle in close enough that you are within your limits.

The Intensity Factor also shows up here. There is a level of intensity at which you can track yourself and a level at which you are overwhelmed. This is not a character flaw—it's neurology. As you gain the skills to speak up for yourself, you become trustworthy in gradually more intense or complex interactions.

THE ART OF ALLOWING: SURRENDER

Vertigo is the conflict between the fear of falling and the desire to fall.
—Salman Rushdie

The art of Allowing is getting really good at tending to your limits, so that you become trustworthy, and then you will automatically trust yourself. Then you become flexible, generous and truly relaxed. Your body becomes softer, looser, more moveable—quite fun!

Surrender implies there is someone or something to surrender to. In Allowing, we surrender to a person, the Taker, within agreed-upon limits. In another use of the word, we surrender to our experience.

Surrender is much sought after and widely misunderstood. The myth is that if it's not easy, there must be something wrong with you (that needs fixing), and all you need to do is trust more. This is terrible advice. By this logic, letting go means getting better at ignoring yourself. Essentially you are saying to yourself: *You don't matter.* If you do this, you remain worried about what might be next, as well you should. You teach yourself you cannot be trusted, so you become even more guarded and feel guilty about it.

Surrender requires an empowered choice. When you give up your responsibility for your no, you cannot surrender. You can only be passive, which is never useful and definitely not delicious. Or you can look for someone who can overwhelm you and make you go along anyway. Then you don't have to be "responsible" for it—you can blame them, worship them, or both.

The question to ask yourself is not, *Why can't I surrender?* Going back to the circle on the ground, the question is, *Within what particular limits does it sound fun to surrender?* Or *Within what particular limits can*

I give with a full heart? Essentially this means, within what limits are you trustworthy to yourself?

The other use of the word "surrender" is the idea that you surrender to your experience. You stop trying to micromanage, and you let your pleasure carry you. You can surrender to your experience in any quadrant or no quadrant. In Allowing, you surrender to the other person, and you might also surrender to your experience. In Accepting, you are not surrendering to a person, but you have an exquisite opportunity to surrender to your experience, because there is nothing to give back. I have seen people in Accepting get confused by wanting to surrender to the other person but also trying to drive the interaction. It's confusing and frustrating for both.

HOW TO STAY IN ALLOWING

Those are the main principles: Adapting Ourselves and the Intensity Factor. Again we'll look at two parts: the agreement and the activity.

Making the agreement

Ninety percent of the success of your Allowing experience is in making the agreement. When you slow down enough to be true to yourself in setting your limits, the experience of it will follow easily. If the doing part is worrisome or you can't relax, it's because there is some limit you have not yet spoken. Come back to the agreement. We talked about this in "The Choosing Is More Important than the Doing."

The limits you set are not negotiable. You set your limits, period—then keep them. You can narrow the options as you go, but don't enlarge the options in the middle of the play. You can enlarge them for the next round if you want.

The instructions say to start with the offer and then pause. Let's look at that.

The offer. You start with asking, "How would you like to touch me for (x) minutes?" I recommend you start with turns of three to five minutes. This gives you an automatic out in case you end up giving more that you feel good about or get overwhelmed. As your skills increase and you gain trust in yourself, you'll probably want to increase the time.

You can, if you like, set some limits right away. You might do this to make it easier for yourself or your Taker or for expediency.

"How would you like to touch me? For now, I am available any place my skin is exposed."

"How would you like to touch me? I'm okay with my shirt off, but I am going to keep by pants on."

The request. Then they make a request: "May I (feel your, play with your, explore your...?)" If they imply it's for you by saying, "However you want," or offering to "give" you something, like a massage, remind them it's for them.

The pause. This is where the magic happens. You need some time to notice whether you can give that with a full heart and to notice your limits, trust them, and value them. In the lab, a twenty-second pause is built in.

The easiest way to make yourself pause is to set a timer for twenty or thirty seconds. Don't answer until the timer goes off, even if you think you know. I've seen lots of times when given more time to consider it, the answer changed.

Even better, commit to waiting for the inner resounding *Yes.* Committing means zip your mouth closed, and wait until the answer within is a clear and unequivocal *Yes* or a clear and unequivocal *No.* The pause can feel awkward; thirty seconds can feel like an hour and three minutes like an eternity. If you think, *Uh, I guess so,* don't settle for that. Wait.

When you are hesitant (you're not necessarily a no but not a yes either), you need one of three things. We mentioned these in the instructions.

1) More information about what is being asked for. You might want to know what kind of touch. Soft, slow? You might want to understand their desires or motivations or what it means to them.

2) Setting some limit such as "This far and no farther." You may be okay with having your face felt but not your eyes. You may be okay with having your legs touched but only up to here. Often there is some variation that works for you.

3) It's an inner no trying to be heard. This one can take some patience from you. There are lots of reasons hearing an inner no can be difficult.

The question to ask yourself is not, *Why can't I give this?* The question is, *What is the thing that I can give with a full heart?* or *What is it about the request, that if it changed, I would be glad to give it?* or *What is the limit that, if I set it, would make me happy to give it?* This is not, *What is it about* me *that would need to change?* It's, *What is it about the* request *that would need to change?*

Another way to make yourself pause is to wait for the sigh of relief we talked about a few pages back. If you are tense at all, narrow the options until you breathe a sigh of relief. Something like this will go through your mind. *Can they feel my entire body?* (Creates tension) Nope. *Can they feel my legs?* (Still tension) Nope. *Can they feel my feet?* (Still some tension) Nope. *Can they feel my left pinky toe?* (Getting closer but still a little tension) *Can they feel my left pinky toe for thirty seconds?* (Tension gone!) Ahh, there it is!

Comfort zone. Start well within your comfort zone. When you push yourself to do something you don't feel safe doing, your protective systems engage. Your body tenses, and you grit your teeth. When you choose something that is within the zone of what is comfortable, you relax.

When you respect your limits, you gain your own trust, which you are going to need. Over time, because you can trust yourself, you naturally and gradually become interested in expanding your options. Things start to look interesting and appealing to you, because you trust yourself to take care of yourself. This is a natural expansion that is a direct result of respecting your limits.

Listen for the pull, not the push. There will be times when something feels edgy but also appealing. (We'll talk about this more in the next lab.)

- This is a push: *I should be okay with this. What's wrong with me?*
- This is a pull: *This is a little edgy for me, but it sounds fun—I'd really like to try it!*

Some examples of answering:
"I need some time to consider that."

"Yes, that sounds great. I'd like to turn around and get comfortable first."

"I'm not sure. Can you tell me more?"

"No, I'm not comfortable with that. What else would you like?"

"Face is fine but not my eyes."

"Thighs are fine, but I have a bruise on the side, so no squeezing there."

"Wow, that's a stretch for me. I think I'd like to try it though. Let me just sit a minute and see how it feels to me...Okay, I'd like to try that. Here's my hesitation. If it's too much for me, I will need to stop. I need you to reassure me that you are okay with me stopping if I need to. Are you? ...Okay then, let's try it!"

If it's extremely difficult. It's common for people to feel awkward with Allowing. Occasionally, they can be nearly paralyzed with fear. If this happens in session with me, I skip Allowing altogether and start you in Accepting. If you want to learn that you have a choice about how you are touched, the best way is to direct the touch yourself—each moment, each stroke. Learn how to choose what you want and what that feels like, and then come back to Allowing. If being touched at all is intimidating, we skip it and start you in Taking so you are even more in charge of what happens.

I gave some examples of setting limits when you make the offer, such as, "For now, I am available waist up." Another way is to first notice what, if anything, you can easily give, and offer that: "You may explore my arms until I tell you to stop," or "You may hold my feet for three minutes, and if you want, you can feel around on them."

The Doing

In the instructions, I said your only responsibility is self-care. Here's how that looks.

I said that in Allowing, ninety percent is in making the agreement. Occasionally, you'll get started and realize you need to change it. The important thing to know about making changes is that you don't need a reason. Often all we know is that it doesn't feel right any more. Trust that. The *why* doesn't need to be clear.

Examples of making corrections:

"I need you to slow down, please."

"Sorry, that's too light—it tickles."

"Ooof, that's too rough!"

Examples of changing your mind:

"I thought that was going to work, but it's not. I need to move."

"That sounded okay at first, but it's not working for me. Please stop and ask for something else."

"I'm getting uncomfortable. I need a pause."

Speak up if your Taker goes beyond your agreement:

"I didn't agree to the arms, just the back."

If your mouth refuses to work, hand signals can fill in. Lift your hand into a stop sign, or put your hand on their hand and hold it still.

As you learn how to say, "Stop," "Slow down," or "I've changed my mind," you are no longer worried or guarded. You can notice the gift you are giving and appreciate the person you are giving it to.

Okay to enjoy it. It's not about you, but it's okay to enjoy it. People often say it's the best touch they've ever had. This is because the Taker's hands are relaxed and don't have an agenda. What you don't get to do is ask for what you think you would enjoy more, because this is not about what you want. It's about what you are okay with.

Notes on moving slowly. In describing intensity, I said one factor is the speed of body movement. In this case, we're talking about the movement of the Taker. This has to do with the rate of neural impulses coming in. When the rate of input overwhelms the rate at which you can process the data, your guard goes up, or you freeze. To relax, you need to know that the activity will stay within what you have agreed to. At what speed can you still feel that it will? At what speed does your alarm system kick in? What do you do when it does?

Here's something you can experiment with. Ask your partner to move their hand up your leg, starting slowly. Then ask them to do so slightly faster and again slightly faster. You will notice that there is some rate of speed that becomes less than pleasant, then a rate at which it becomes unpleasant, and then a rate at which your body responds with a swift kick. There may be a rate at which you can no longer speak up. You can set a "speed limit" on your Taker's hands: "Yes, you can feel my back, and I need you to move slowly. I'll tell you if I need you to slow down."

Forgive yourself. At some point, you will endure or tolerate something that you are less than happy to give, maybe even unwilling to give, but you don't know how to stop. If you go slowly and consider your agreements as instructed, it is less likely to happen, but given that you are both exploring, and given that the touch itself is likely to speed up, and you and your Taker are likely to get excited, it may happen. Regroup and forgive yourself. You will learn something about yourself and your limits, and you'll come back to it again with more clarity and understanding. Again, this is why it's best to start with short turns and nonsexual body areas. Your capacity to keep up with yourself grows gradually.

Neutral. Another part of the art of Allowing is remaining neutral. Taking is often difficult for people to explore; they will tend to slide back into trying to Serve. It helps if you remain neutral. If you moan and sigh, the Taker will try to please you more. Outside the container of the practice, let yourself respond. It's only inside this container that it's helpful to stay neutral at first. Though it's often more challenging for the Taker, the less you do, the more they will discover. Once you are both secure in the quadrants, this is less needed, and you can let yourself moan and sigh to your heart's content.

The experience. Allowing can be luxurious, delightful, rich, relaxing, and often pleasurable. The mood of it will depend largely on the Taking partner. You are following, not leading. The mood can be contemplative, meditative even, or tender, cozy, silly, or sexy. It can be like a couple of kids roughhousing. It can become lusty and passionate. It often feels intimate or tenderhearted. There can be times when things are moving quickly and you have to stay on your toes, and other times when you relax into a sweet, trance-like surrender. There will be times you feel self-conscious or embarrassed, and other times when you feel comfortable and generous. You don't have to micromanage, and you get to be surprised.

ALLOWING EXAMPLES

What some people have said

"Am I supposed to enjoy it?"
"Am I allowed to enjoy it?"

"That feels like tolerating."

"Wow—I love not being in charge!"

"I thought that was going to be okay, but it actually wasn't, but I didn't know how to stop it gracefully. I'm glad it's over."

"I learned that if I don't say, 'It's enough now,' I'll find some other way to leave."

"Because of the structure of the game, I knew that what I had agreed to was the only thing that would happen. It was a profound experience for me."

Saved by the bell

Once when playing with a partner, they were in Taking and I was in Allowing. We were moving quickly, kind of a play-wrestle, and having a great time. At one point, I could feel myself step over a subtle threshold. The movement became just a little too fast, and I became uncomfortable, right at the edge of okay-not-okay. This went on for a minute or two, while I was trying to gather up the courage to speak, when the timer went off. Saved by the bell!

Blissed out

Another time, with a client, he was learning Taking and really sinking into it, moving his hands very slowly, up and down my back and legs. He became more and more relaxed and so did I. This went on for probably fifteen minutes, but it felt like time stopped. This was one of the most relaxed states I have ever been in. After, while driving home, I noticed my voice had deepened about three notches.

I didn't know

Another time with a client, I was role-playing Taking so they could learn Allowing. When I do this, I am always careful to move slowly so the client does not get overwhelmed, but I still actually Take. That is, I choose and ask for something that is within their limits but also enjoyable for me. This time, I was feeling their arm and hand and settled into enjoying it. They became tenderhearted and said, "Wow. I can tell you are enjoying it. This is totally different. I don't think I ever knew that anyone could enjoy me before."

Do whatever you want!

I told this story in the first chapter, about the man who thought "How do you want to touch me?" meant "Do whatever you want!" That's a great example of the Adapting Ourselves principle.

PRINCIPLE:
ADAPTING OURSELVES

I had a good aha moment during a Take/Allow practice...I realized I did not have to endure when I am Allowing...it was like, "Wait a second, how did I not notice this before?" I could literally shift my hand, get comfortable in my seat, change positions and not endure!! The cool thing was I felt it in my body... amazing! :)

—A student

We will adapt ourselves unnecessarily to whatever is happening, and this feels so normal that we often don't notice we are. We are going to reverse that dynamic. Instead of changing ourselves to suit the action, we are going to change the action to suit ourselves.

A young woman came up to me at a conference where I had spoken. She was "receiving" from her boyfriend but not enjoying it much. Because we had been talking about the quadrants, I said, "Maybe it's because you are not receiving." What I meant was that maybe instead of being in a receiving dynamic (Accepting), she was actually in a giving dynamic (Allowing). Her response was revealing. "Ooooh yeah, right, I get it—I should open up my heart more and take it in, receeeeive it more." It showed me that what she thought I meant by receiving was that she needed to change her attitude. She was essentially saying that the activity was right, and the problem was with her. Here are some other common statements:

"I feel guilty for not liking something that is being done."

"It didn't occur to me that it didn't actually have to happen."

"Why don't I like this? There must be something wrong with me."

"I had a tantra massage, and I was gritting my teeth all the way through it."

"I'm not really comfortable with that, but I feel like I should be. Are other people okay with that?"

"It's not what I wanted, but she didn't ask, so I figured I'd make the best of it."

I've heard countless statements like these, and there are more examples scattered through the book. I began to notice that what these had in common was that they assumed the activity was right, and the problem was how they felt about it. Their job was to somehow change how they felt so that the activity could continue. I began to wonder why on earth we do that.

Touched against our will. I eventually realized that there is one fact that colors every experience we have of being touched. That is that every one of us has been touched against our will in ways we did not want or like and were unable to stop, and it happened before we could talk. In the best of circumstances, it was only when necessary and with kindness, like being picked up to be bathed, fed, or played with. In the worst cases, we may have suffered terrible violence. Most of us are somewhere in between, but wherever we are on the spectrum, these early experiences are embedded deep in our nervous system.

It's a fact of life that as a child, things happen we don't want, but here's the rub: the fact that it happens so early in our neurological development means that we come to feel that this is the *nature* of touch. We learn that touch is something that just happens, and we have little choice about it. If we're not thrilled with it, we have to change ourselves. We have to try to make ourselves like it or at least try to be okay with it. It teaches us that what is happening is more important than how we feel about it.

At the same time, we didn't get the touch we wanted (and often still don't). We put up with touch we didn't want and set-tled for the crumbs of what we did want—and this feels normal. You may think this applies only to those who suffered abuse. Not at all. It's every one of us; it's just a matter of degree. We believe it's not the touch that's the problem—it's us.

When your partner asks you how you would *like* to be touched, and you answer with how you *don't mind* being touched, this is what is happening. When you are being touched in some way you don't like but think you are supposed to like so you try to like it, this is what is happening.

After childhood, we sometimes have opportunities to learn that we do have a choice. Sometimes we don't. Mostly, it seems, we know it in our heads, but our bodies must learn it by experience.

The effects of adapting. The obvious effect of this is that when we are being touched, we go along with what we don't want (in Accepting) or what we don't feel good about giving (in Allowing). We miss the fact that it is possible to be touched in ways we want. It just does not occur to us. Or we push ourselves to be okay with something we're not and blame ourselves for it. For the most part, we don't notice that we are doing it—again, because it feels normal.

Adapting also affects us in the Doing Half. We think that what we're doing is the magic bullet (if only they would stop resisting!). We think that we are supposed to be able to do anything, and even if we don't feel good about it, we keep going.

The real problem with this adapting pattern is more insidious. We forget to notice what we want, and we confuse that with what we are Willing-to. We stop valuing our desires, stop trusting them, and worse, stop noticing them. Eventually we forget that there is in fact something we want. This leads to deep passivity and hopelessness. This is where we become dangerous to others and to ourselves. We forget that our boundaries matter. We tend to put ourselves in situations in which others take advantage of us, and when we don't value our own boundaries, we stop valuing (or noticing) the boundaries of others. This too is where we become dangerous to ourselves and others. In the introduction, I gave the example of not knowing what we want and allowing dioxin and the loss of salmon, songbirds, and more.

Reverse the sequence. Instead of trying to change yourself to suit that activity, what might happen if you change the activity to suit yourself? To do this, it helps to reverse the sequence of what happens. In the old sequence, the touch happens first, and then you figure out how to feel about it. In the new sequence, you choose what you want, and then the touch happens.

When the touch happens first, you have to ask yourself, though not usually consciously, *Do I want this? If I don't, now what?* When the choosing happens first, you notice what you want and ask for it, and as long as the resulting touch is reasonably close to what you requested, your body is looking forward to it and drinks it in. This is an entirely different experience.

This is why to learn Accepting, you must take the time to notice what you want and request it. If someone else chooses for you, no matter how tuned in you think they are, you're back to adapting.

The impact of this cannot be overstated. Sadly, it seems we cannot completely override our tendency to go along, but we can minimize the opportunity to fall into it, and this is what the labs do. The structure itself reverses the sequence. Nothing happens until you request it. To help, there are speed bumps built in, pauses to notice your desires and limits.

This principle is particularly important for hands-on practitioners, because your clients will tend to go along with what they think you think is right, when generally what they need, to become empowered, is to learn to choose. See the online notes.

CHAPTER 12

Lab 2:
Exploring the Serve-Accept Dynamic

E xploring the Serve and Accept Quadrants tends to be a little more straightforward. The challenge is in finding out where you are not quite clear about who it's for. The joy of exploring them is the profound, luscious, and just plain fun experiences that are possible.

Like the Take-Allow Lab, the parameters open up: which body areas are potentially available and how much time you spend here. Again, that may be a big relief or a whole new kind of intimidating. The instructions show you how to slow down so you can stay in the quadrant and explore it.

You might think that your job as Accepter is to like and appreciate whatever is done to you or to change your attitude somehow so that you like it better. It is not. The point of Accepting is to notice what you want and to communicate that. There is a vast difference between those two. Still, you will likely think there is something you are supposed to want, supposed to like, or supposed to ask for, so I'll be coaching you about that.

As the Server, you might think your job is to create a pleasurable experience for your Accepter so they respond in some way that seems right to you. It is not. The point of Serving is to be clear with yourself about your limits and, within those limits, to do what was asked for as best you can, knowing that the Accepter gets to experience their enjoyment in whatever way they do. I'll be coaching you about that.

In the lessons, we started with the Accepter's request: "Will you massage my hand?" In the labs, we start with an offer from the Server: "How do you want me to touch you for (three, five, ten, etc.) minutes?" This opens the door for the Accepter to pause to notice what they want and ask for it. "Will you (touch, caress, massage, tickle, stroke, etc.) my (hand, head, chest, belly, etc.)?"

This is the other question of the Three Minute Game with, like the previous lab, a couple of speed bumps added: 1) the Accepter pauses to consider what they want, and 2) then the Server pauses to consider if they are willing to give that.

As before, I'll give you the steps, and then we'll look more closely at each quadrant.

THE PARAMETERS

- Start with short turns of three to five minutes. Later, when you feel ready, you will naturally start to ask for longer turns.
- Accepter, start with asking for things that are relatively comfortable for you. Later, you will naturally start to experiment. You'll become able to stay in your quadrant in gradually more intense and complex interactions.
- Do this lab for twenty or thirty sessions, and then play with it for a lifetime.

THE STEPS

 Open your container.

Decide how much time you are going to spend, and open with your dedication or ritual. Divide the time in half, so you each get a turn. One person today and the other person tomorrow is also fine.

2. Make an agreement.

First the Serving partner:

1. Preferably, make eye contact.

2. Then make the offer: "How would you like me to touch you for (three, five, ten, etc.) minutes?"

Then the Accepting partner:

1. Take a twenty-second pause or longer.

   - If you think you already know what you want, take the full twenty seconds anyway. Sometimes it changes.

2. Make a request.

   - As in the lesson, don't tell them what they can do; tell them what you want them to do.

   - Use the words, "Will you...?" There are two ways to do that:

     "Will you...?"
     "I would like...Will you do that?"

   - Not this:

     "I usually like..."
     "You can..."
     "Whatever you want is fine with me."
     "How about...?"

   - Some examples:

     "Will you scratch my back, slow and firm?"
     "I'd love for you to hold me. Will you do that?"
     "Will you rub my feet, and hold them in your lap to do it?"
     "I'd really love my head scratched. Will you do that?"

   - If you don't know how to describe it, demonstrate: "Will you do this, like this?"

Then the Serving partner again:

1. Ask anything you need to clarify.

   - Do they mean soft, light, firm, slow, or deep? Ask.

2. Take a twenty-second pause.

- Ask yourself, *Is this something I can give with a full heart?*
- Wait for a resounding inner *Yes!* and include any limits. If you hesitate or hear an inner *Maybe*, that means:
  - You need more information. Ask for whatever you want to know. "I think so, but can you tell me a little more of what you have in mind?"
  - Or you are a yes but with certain limits. "Yes, I'll need to sit over here on this side to reach you."
  - Or an inner no is trying to be heard.
  - If you wait a little longer, it will be clear which one it is.

3. Answer

- Some examples:

  "Yes!"

  "I'm not sure. What do you mean exactly?"

  "Yes, as long as I can move over this way."

  "Yes, part of it. I'm glad to do the back part but not the shoulders part. Does that work for you, or would you like something else?"

  "Wow, that's a stretch for me. I don't think I'm up for it. What is something else you might like?"

3. Lean back and get comfortable.

The Accepter does not adjust to the Server's position; the Server adjusts to the Accepter's position.

The Accepting partner:

- Get comfortable first—*before you begin.* Same reasons as before. Lean back, stretch out, wrap yourself around, and put pillows where you want them. Often it takes a little figuring out together.

The Serving partner:

- Put yourself in a position that is reasonably comfortable for you too, using lots of cushions.

Do what has been asked, as best you can.

The Serving partner:

1. Respect your own limits and comfort; move as you need to.

2. Do what has been asked as best you can and no more.
   Don't make up things they did not ask for.

3. Check in.

   > "How's this pressure?"
   > "Are we on the right track here?"
   > "Anything you would like different?"

4. Change your mind if needed.

   > "I thought that would work, but it's hard on my knees.
   > I'll need to move."
   > "I thought I would be comfortable with that, but I'm not.
   > What else would you like?"

The Accepting partner:

1. Settle in and enjoy it as much as you like.

2. You may change your mind. Just say so. Sometimes things don't
   work as well as you thought they would. Sometimes you have
   enough and would like something else.

   > "Slower, please...Slower...Reeeeally slow...Yeah, that's great."
   > "Wait a minute, I have to move over this way."
   > "That's not working as well as I thought it would.
   > Would you do this instead?"
   > "That's great, now please…"

 ## Thank you/You're welcome.

Sit up facing each other.

Accepting partner:

- Say "Thank you."

Serving Partner:

- Say "You're welcome" and nothing more. No matter how much you enjoyed giving, do not thank your Accepter. (See Lesson 3.)

6. Switch roles.

If you have time, you can start again, and give yourselves longer to sink in.

7. Talk about what you noticed.

Talk about what you noticed *about yourself,* not about your partner. Do not give a review of their performance (because it wasn't one). This might include sensations in your body or emotions or thoughts that arose. What was challenging? What was a relief?

- As the Accepter: *Did I remember it was for me, or did I try to take care of my partner?*
- As the Server: *Did I do something I was not comfortable with? If so, why?*

8. Close your dedicated time.

This is where you can thank each other if you like.

9. Come back to it.

Return a dozen or twenty or thirty times—or for a few decades.

NOTES ON HUGGING AND BEING HELD

If you ask for a hug, are you "giving" a hug or "receiving" one? Usually both people have their arms wrapped around each other, so it's hard to tell, even from inside the hug. Experiment with this: Instead of asking for a hug, ask to be held. This is usually more vulnerable, because you can't hide behind partially "giving."

In being held, you are receiving (Accepting). Alter your position so you are not holding up your weight. Don't hug back—that is, have both your arms inside theirs. What do you notice?

In holding, you are giving (Serving). It may not seem like you are doing much, but you are. If you notice the Accepter is holding up some of their own weight or holding on to you, invite them to change that if they want.

FEELINGS, EROS, AND TURN-ON

Like the Take-Allow Lab, play with this a few times, and you'll notice a range of moods and feelings, and at some point you may find yourself getting turned on. In fact, you might be surprised at how turned on you can get without genital contact. Or maybe you're not surprised at all! Like the Take-Allow Lab, this is a great place to explore your arousal, because it's not leading to different activity. We'll talk about eros and sexual feelings in the following sections about Accepting and Serving.

A FEW FUN THINGS TO ASK FOR

When people think of Serve-Accept, they often focus on sexual touch with an emphasis on erogenous zones, but erogenous zones are learned and largely cultural. With real presence, any body part can elicit any feeling, depending on the context. There are a larger number of nerve endings in some areas than others, but this is not the primary factor. A visit to the urologist or gynecologist is rarely enjoyable. The back has relatively few nerve endings but can be a very sexy place to be touched. There's hardly anything more boring than skipping the body and diving straight for the erogenous zones you read about somewhere. Here are a few fun things to ask for.

- "I want to put my head in your lap and have you run your hands through my hair. Will you do that?"

- "Will you listen to me talk about my day? Something happened that was upsetting…Thanks, and now will you hold me?"
- "I'd like you to sit behind me, let me lean up against you, and wrap your arms around me and stroke my chest. Will you do that?"
- "Will you spank me? Gently at first, and I'll tell you if I want more."
- "Will you kiss my eyelids?"
- "Will you nibble my ears? But don't stick your tongue in them!"
- "Will you kiss all around my neck, wherever my skin is showing? Yeah, and lift my hair up there and get right up next to my hairline…Oh, yeah!"
- "Will you rest your hands on my heart and my belly and hold them there, not moving?"
- "Will you hold me and tell me a story?"
- "Will you get me a cup of tea and then come back and ask me what I want next?"
- "Will you scratch my back, from the top to the bottom, slowly and firmly?…Yeah, like that, but slower, really slow."

EXAMPLES

These are examples of people in session with me that show some negotiating.

Hold me

Me: How would you like me to touch you, right now, for a few minutes?

Lake: Hmm…would you hold me?

Me: Sure. How would you like that?

Lake: I used to have a girlfriend who would sit on my lap facing me, straddling. Are you comfortable with that?

Me: Yes, I am, as long as I can get my legs comfortable. Are you okay on a chair for that?

Lake: Yes!

Weight

Me: How would you like me to touch you, right now, for a few minutes?

Sara: I really miss having someone's weight on me. Would you lie down on top of me?

Me: Sure. Front or back?

Sara: Either one is fine.

Me: This is your turn. You get to choose. I'm okay either way.

Sara: Then back. That's not too weird?

Me: Not at all. It's one of my favorite things too.

Sara: It is? Awesome…ahhh…yeah. That feels great.

EXPLORING ACCEPTING

In Accepting, you explore being touched in exactly the way you want. When you do that, the difference between Allowing and Accepting becomes clear and liberating. The key is to slow down enough to notice what you actually want instead of what you think you are supposed to want.

The Adapting Ourselves principle shows up here as it did in Allowing. We tend to go along with, settle for, and make the best of however we are being touched. When we are asked how we want to be touched, we answer with how we don't mind being touched. We are acting like the whole thing is for someone else. This is complicated by the fact that we tend to think there is something we are supposed to want.

The other principle that shows up here is Follow the Pleasure. Instead of telling the pleasure where you think it should be, follow it where it already is. For example, we may think we are supposed to want something dramatic, but what we really want may be to have our hand held.

To experience the Accepting Quadrant, you must make a request. You cannot learn Accepting by having someone choose for you, because as soon as they choose (guess), you will tend to try to make the best of it. Instead of changing yourself to suit the action, you learn to change the action to suit yourself.

The secret to ease and joy in Accepting is not in the Doing (or in this case, the Done-to). It's in the asking. As you become clearer about

169

what you want, stay true to that, and ask for that, the ease and joy follow naturally. When it's what you want, the enjoyment of it is automatic.

Another way of saying this, which I said in chapter 1, is that the Accepting Quadrant is inherently wonderful. If it's not wonderful, it's not because you're not a "good receiver." It's because it's not the thing you want (or it's more of it than you want). The question to ask yourself is not, *Why don't I like this?* or *Why can't I relax?* The question to ask yourself is, *What is it I actually want? What sounds wonderful right now?*

THE ART OF ACCEPTING: BELIEVE IT'S FOR YOU

If you believe it's for you:

- You take as much time as you need to notice what you want.
- You ask for it directly and clearly, with a question, not a hint or apology.
- You get yourself comfortable before you start; you don't settle for good enough to manage.
- You change your mind any time you want and communicate that.
- You ask for refinements such as "Slower, please."
- You let yourself express your pleasure in whatever way is natural and spontaneous.
- You let your giver tend to their own comfort and have their own experience.
- If/when you have enough, you stop.

If you believe it's really (secretly?) for the benefit of the Server:

- When asked what you want, you answer with what you're okay with.
- You worry about taking too long to answer.
- You ask for what you think your giver wants to "give."
- You position yourself so it's easier for your giver.
- You try to make your giver feel good by:
  - acting like it's okay (you don't ask for changes you want)
  - silently going along with something you didn't ask for

- listening to them talk about themselves
- faking your pleasure: sigh, squirm, breathe hard, fake orgasm
- keep going after you've had enough

If you are doing anything on that second list, ask yourself, *Who is this for?*

HOW TO STAY IN ACCEPTING

Those are the main principles. The first step is to notice there is a difference between what you are *willing* to have done to you and what you *want* to have done to you. Once that is clear, the rest of it falls into place. The basic instructions are in the steps. Here I give you more detail.

Making the agreement

Asking for what you want (and getting a yes) creates the dynamic. Without it, there is no Accepting Quadrant. The instructions suggest you pause after being asked what you want.

The two big challenges of staying in Accepting are knowing what you want and then asking for it. It is strange that being asked what we want can bring up such discomfort. Having plenty of time to ask for what you want is a luxury. It's not an option in every situation, but it is here. If it feels like anything less than a luxury, ask yourself why.

Every infant is born knowing how to ask for what they want. That's pretty much all they do! We had to learn how *not* to ask, because we were shamed or punished or it didn't work. Now we are learning how all over again. It's challenging. *Aaack! I have to ask?! I can't do that!* It's not vulnerable because there's something wrong with you—it's *inherently* vulnerable. When we reveal our desire, we can be denied, laughed at, or criticized. We can bump into our self-doubt, shame, fear, confusion, and guilt. What to do? Start small and well within your comfort zone of what to ask for.

Now we're back to the magic four: notice what you want, trust it, value it, and communicate it.

Notice what you want. People often say, "I don't know what I want!" as if it's a problem. Of course we don't always know! It's not a problem—unless you are in a hurry to get going.

Clear the roadway. There is a roadway that travels from the body's knowing up to conscious awareness, and along that road travels the information of what we want. The road is full of potholes and fallen logs, and it takes some time for the message to slowly climb over the logs and finally arrive in your awareness. Often it comes through as just a whisper. When it finally arrives, you believe it, trust it, and value it. You request it from your partner, and lo and behold, you receive it.

The next time you are asked what you want, the roadway is a bit clearer and the next time clearer still. Clearing that roadway is a lifelong process and harder for some kinds of desires than others, but clear it does. Sometimes big logs are cleared away in one swoop. Mostly it's gradual, and often it's tenderhearted.

Clearing that roadway is perhaps the most empowering and crucial thing you can do personally and for the good of the world. As we learn to listen to our bodies, we regain our inner compass. It guides us to notice what we want in the moment, but more important is noticing what we want in the world. In the more immediate range, within the labs and in your touch relationships, you gradually clear the logs off the roadway, the messages arrive faster, and you become creative. Things pop into your mind that never would have occurred to you before. *Because the roadway is clear.*

I can give you a list of ideas a mile long, but it can never replace clearing the roadway. Clearing the roadway takes time, courage, and coming back to the question "How do you want me to touch you?" many times. You stop trying to get your partner to guess correctly and blaming them for not being able to. Eventually, when you feel disappointed or resentful, you ask yourself, *What did I want that I did not ask for?* This is powerfully liberating.

Commit to waiting. The secret to noticing is to give it time. That's it. It doesn't matter how long it takes; what matters is that you give it the time it does take. It almost always comes within sixty seconds, but it *feels* like forever. I have seen it take several minutes and once forty-five minutes in a session with me. This means commit to waiting for the inner *Hell yes!* It can take all the courage you have. Wait until the message arrives and whatever you are thinking of lights you up: *Oh! Yeah! That sounds wonderful!* A useful script is "Thank you for asking. I'm not sure yet, so I'm going to think about it a bit."

Things that might help. Start with something that feels well within your comfort zone. If you spend a whole year asking for nothing but foot rubs, if that is true for you, you are feeding some part of yourself that has been hungry for a long time. This way you learn to trust that you will listen to yourself. You feel safe, and when you have enough foot rubs, you will naturally want to explore more. If you're at a loss, you might find it helpful to scan your body: Ask your shoulders, *Is it you?* Ask your arms, *Is it you? Who wants touch right now?*

In Taking, we talked about keeping underwear on as an option. The same thing is an option here, whatever lets you relax the most. Also an option is the level of dress of the Serving partner. Maybe you want them naked, wearing underwear, or fully clothed. Ask for that, and then they get to choose if they can give you that.

If you want, you can experiment with having them wait until you tell them to start. This can help you notice that you are in charge and give you time to settle. "I'm going to lie down here, and I want you to wait—don't touch me—until I tell you to start."

Listen for the pull. There may be times when you want to try something a little edgy for you, or you feel like you should. We talk about this in Follow the Pleasure, in a few pages. Listen for the pull: *This feels edgy but also fun, and I really* want *to try it.*

What doesn't work. Asking for a feeling or an intangible: "Make me feel special" or "Touch me with love and respect." First, no one can give you a feeling. It happens within your own physiology. Second, no one can know exactly what makes you feel special, loved, or respected. For one person, love and respect mean soft caresses. For another person, love and respect mean whips and chains. If you want a feeling, ask yourself, *What is the action that will help me feel that?* and ask for that. It's okay to include that in your request. "I want to feel special. Will you…?"

Then trust it and value it. Once you have waited for the inner *Hell yes,* trust that the information bubbling up to you is accurate. Many of us have never felt that what we wanted mattered. It does. We don't always get it, but it matters.

Then the instructions say to make your request.

The words. There are two ways to make a request for the Accepting Quadrant. They both include the words *Will you.*

- "Will you…?"
- "I would like…Will you do that?"

Why so strict? I have noticed that being simple and direct brings up the most feelings. It's easy to avoid the raw vulnerability of asking if you fluff it with lots of words, hint, add flourishes, or suggest what they can do or what you don't mind them doing or state what you usually like. Asking in the simplest way possible makes it difficult not to notice that you are asking for a favor with all the vulnerability that engenders. Asking prevents you from giving away your responsibility for choosing.

As we said in the lesson, the words you use both reveal what it is you are thinking and set you up to be able to experience what you just said. If you say, "You can…," you set yourself up to Allow instead of Accept.

Listen to the answer, and take it in. When they say yes, pause a moment with eye contact, and take it in. Wait there until you believe them, even if it takes a while. I have seen this take a full minute, but by the end of that minute, the Accepter had no doubt and was able to take in the gift wholeheartedly.

You may be hypervigilant for this. You might be worried your giver doesn't want to. Maybe you haven't experienced much generosity in your life. If you notice you are tense at all, there is something still on your mind. What do you need to hear that would put your mind at ease? Ask for it: "Are you sure you're okay with this?" or "Will you please reassure me that you will take care of your boundaries and stop if you need to?"

Respect the limits of your giver. Of course, if they say no, no whining or pressuring: "Oh, c'mon, it'll be fine!" If you do that, you encourage them to ignore their limits. Never useful. You may worry that asking for what you want will make you more selfish, but what actually happens is that you become more respectful. Your sensitivity will go up, and you will be able to tell when the giver is clear.

The Doing

Then the instructions suggest you lean back and get comfortable.

Lean back. Same reason as in the lesson. It's amazing how often people will put themselves in the position that they think makes it easier on their Server (sitting up, for example) and don't notice it. I often say in workshops, "If you looked at yourself from over here, who would it look like is working?" They invariably say, "Oh, yeah, it looks like I'm the one working."

If it's hard to relax. If you are having trouble relaxing, something is still on your mind. It may be concern about the Giver. It's okay to check in. You can ask, "Is this okay with you?"

More common is that it's not the thing you want, or it's more of it than you want. You may have asked for a back rub, but what you actually want—what would allow you to relax—is one stroke down your back and then a pause to wait and see what you want next, but you are trying to make yourself be okay with (relax with) a back rub. It could also be that the touch is happening faster than you can notice what you want, so you have to scramble to keep up with yourself. It outruns you. Slow down the activity so that instead of the activity leading, your noticing leads and the activity follows.

Here we are back at this question: The thing to ask yourself is not, *Why don't I like this?* The question to ask yourself is, *What is it that I actually do want right now?* or *What sounds wonderful right now?*

It could be that what they are doing is lovely, and what you are tense about is trying not to feel vulnerability, pleasure, gratitude, or the guilt that arises. If it's extremely difficult to relax, stop. There is something that would help. What is it? Maybe asking for something simpler or a shorter time? Reassurance? Changing your position? Fewer clothes on, more clothes on?

Make refinements and change your mind. Your tendency will be to adapt yourself to suit what is happening (we're back here again!). What you need to do instead is to change what is happening to suit yourself.

"Slower, please...slower, really slow...yeah, that's great."

"Wait a minute, please. I have to move over this way."

"That's not working as well as I thought it would. Would you do this instead?"

"That's great. Now please…"

"That is fabulous…now stop and let me rest a bit."

"Thank you, that's enough for now…I still have five minutes left? Great…let's see, what do I want next?…nothing quite yet…okay now will you…?"

Or tears come up: "Stop please…now start again…stop again and hold your hands right there. Okay, start again please."

The pleasure ceiling. We talked about this in chapter 4 (About Pleasure). Your pleasure ceiling is the point just behind which lies your shame, guilt, tenderness, gratitude, and your tears. You are going to hit that. Everyone has one, and it doesn't matter where yours is; what matters is that you respect yourself. When your feelings arise, follow the pleasure again. Does it sound appealing to have some support for that? To pause and back up? To keep going and let the tears flow? To take a break? You get to decide—because it's your turn. This teaches you to trust yourself, and your pleasure ceiling will naturally rise.

Your body is going to express what you feel. You'll want to make sound, move, maybe shake. You may feel self-conscious, and you get to decide what to do with that. Every relationship has a level of comfort around showing emotions, especially sexual ones, and the feeling of being free to let it out is rare. You can start small, and your level of comfort will grow. Shaking and trembling can be a release of joy or fear. Check with yourself. Your partner should also be checking your face and noticing if you look happy or scared. If it's fear, stop. There is no need to overwhelm yourself.

Let your Server have their own experience. You may think your job is to appreciate what happens and feel thankful. It isn't. Your responsibility is to communicate what you want and abide by your giver's limits. That's it. You are not there to make your Server feel good. They are there for the experience of Serving. If you are trying to keep them happy, you are not receiving, so there is no one for them to give to. When you stop trying to please your Server, it's the highest kind of respect, as they get to have their own experience.

176

I have seen the Server become judgmental and disapproving. Sadly, it happens, and it will affect you. Once again, you get to decide what to do with it. You can stop or ignore it, or you can keep going and let them deal with it. You can check in: "You look tense. Are you okay with what I'm experiencing?" It's possible you may have been misreading them.

The trap. The trap in Accepting is performing a response you think the Server wants to see. This is easy to fall into—I'm not sure any of us is free of it. This is related to giving your giver a good experience and is a reflection of not understanding that it is for you. Performing and bliss are mutually exclusive. You can't do both at once.

Eye contact. Being openly seen in your pleasure can feel vulnerable. You can experiment with eye contact. Hiding feeds your shame. You may be closing your eyes as you melt into bliss, but if you feel embarrassment, experiment with making some eye contact. Peek out now and then or at least after. Let yourself notice that you are still here and still accepted.

Sexual feelings. What you are doing here, among other things, is de-conflating touch and sex. You are finding that touch can express and satisfy a whole range of care and affection, and you get to explore touch that is not about sex at all. You can have touch that feels sexy but is not leading anywhere else, which lets you completely fall into the turn-on of the moment for three minutes or ten minutes. There is a tremendous freedom here. What does it feel like to revel in your turn-on?

Stop when you have enough. It may seem obvious, but I have not found it to be. Continuing on when you don't want to is another form of going-along-with. One student said, "It felt really great, and then it didn't, but I didn't know it was okay to stop."

Aftercare. If you have blasted past a current edge, expect some inner backlash, which can be a mix of liberation and self-doubt. You may think, *What the heck was that? Why was I so selfish?* Partners often find new territory here, both erotically and emotionally. It makes a big difference to have some quiet time cuddling or maybe sleeping. Aftercare means time and gentleness. Don't rush off.

The experience. It can be tenderhearted with relief, misty eyes, self-acceptance, or gratitude. It can be rowdy, playful, silly, sexy, and sensual. It can be all about you, and there may be moments of guilt, shame, awkwardness, and exposure as well as moments of prolonged arousal and bliss. Being the center of loving attention is not always easy, and pleasure may bring up self-doubt (whether you are enough, too much, deserving, selfish, spiritual enough, etc.). It is ultimately a bonding experience, and at the same time, you distinguish your experience from your partner's. What happens inside you is different from what happens inside them! Pleasure is a powerful healer, and a receiver who falls fully into their own pleasure is a joy to serve.

SUCCESS!

Oh, great. I got all the way through it! If you believe that success at Accepting means not quitting, you will ignore your signals of whether or not you like it.

Oh, succeeding means enjoying it? If you believe this, if you don't much like it, you will have to *try* to like it (and feel guilty if you can't).

Oh, succeeding means knowing what I want right away? If you believe this, you will jump into whatever you can think of and won't give yourself the time to notice what it is you actually want.

Success at Accepting means waiting for the inner *Hell yes!*—as long as it takes. Once you do that, the enjoyment happens automatically.

EXAMPLES

For me

I had a big aha about Accepting some years back (at the women's workshop I talked about in the first chapter), long before I began thinking about the quadrants or knew they existed. I was on the massage table, tended by another participant, and I sank right into pleasure. At some point, I realized that this pleasure was all for me. That is, I realized that this person was not doing this in order to get something back from me. It really was all for me. The realization hit me so hard it made me wonder what I had been feeling all the times before that, and I realized how much of my experience of being touched had felt like it was someone trying to get something from me. That moment changed my life and was one of the moments that led me here.

Even after all this time

One person described her experience at a workshop this way: "Even after all this time of practicing, it was hard to ask for what I wanted. I said, 'You can such-and-such.' The facilitator heard me and came over and said, 'Is that an attempt to make a request?' I said, 'Yes,' and she said, 'Try that again.' This time I asked, 'Will you such-and-such?' Then they started doing it, and it wasn't quite what I had asked for, so I had to struggle again and make myself ask again. This happened two or three times. Then, finally, my giver got it exactly right. Then I realized I was not settling for, not tolerating, not trying to make somebody else feel good. I got exactly what I wanted, and I started sobbing. *Oh, this is what it feels like to really ask and get what I want!* Then the floodgates opened, and I cried."

Taking the time to choose

This was in a session with me, and it shows the principle of The Choosing Is More Important Than the Doing.

Me: How would you like me to touch you, right now, for a few minutes? (The person across from me pauses, unsure. Moisture comes to their eyes as they look into mine and take a slow, deep breath.)

Ten: I have no idea.

Me: That's okay, we have plenty of time.

Ten: No one has ever asked me that before. It's hard. Why would it be so hard?

Me: I don't know. Maybe because no one has ever asked.

(Pause)

Ten: Well, what do you suggest?

Me: This is for you. You get to choose. Don't worry, it will come.

Ten: Well, I always like to have my head scratched.

Me: That's nice, but this is for right now. Is that what you would like right now?

Ten: Well, actually, no. I think I'd like to have my shoulders rubbed.

Me: Do you want to think about it a little longer?

Ten: No, that's what I want.

Me: Great. Would you like that firm or soft, or how?

Ten: Whatever you are okay with.

Me: I'm okay with anything. This turn is for you. You get to have it the way you want it.

Ten: My God, why is this so hard? (tears) I just don't know! Am I supposed to know?

Me: Sometimes people know, and sometimes it takes a while. Either way is fine. Your body knows what it wants. If you sit a while, it will tell you.

Ten: Okay. I have it. Will you rub my back and shoulders, deep like a massage?

Me: You bet. Would you like to sit up or lie down?

Ten: I'd like to lie down. (I rub their shoulders.) God, I can't believe that was so hard...Are you sure this is okay with you? You don't mind doing this?

Me: No, I don't mind. I'm glad to do it. How's this pressure?

Ten: Perfect. It feels great. Thank you so much.

Me: You're welcome.

Ten (more tears): This feels really good.

Simple

Here's another example from a session with me that shows how simple it can be.

Me: How would you like me to touch you, right now for a few minutes?

Pat (deep breath, sigh): Would you just hold me? Let me lean my head against your chest?

Me: Yes, I'd be glad to. This way?

Pat: Yeah, oh, yes, thank you. That's exactly what I needed. I can hear your heart.

PRINCIPLE:
FOLLOW THE PLEASURE

One result of the tendency to adapt to what is happening is to think there is something that *should* be pleasurable (because, you know, everyone says it is). Often that means trying to push through our resistance, hoping that it will miraculously *become* pleasurable. This is the worst advice I've ever heard.

We have probably all been here: we are being touched, and it's less than inspiring, and we try to make ourselves like it. Our muscles tense just a little, we hold our breath just a little, and we clench our jaw just a little. Our defense system engages, and when that happens, the pleasure system shuts down. Sadly, for many people, this is pretty much their main experience of being touched.

What to do instead? If you want the pleasure system to engage, you can't put a leash on pleasure and drag it along behind you. Don't start with what you wish you could enjoy or think you should enjoy. Start with what you already enjoy. Follow it. Ask yourself what sounds wonderful to you right now.

Then a couple of things happen. First, the defense system is no longer needed so it settles down, and that allows the pleasure physiology to engage. *You then have an experience of actual pleasure, and that teaches you how it feels.* Not a few crumbs of pleasure amidst the tension but full-bodied settling into pleasure. That experience leads you somewhere else, into more coziness, more emotional tenderness, more playfulness. Then it leads you somewhere else.

Second, and perhaps most important, you learn to trust that you won't abandon yourself, which creates a sense of safety. You breathe a sigh of relief. Then the sense of safety automatically leads to new interests. You notice there are options you didn't see before, and you begin to ask for new things. The change in physiology changes your perception; the world looks different.

Two Scenarios

These two scenarios offer a deeper description of how following the pleasure could potentially play out.

First scenario. Some kind of touch is offered that puts you in the Accepting Quadrant. You don't know how to notice what you want, because it didn't seem to matter before. You want to get through the awkward phase and just get going. You try to think of something your partner would like to give you or something you heard about that everyone else seems to think you should want. Feeling under pressure, you come up with an old standard: a back rub, but it's not a back rub you really want. You want to be held.

You submit to this back rub. You tell yourself, *Well, back rubs are supposed to feel good, so I'll make it feel good.* Maybe it's a real struggle and you can't wait for it to end, or maybe it's reasonably tolerable. Maybe it's even pretty good. When it's over, you notice that you breathe a sigh of relief. You wonder what is wrong with you. You ask yourself, *That's where the pleasure should be, so why wasn't it there?*

Second scenario. Some kind of touch is offered, and you're in Accepting again. You feel uncomfortable, because you don't know what you want or how to ask. This time, you have compassion for yourself and wait. *Hmm...maybe a back rub? Nah, that's not it. Maybe a butt rub? Interesting, but nah, that's not it.* You wait. You remember to follow the pleasure. *What sounds wonderful? Oh, I want to be held, but that doesn't sound right. Surely I should want something sexier! Nah, what sounds wonderful? It's holding. That's what I want.*

You ask to be held, and the giver agrees. After a few minutes, you've had enough holding. Now you have the same question again. *Maybe I should stay here because I don't want to bother my partner. Maybe I can make myself continue to like it.* You take a breath, and you remember to follow the pleasure. You thank your partner for holding you and ask them if they'll rub your feet. They agree, and you both get comfortable.

You enjoy that for quite a long time. Maybe too long? You're back to the question again. *Shouldn't I be wanting something else now? Maybe if I have my legs rubbed I can make myself like that too? Nope—follow the pleasure, where it already is.* You stay there as long as you like. Maybe it changes; maybe you want it deeper or slower, maybe you want to move so your back is more comfortable, or maybe you want to keep going exactly like you have it. Maybe you're feeling finished and want to stop.

So follow the pleasure. Don't try to get it to follow you.

The feelings. Following the Pleasure also includes what to do when feelings arise. In the Receiving Quadrants (Taking and Accepting), guilt, shame, or awkwardness are likely to arise. Now what? Does it sound appealing to have some support for that? Does it sound appealing to pause and back up? Does it sound appealing to keep going and let the tears flow? Does it sound appealing to take a break? You get to decide—because it's your turn. In the Giving Quadrants (Serving and Allowing), it's not about your own pleasure, but tension or worry may show up. Does it sound appealing to stop? Does it sound appealing to stretch a little? You get to decide.

Listen for the Pull, not the Push.

What about those times when you want to stretch beyond your comfort zone, when something sounds appealing but it's edgy for you? Great question. The key is right there—it's appealing. It's at the edge of your comfort zone. Don't push yourself. Listen for the pull.

The Push:

- *Everybody else likes it. Why don't I?*
- *I'm going to make myself do this, because it's good for me.*
- *I really should be okay with this.*
- *Well, I should give it a chance.*

The Pull:

- *It sounds scary, it's a little edgy, but it also sounds really fun!*

- *Wow, that looks vulnerable. And it's something I really want.*
- *That looks edgy, I'm totally out of my comfort zone—but it also looks great. I want that!*

In the Push, you are telling your heart, *You don't matter. Just shut up and get with the program!* In the Pull, you are telling your heart, *Like that idea? I believe you, and I will take care of you.* The real edge is not the activity in question. The real edge is *How true can I be to myself?* This is much harder to do. Then we trust ourselves, and our interests naturally expand.

There is a certain flavor of fear that is exciting, and there are some wonderful ways to play with that excitement from a delicate spark to deep, transporting, inner shadow play. Even so, it is still within the range of choosing how to play with it, so Listening for the Pull still applies.

One student said, "If all I do is push through everything, I never learn where my real baseline is, because all I do is walk right over it. I don't know what my innate preferences are. What I'm doing is noticing where my baseline is."

EXPLORING SERVING

The Serving Quadrant is the one that everyone seems to want to get better at with better technique, smoother strokes, and newer tricks. What makes for excellent Serving is not the strokes; it's the art of finding out what the Accepter wants.

To review from the lesson, the gift you are giving is your action. You learned to ask how they wanted to be touched and how to wait until they tell you. You learned that you do not *cause* their pleasure, you *contribute* to it, and understanding that their experience belongs to them (not to you) frees you from trying to create a response, so you can enjoy giving the gift. This lab is about how to do that really well.

THE MYTH OF TECHNIQUE

The myth is that there is a right technique (or a right body part) that would light up the heavens if only you could figure out what it is. What's true is that the right touch is the one they ask for and nothing else. To Serve, you have to replace the idea of the right technique with finding out what they want and trust that they know what they are talking about. Give up everything you think you know about erogenous zones and strokes, about how they are supposed to feel, what they are supposed to want, how they are supposed to respond, and what kind of pleasure is supposed to be happening.

This is not easy. The hardest part can be noticing that you have these expectations. If you have ever watched a technique video, porn film, or even a romance movie, the images are in there. If you have ever read a novel that describes taking your lover (usually a woman) to heights of an explosive orgasm in fifteen seconds or read a magazine about taking your lover (usually a man) to two hours of ecstasy, you have these images in your mind. How about a tantric massage video that sets out the strokes for you, step by step? Throw it all out. Find out what your receiver wants at this moment with you.

The degree to which you are guided by the images, you cannot be present with your partner. You will be trying, however subtly, to get the action to look like that one you saw or read about. This is not because you are an insensitive dolt; it's because the assumption is so embedded in our culture that we can't avoid it.

LIMITS, GENEROSITY, AND JOY

This is the same principle we saw in the Allow Quadrant. The misconception about generosity is that you should be willing to do pretty much anything, and if you aren't, you need to change your attitude and expand yourself somehow. This is backwards.

The secret to generosity is to tend to your limits. When we can say no, we no longer have to guard against what someone may ask us for, so we relax and become generous within our limits. It's limits first, and then generosity and joy arise from there.

Like any form of giving, if you feel resentful or hesitant, you have not yet noticed or communicated your limit. When you feel tense about giving, look to your limits. Ask yourself, *What am I afraid they will ask me for? Which is to say, What am I afraid to say no to?* You also might find that when you trust yourself to stay responsible, your limits themselves relax somewhat. You learn you don't have to keep your guard up and that you can change your mind at any time.

There may be something you are asked to do that feels a little edgy for you but interesting anyway. This is where you listen for the pull, not the push, which we talked about a few pages back.

THE TRAP

There is a large trap in Serving, easy to fall into. The trap is doing something *so that* you get a response. You want them to moan and melt, so you do this technique you think will make that happen. It's a trap because it seems like it ought to be the right thing to do. After all, don't you want to make them feel good?

The belief is: *If I take the right action, I'll get the right results.* It's true for designing bridges that stay up. For playing and affection, not so much. The trap can also arise from the indirect route to pleasure that we talked about in the Taking lesson. When the direct route is closed, the indirect route is all you have left, so you'd better get that response, or you have nothing.

Why is it a problem? First, their response is not an accurate indicator of enjoyment. They may be panting and moaning or be in quiet bliss. Some of the most blissful states are entirely quiet; they look like nothing. Or they may be laughing or falling asleep.

Second, you become determined to do whatever it takes to get there. This makes it hard to notice the real person in front of you and what they want. When your attention is on the result, it brings tension into your hands.

Third, it makes them perform for you. It puts the Accepting partner in the position of providing you with a response, and if they don't, you think you have failed. They think they have failed, and everybody tries harder. This is where faked orgasms come from. Women are famous for this, but men and nonbinary folks are not exempt.

Mainly, though, it's manipulative. If you look more closely, you are using your "receiver" to satisfy yourself. You are telling them, *The experience you are having is not good enough for me. I want you to have this other one,* or *What you feel does not match my self-image of the effect I think I should have on you.*

Of course, this is not giving at all. Nothing real is happening. The "giver" is trying to get something, the "receiver" is trying to give something, and everybody is faking. It can't satisfy, but nobody knows why.

Why do we do it? It helps us feel good about ourselves and prove our worth. We think it will bring us connection and safety. We want acknowledgement, gratitude, and affection. We want to get them turned on so we can do more. We want them to think we are sexy, desirable, generous, or skilled. It fits with our self-image as a giver. It keeps us in power and them in our debt. If we are unable to internalize our own experience, seeing someone else in pleasure is as close as we can get (the indirect route again), or we don't know anything else to do. We follow the images we've seen in porn, sex ed videos, or romance movies. Are any of us ever free of these? Probably not. One person said, "As long as I'm in control and orchestrating the other person's experience, I don't have to put myself out there too much."

How do you notice you are doing it? It's so natural you're not likely to notice at first, but you do become more aware of it. It's mainly an inner awareness, but there are also a few outward signs: you're glued to their face to track their reaction, your hands move in repetitive, rhythmic ways (unless they have asked you to), or you have watched technique videos.

The easiest way to notice is if you are disappointed. If you think, *That worked*, or *That didn't work*, that signals that you were hoping for something. The purpose of effort is to create an effect; if you don't need an effect, there is no effort. If it feels like an effort, ask yourself, *What is the effect I am hoping for?*

In true giving (in this case, Serving), you care about giving them what they desire. You don't care what they do with it. One person said, "Yeah, that happened to me. I could tell she was acting. It made me sad to think she thought that was what I wanted from her."

When you leave the trap and really Serve. It tends to be humbling. Getting a result satisfies the ego; contributing satisfies the heart, and when you can let go of the result, it's a big relief. You no longer have to make it turn out right. Freedom for you, freedom for them. You really see your partner, so they are no longer an extension of you, and they are exquisitely beautiful to witness. You feel humbled, generous, and appreciative.

THE ART OF SERVING: SPACIOUSNESS

The art of Serving is creating spaciousness. You already know that the Accepting Quadrant is challenging, and often the biggest challenge of it is noticing what you want and asking for it. Almost everyone will distrust their impulses, ignore their desires, and go along with what you, the Server, seem to want to do and try to make the best of it.

In the Serving role, you want to reverse that dynamic. When you keep your desires out of the way, it makes room for them to notice what their own desires are and bring them forward. Creating spaciousness is not a lack of an action, like not pushing or not shaming; it's an action on its own. It's like building a fence around a spring so you don't step in it. Spaciousness protects them from you.

You get good at asking what they want, gently and without grilling them. You slow down so they don't feel pressured, and you are relaxed and confident in letting them take all the time they need. You don't make suggestions, no matter how brilliant you think the ideas are. You don't allow them to defer to you but remind them, if needed, that it's for them. You wait for their request and never start without it. You do only what was asked and don't make up extra things to do (again, no matter how brilliant).

You might feel you want to rescue them from their awkward moment of noticing what they want, but what is more helpful is to be there with them, creating the spaciousness that allows them to find their desire and voice. This is ultimately the biggest gift, and it is an example of how using the container creates options that you would be unlikely to find otherwise.

ABOUT TAKING AND SERVING

I used to say learning Taking makes you better at Serving. I have come to see that learning Taking makes Serving possible. Learning Taking teaches you the difference between Serving and Taking. In Taking, you learn to put yourself first, and until you can put your desires first, you can't put them last, because you don't know what they are. Until you learn Taking, you cannot Serve with integrity. We'll talk more about this in the Wheel section in the chapter on Serving.

HOW TO STAY IN SERVING

Those are the main principles that show up in Serving: that the communication is the real art here, not the strokes; that you don't cause their pleasure, you contribute to it, and they get to do with it what they want; that owning your limits lets you be generous within them; and that trying to get a result is not a real gift. That's a lot to keep in mind, but different aspects of it will come to mind at different times, and over time, they will all become more natural to you.

The steps to stay in Serving are in the lab instructions; I expand on them here.

Making the agreement

We're back to "The Choosing Is More Important Than the Doing." In particular, you want to not let your Accepter acquiesce to what they think you want to "give" them. This is for them. Then you want to be clear about your limits so you can relax and enjoy giving.

You have asked how they would like you to touch them. Now they are taking a pause.

Wait. Your partner is waiting for their inner *Hell yes!* It is important that you wait with them. It can be uncomfortable for them, so you want to create space for them. Don't make suggestions, look at the clock, or make a face. Don't pressure them: "Okay, so what do you want already!? You never know what you want, do you?" There is no time limit. If your partner takes twenty minutes to ponder, that is part of what you are giving by Serving. I have seen it take forty-five minutes. I often hear, "What if they don't know what they want?" They might not. Why is this a problem? It's only a problem if you are in a hurry to get going. Given some time and some spaciousness, they will eventually notice what they want.

About patience. Often people say of the Serving role, "Be patient while you wait." The thing about patience is that if you are happy with what is happening, patience does not apply. If you feel you need patience, what do you believe is supposed to be happening? You are not waiting for something to happen. Quite a lot *is* happening inside your Accepter, and that something is important and powerful, so value it.

If they ask you what you want. If they ask you what you want or give you permission to do something ("You can…"), remind them this is for them, not for you. Do this gently with good humor.

If needed, clarify what they are asking. This can be awkward for either of you, but as the Server, it's your job to get clear. Hurrying ahead to get out of the awkwardness does not serve anyone. For example, if your partner says, "How about my back?" you have very little information. You will need to ask, "You bet! How would you like that? Caresses, massage, fingernails? Soft, more firm?" or "Would you like your shirt on or off?"

If your partner says (and I have heard this from many), "Touch me in a way that is loving and sexy," you have even less information. Try something like this: "I'd love to do that for you. What kind of touch would make you feel loved and sexy right now?" Don't give up until you know what your partner wants.

This humorous example from a workshop highlighted that the simple act of hearing what they ask for can be foreign. Len was Serving, and Marta was Accepting. Marta asked for how she wanted to be touched. Len listened and asked, with good intention, "Do you have any limits of what you don't want me to do?"

(I interrupt) Why are you asking that?

Len: I want to be sure I don't do anything she doesn't want.

Me: She just told you what she wants.

Len: You mean, just do what she asked?

Me: Yes.

Len: Ooooh, I get it!

Then the instructions say that once you're clear on what they want, pause and consider.

I used to say it's okay to have limits here. What is true is that you do in fact *have* limits to what you are willing and able to do. Now we're back to the magic four—your job is to notice, trust, value, and communicate those limits.

Wait for a full-hearted *Yes!* When you hear yourself say, *Uh, I guess so, I don't have any reason to say no,* don't settle for that. Wait for a full-hearted *Yes! I'll be happy to do that!* This is the same principle we saw in Allowing.

If you are hesitating. If you're not a *No way!* but not a full-hearted *Yes!* either, you need one of three things (also listed in Allowing):

1) More information about what is being asked for. You might want to know what kind of touch: soft, slow, or deep? You might want to understand what it means to them.

2) Setting some limit: "I'm happy to give you this but not this." You may be okay with massaging their shoulders but not their back or massaging their back but only if they keep their shirt on.

If your heart is heavy, stop and ask yourself, *What do I need to change?* It's not your attitude; it's your agreement. What part of the agreement needs to be different so that you can easily and gladly give with a full heart? Maybe it's a different body area, a different kind of touch, level of clothing, or less time.

3) An inner no is trying to be heard. Saying no can be difficult for reasons such as wanting to keep our self-image as a giver or wanting to be perceived as confident and easy going, or we want to be perceived as skilled, or we think we should be okay with that and can't let ourselves notice that we're not. A big one is that we don't want to lose the connection. We don't realize that we can say no and still feel connected.

Sometimes we hesitate to listen to our inner no because we don't have a "reasonable reason." There is *some* reason in there; you don't have to know what it is. One of the most valuable concepts I've learned comes from Cuddle Party: "If you're a maybe, say no."

When you do say no or set a limit, you want to maintain connection and respect. Acknowledge that it's okay to ask for it, and then respect your limits. "Hmm, that sounds fun, but I'm not up for it. Would this work?" or "I can't sit that way, so whatever I can do for you this way works for me." If you need more time, say, "I need some time to consider that."

We're back to the questions again. The question to ask yourself is not *Why can't I give this?* The question to ask yourself is *What is the thing that I can give with a full heart?*

Listen for the pull, not the push. We talked about this a few pages back. This is a pull: *This is a little edgy for me, but it sounds fun too—I'd really like to try it!*

The Doing

Now the instructions say to do what was asked for and nothing else, as best you can. Set aside whatever you think it's supposed to look like, and let them have their own experience. That's it.

Get comfortable. It's for the Accepting partner, so their comfort is most important. Help them get comfortable first, and adjust yourself to them as best you can. If you are bending over at an awkward angle, your attention will be pulled elsewhere, and you won't be able to Serve as well. Change as needed.

Do nothing except exactly what was asked for. This can be so tempting! You are going along, and you have some idea that you are sure they would love. You just know it! If you are tempted to do more, ask yourself why. Are you trying to impress them? Do you not believe them? Why not?

Are you bored? Do you want to see a different response? This is part of creating spaciousness. A good way to start is to place your hands where they have asked, and wait there until both of you are breathing easily, or say, "I'll wait here until you tell me you'd like me to start."

Again, this is not a prescription for everyday life—by all means, give each other surprise gifts! In the labs where you are both learning, do exactly what was asked for and nothing else. You can decide later how it applies to your life.

Check in. When Accepting, it can be hard to speak up and ask for changes, so as the Server, you can make that easier by checking in.

Some things you can ask:

> "How's this for you?"
> "How's this pressure?"
> "Is there anything that would make this even better?"
> "Something more or different that you would like?"

Don't say:

> "Does this feel good?" That invites a yes/no answer in which "good enough" counts as a yes, but good enough is not the point. Fabulous is the point. Your Accepter is likely to reassure you even if it's mediocre.
>
> "Am I doing a good job?" This question is you wanting reassurance.
>
> "Is this okay?" This means *Is it acceptable enough that you are willing to tolerate it?* Again, that's not what you actually want to know.

Does your receiver look tense (holding their breath, have a tense face or jaw)? If so, **stop what you are doing** and check in.

> "You look a little tense. I'm going to pause for a moment."
> "How are you doing?"
> "Is this what you had in mind?"

When your Accepter asks for a change or correction, if you want, you can say "Thank you." You are thanking them for the information that lets you do a better job. This reminds the receiver that requests are welcome and not a burden. I once heard a Server say, "Don't tell me what to do. I know what I'm doing." *Aaaackk!*

193

About confidence. You may think confidence comes from having the right stroke or getting the right result. It actually comes from an open inflow, the ability to notice with your hands, eyes, and ears. When you are able to respond and change, that is the source of confidence. If you are feeling unconfident, pause, and bring your attention back to what you notice: what you feel with your hands and what you see and hear.

Inflow and outflow. Your hands remain open to taking in information. You are feeling the temperature of their skin, the tension or relaxing in their muscles, their rate of breathing. Much of this may be out of your conscious awareness, but the data is arriving nonetheless. The inflow is open for information and possibly pleasure, and the outflow is open for giving the gift.

You are allowed to enjoy it! It doesn't mean you are "taking." In the Taking Quadrant, you learn to notice with your hands and enjoy with your hands. You carry that skill with you into Serving. What makes it Serving is that you set aside what you would prefer to do and are doing what they requested.

Listen for the timer. For turns longer than five to ten minutes, give them a heads-up: "We've got a couple minutes left. Anything you'd like more of before we stop?" Do not extend the time past what you have agreed on. You may think you're being generous and that they will love the extra time (they might), but you are eroding your and their trust in the container, and that diminishes your ability to relax into it. Close their turn on time, and later, after you both have turns, you can choose again what you'd both like. It might be more of that, or it might be something else entirely.

Your own arousal. What if you get turned on? That depends on your relationship. Even if you are intimate partners, don't expect that mutual arousal is the point, as it is in sexual play, or that your arousal will inspire your partner. Neither do you have to hide it (as if you can). In general, it helps to admit it, so they don't have to wonder and worry. Reassure them that you are still here to Serve. Hopefully you are.

The danger is that if you get turned on, your receiver may try to perform for you. They may resent that they are no longer receiving the attention you promised. They may enjoy your turn-on; that's fine too. It can be fun to ride their turn-on, and it pretty much happens automatically. The difference is you are not using it to get yourself going.

The experience of Serving. In Serving, you are following, not leading, so the mood will depend on the Accepter. It can feel quiet and meditative, sensual, silly, raucous, or erotic. You may melt into the bliss of the moment; you may get tired, distracted, or bored. You may get turned on and ride your partner's pleasure. It can be focused on communicating and the connection between you, or your Accepter can focus on their own sensations, settling into a trance-like state. You may feel well used, grateful, or honored to have the chance to contribute. You may notice where you are attached to your self-image as a giver. When you finally, blessedly, let go of getting a result, it's a big relief.

EXAMPLES

What some people have said

"I always thought that it was up to me to figure out what to do or not do."

"I am sooo much more comfortable here than in Taking!"

"This is so gratifying!"

"Oh! I can feel the difference now! This is not Taking! This feels really good."

"I can feel the difference in my hands after learning Taking. I can feel her relax."

It's okay to ask

Sam was massaging Gina's shoulders.

Sam: This feels vulnerable, like I have to get it right.

Me: What would help allay that fear?

Sam: I don't know.

Me: How about finding out if it actually is what she wants?

Sam (to me): Oh yeah, I could do that!

Sam (to Gina): Is this what you want?

Gina: Almost. Can you go a little slower?

Sam: Yes, like this?

Gina: Yes. Ahh, that's perfect.

Sam (to me): I get it. It's okay to ask.

CHAPTER 13

Lab 3: Play

If its purpose is more important than the act of doing it,
it's probably not play.
—Dr. Stuart Brown

Back in my chiropractic days, I attended a seminar on using chiropractic with animals. The presenter asked, "How can you tell if an animal is healthy?" The answer: "It plays." I thought, *Well, then we humans are in trouble!* Play is a fundamental human need to do something for enjoyment with curiosity and no need for a result. This need is something we are born with. We seem to outgrow the *ability* to play, but the need for play we never outgrow, and most of us have to learn it all over again.

In this lab, I talk about what play has to do with the quadrants and a few skills it takes to recover it. Then I'll introduce an experiment.

THE ELEMENTS OF PLAY

The key elements of play are that 1) something changes, 2) you respond to the change, and 3) you are open to the outcome.

Change. An example is puppies playing in the yard. One puppy changes direction, and the other responds. One rolls over, and the other responds. The change is moment by moment, and each change invites another change. The changes may be fast, slow, or anywhere in between. Even in a slow-moving game like chess, you have to wait for something to respond to.

Responding to change. That's where it gets fun. When puppy A turns south, puppy B follows. He doesn't keep going and wonder why his technique didn't work. Within limits, the more change there is, the more play is possible. Not enough change, and it gets boring; too much change too fast, and it gets scary.

Responding means improvising; it arises from somewhere within, and we don't always know where. It's easier to improvise when you know what the constraints are. In sports, there are the constraints of the playing field and rules of the game. Within those constraints, you improvise moment by moment.

Open to outcome. It has to be an open-ended outcome, or it's work. Trying to make something happen is not play; it's outcome management. The more determined you are to get the result, the more tension you feel. Sadly, this is how many people experience sex.

It's possible to have a goal that is part of your play, like a neighborhood soccer match, but soccer pros are not playing; they are working. It's also possible to enjoy your work by bringing some element of curiosity and play into it. Otherwise it's drudgery. Play requires a certain kind of curiosity. *Let's see what happens if...*

Play is satisfying *as it is.* There is no need for an outcome.

A few more things about play. Play depends on both (or all) people choosing to engage. Otherwise, it's imposition or assault. If you are wanting to play and the other is stuck on a script, it's going to get frustrating pretty quickly. Play requires that people engage in a way that does not harm themselves or the other and nourishes them in some way. Play lifts both people up; it does not exploit. The play itself generates interest and engagement. It has a way of grabbing your attention, which is enlivening.

Play requires you to bring your desires forward. It relies on the impulses that arise. Play requires the ability to choose what satisfies. In order to engage in play, we need a sufficient sense of safety. We need to know we are seen and heard and our boundaries are respected. This is one reason why you make eye contact and slow down in the labs. One way we create safety is to create a container. In the labs, the container is the limits that allow you to not worry about where it will go.

Play can take many moods. It's not necessarily a lighthearted "playful" mood. It can be physical tumble like the puppies; serious, deep and passionate; sensual, soulful, soft and slow; raucous, wild and fast. It could be more mental like playing with power and submission or fantasies. What makes it play is responding to change and being curious and open to outcome. See the online resources for more about play.

PHYSICAL PLAY AND THE LIMITING FACTOR

I think of play in its simplest form as being open-ended, improvisational, affectionate physical play. You allow your body to be curious and respond to what the other's body does, letting it take you wherever it does with no need for a goal. This kind of play can be challenging to access and is profoundly liberating.

Much of what I understand about play I learned in Contact Improvisation (CI). CI is something between a dance and a sport. It's based on contact between two or more people, playing with gravity, weight, and momentum. There are no steps. Everything is improvisational, and you don't know what's going to happen next. I learned that you can't use a recipe, so you have to rely on yourself. To do that, you have to be able to notice yourself (where you are in space, where your body is in contact with your partner, and what impulses arise) and your partner (where they are in space and how that is changing). You can't plan even one or two seconds ahead, because in those seconds, your dance partner has moved. You have to notice *constantly*. It's challenging because it requires extraordinary focus. Responding to change is true in all forms of dance that include a partner, but in most other dance, there are at least some steps to start with. In CI, there are no steps, just noticing and impulse.

There is a limit to how much change we can track in any given moment, and this, not your repertoire of cool moves, is what limits your dancing. The cool moves don't matter. *You can respond only as quickly as you can track what changes.*

This is clear to me when dancing with people who like to move more quickly than I can track. The sense of overwhelm is awful! There is a rate of change that is too much for me and a slower rate that allows me to track it. Then I can lose myself in the flow. It's exquisitely pleasurable and feels as if my body is moving, responding, playing, and I am following along. It might sound like getting good at CI means being able to go faster. Not true. Getting good at CI means getting good at noticing, and the noticing itself is pleasurable. You may be moving slowly, but it's completely engaging because you are so focused.

The ability to notice develops with practice. You've been developing it through the lessons and labs. You do get better at it, both in the quality of attention you can bring to it and the rate of changes that you can track. This is what allows you to gradually play with more intensity and still stay in your quadrant.

Noticing. The foundational skill that allows you to play is not your moves, it is noticing. As you develop your ability to notice, you begin to trust yourself. The more you trust yourself, the more you enjoy change. Unpredictability becomes enjoyable. You play with it.

The less you are able to notice, the more you have to rely on a recipe, because that's all you have. A recipe cannot meet your need to express what you feel. Play is expressive, so it's always real and cannot get boring. If you are bored (and this is especially true in sex), the problem is not that you are not doing enough; it's that you are not noticing or are not responding authentically, meaning you are planning ahead or holding back.

Based on that ability to notice, self-care shows up, the ability to take responsibility for your limits. The less skill you have at self-care, the more you need to try to control what happens. The more skill you have at self-care, the more fun it is to improvise. True in touch, true in sex, true in life.

There is no question that it often feels safer to use a recipe. The terrifying question of improvising, and also of sex, is *How do I know what to do?* Change the question to *What do I notice right here in front of me, in the other person, and in myself?*

SEXUAL PLAY

Sexual play is play in which sexual arousal is welcome. It may include the genitals but doesn't have to. Some of the hottest sexual play doesn't include them at all. If sex equals doing stuff with genitals, you can do that alone. To play, you need someone to play with. To enjoy each other, you want to learn how to show up in the moment, open the inflow, notice what you want, and learn how to express what you feel. This is a very different thing.

Sometimes we may know how to play, but when sexual activity begins, we forget to play. We forget how to be open ended about the outcome and become determined to get somewhere. We stop being authentic in how we respond, and we get on the program. It shows up mostly in focusing on technique and forgetting to notice what is here in front of you. Relying on the technique video or what worked last time is like trying to play soccer by responding to last week's game. It's not only useless, it's dangerous.

PLAY AND THE QUADRANTS

The quadrants separate receiving and giving, which creates amazing and rich possibilities you would find no other way. Play is different. In receiving, you ask your potential giver to set aside what they might prefer in order to go with what you desire. In play, you don't want the other person to set aside their desires; both of you bring your desires forward. Indeed, if either of you can't, there is no one home to play with.

By desire, I don't mean necessarily sexual desire. I mean the impulse to move and touch and do. It is likely that much of your impulse to do is wrapped up in Serving—that is, when you start doing, you automatically tend to try to Serve. If you are stuck in Serving, you are trying to manage the outcome, which kills your play.

Bring a sense of playfulness to any quadrant by bringing curiosity and being open ended. If you want to step out of the quadrants and into open play, stop trying to give, and bring your desires forward, both of you at once.

The Taking Quadrant is the key. Taking is where you learn how to locate your experience within yourself and how to notice and trust your impulses to move. You learn how to ask permission, trust the yes you hear, and trust your ability to stay within the limits of that yes. You learn how to not be afraid of your own feelings as they arise. As all of those develop, play becomes possible. Then you can cut loose; you stop planning, performing, and working at it and respond in the moment. You have a tremendous sense of freedom. If any of those steps are not working, it will be difficult to play. You may find it accidentally, in fits and starts, but won't be able to sustain it. Come back to the Taking Quadrant. Taking is where you break your compulsion to try to Serve. It could even be said that the purpose of the quadrants is to get you to the point where you can play.

Here are your experiments for this lab.

HAND DANCE

Experiment 1. Take a minute to recall what it feels like to Serve. Sit side by side, and both people bring one hand into the middle. One person gives the other a hand massage for about half a minute. Then switch.

Now, try to give each other massages at the same time. Oops! You can't give a massage if the other person is moving. It can be infuriating or comical. You want them to be still and let you massage them! Sound familiar?

Experiment 2. Take a minute to recall what it feels like to Take. One person explores the other person's hand for half a minute. Then switch.

Starting slowly, begin to explore your partner's hand at the same time. Your partner is moving, but it doesn't matter. You can still feel, but the thing you are feeling is moving. It may be even more interesting. Soon it becomes a kind of dance. It becomes play.

What you'll notice. When you both try to Serve, it can't be done. You're just trying to get the other person to sit still long enough to accept your Serving. With both of you in Taking, it becomes a dance. (You are both Allowing too.) Both of you follow your impulse as you learned to do in Taking, and you can do this at the same time. If what they are doing becomes unpleasant, you easily just move your hand out of the way. The arms will want to get involved and, eventually, the whole body. How long can you stay there in that mode without flipping into trying to Serve? Set a timer, and stop every three minutes to check in. *Are we still in Taking?*

YOUR DEFAULT SWITCHES

If you have been with a person who is selfish, switching to constantly being served can sound wonderful. Having someone focus only on you *is* wonderful sometimes, but if they are stuck in Serving and never bring their own desires forward, there is a certain level of play (and passion) that cannot happen.

Here is what happens over time with the practice. Your default starts out as Serve-Accept, because that is what feels normal. When you touch, you try to Serve, and your partner assumes that is what you are doing. If you want to try Taking, you have to communicate it clearly. Otherwise, it can feel creepy.

As you get comfortable in all quadrants, your default will gradually switch to Take-Allow. This happens pretty much automatically. You reach out and stroke my hair or caress my shoulder, and I assume that it arises from your own desire and can be trusted. I know that you're not trying to produce a result or get some response out of me, so we both relax. It becomes completely natural.

Now if you want Serving or Accepting, you have to ask for it. Both of you are rolling around, feeling, moving, exploring, and enjoying each other's bodies. Both are in Taking mode. Both are improvising and responding—you are playing. They touch a particularly wonderful spot in a particularly wonderful way, and you ask for Serving. "More of that, please, right there. Yeah." You hang out there a while. You are now able to communicate about it.

So you start out with a default of Serve-Accept, and if you want Take-Allow, you ask for it. You gradually switch to a default of Take-Allow, and if you want Serve-Accept, you ask for it. In this way, you learn to trust your impulse and desire, learn to trust expressing it, and learn to trust that you will both be true to yourselves first. This is the route to freedom when free play and wild abandon become possible. Performance ends and genuine expression of love opens up. This is what satisfies the heart.

PLAY AS AN APPROACH TO LIFE

What if you took play as an approach to life? What would it take? It would take not trying to control the outcome. This depends on a certain kind of deep acceptance of the inherent uncertainty of life. Sounds like a spiritual practice. One way to play with this is to consider everything an experiment. With an experiment, there is no wrong answer and no failure. When everything offers something to respond to, when you get curious, play is possible.

PART 3

The Wheel of Consent

CHAPTER 14

The Wheel of Consent

Their door was open at all times to offer shelter;
their house became a kind of stepping stone for new immigrants.
"Today, you; tomorrow, me," Inmaculada always said.
"There's a time to give and a time to receive,
that's the natural law of life."
—Isabel Allende

The practice of the Wheel of Consent lets you experience each quadrant. The model helps you make sense of your experience. In this chapter, I'll diagram the Wheel and show you how it works. In the chapters that follow, we'll look at each half and each quadrant. Some of the ideas in this chapter we have talked about in other places; here we put it together.

We've seen how when you ask each other the two questions—"How do you want to touch me?" and "How do you want me to touch you?"—you create four interactions, and in each interaction, you are either touching or being touched, and it's either for you or for the other person. The two factors, who is doing and who it's for, combine in four ways, and those combinations are the quadrants. Each quadrant offers a particular set of potential experiences, challenges, insights, pleasures, and erotic themes.

For example, I offer to give you a back rub, and you say, "Yes, please," or I ask permission to feel your back, and you allow me. In either case, my hands are on your back, but who it's for is different. The difference is significant and is part of creating consent.

Like any model, the Wheel of Consent can help you see where you are, what you're missing, and where you spend most of your time. It can help to normalize an experience and make it more accessible. It can clarify dynamics that are confusing: "Oh, no wonder! I knew what it felt like, but it didn't make sense before!"

There are a couple of things to know about the model.

1) You don't actually need it. What changes you is not the concept— it's the experience. For some people, seeing the diagram helps them find the experience, and for some, the experience comes first before the model makes sense. Generally speaking, once your hands *feel* the difference between Taking and Serving, the model falls into place and becomes obvious. If you find yourself hunched over the diagram with furrowed brow trying to wrestle it into submission, drop it and come back to it later. Go back and play with the lessons; they are more fun anyway.

2) The Wheel is a diagram of what happens when two people play the Three Minute Game. That's all it is. As you notice the underlying principles, you may notice how they play out in relationships, community life, and international politics. Not every *interaction* fits the Wheel, thank goodness, but the dynamics that the Wheel demonstrates are fundamental to all interactions. Once you get going on it and start analyzing everything, it's helpful to remember that it's only a diagram of what happens when two people ask each other those questions: "Will you...?" and "May I...?"

So you don't actually need the model, but if you are geek-ish on these things, as I am, you will find that the Wheel and its implications will keep you happily occupied for decades. I wish you luck.

THE OLD MODEL AND THE NEW MODEL

Receiving and Giving. In the opening chapters, I defined receiving and giving like this. The words are often used to describe the direction of an action that is delivered but not whether it is wanted or not. The other way the words are used describes a gift that is wanted but not who is doing the action. (It may be an action done for you or an action you are allowed to do.) One meaning refers to the action, wanted or not, and the other meaning refers to a gift no matter which way the action goes.

No wonder it's confusing! Here I use "receive" and "give" to describe not the direction of the action (who is doing) but the direction of the gift (who it's for).

The old model. Because of the dual meanings of both words, "receive" is conflated with "done-to." That is, when we mean "done-to," we say "receive." That makes us subtly assume that when we are being done to, we are receiving (or are supposed to be receiving) a gift of some kind. Likewise, "give" is conflated with "do." When we mean "do," we say "give." That makes us subtly assume that when we are doing, we are giving (or supposed to be giving) something.

In the old model, only one dynamic is possible. More accurate is that our language admits of only one dynamic; our bodies know the difference and endure some confusion. Here's the old model.

DO / GIVE ⟶ DONE-TO / RECEIVE

The new model. Once you understand that the two factors are distinct, you can see how they combine and create four quadrants.

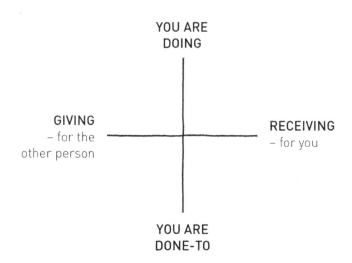

When we name the quadrants, it looks like this:

Once it's on paper, it's easier to see a few things.

The Four Halves

The Receiving and Giving Halves are focused on the gift—who it is for.

You can see that in the Giving Half, there are two ways to give:

- In Serving, you give your action (what you do to them or for them)
- In Allowing, you give access to you (your body, attention, belongings)

In the Receiving Half, there are two ways to receive:

- In Accepting, you receive the gift of the other person's action (what they do to you or for you)
- In Taking, you receive the gift of access to them (their body, attention, belongings)

The Doing and Done-to Halves are focused on the action—who is doing.

In the Doing Half, you are the one doing:

- Either it's for you (you are in Taking)
- Or it's for them (you are in Serving)

In the Done-to Half, you are the one being done to.:

- Either it's for you (you are in Accepting)
- Or it's for them (you are in Allowing)

2. The Four Quadrants

Each quadrant is a combination of the two factors:

- You are doing, and it's for you (you're receiving a gift)—The Taking Quadrant
- You are doing, and it's for them (you're giving a gift)—The Serving Quadrant

- You are being done to, and it's for you (you're receiving a gift)—The Accepting Quadrant
- You are being done to, and it's for them (you're giving a gift)—The Allowing Quadrant

Even simpler:

- You do what you want (Taking Quadrant)
- You do what they want (Serving Quadrant)
- They do what you want (Accepting Quadrant)
- They do what they want (Allowing Quadrant)

3. The Two Dynamics

The Serve-Accept dynamic. The action moves from Serve to Accept, and the gift moves the same direction, also from Serve to Accept. The gift is the action of the Server. This dynamic is created by the Accepter asking "Will you…?" and the Server answering "Yes, I will."

The Take-Allow dynamic. The action moves from Take to Allow, but the gift moves in the opposite direction, from Allow to Take. That is, the Allowing partner is giving a gift to the Taking partner. The gift is access. This dynamic is created by the Taker asking "May I…?" and the Allower saying "Yes, you may."

4. The Circle

The circle represents consent or your agreement. I'll talk about that shortly.

ABOUT THE QUADRANTS

Each quadrant is half of a dynamic; the agreement creates the dynamic. Your quadrant is one end of that dynamic; your partner's quadrant is the other end. That's the structure, and then there is the experience of it, what it feels like to be there. The agreement sets up the *possibility* of the experience but doesn't guarantee it. We usually have to learn what each quadrant feels like. This is what you experienced in the lessons.

Each quadrant is distinct. No two are the same. They may feel the same at first, but when they click, the difference is clear. Again, this is what the lessons do. No quadrant can substitute for the others. Each one can only be found one at a time, and you cannot learn any quadrant by trying to combine them.

Each one is enjoyable in its own right. Different kinds of satisfaction will be found in each of them, but all are enjoyable in their own way. It's one of the signs you are there. If it does not feel enjoyable, you are not in it. It's not because there is something wrong with you; it's because we haven't set it up quite right so you could find it. The thing that is not enjoyable is not actually the quadrant; it's something else.

Each one will challenge you in different ways. It varies by the person, but certain themes tend to characterize each one. They can be challenging to find the first time, and they can bring up uncomfortable feelings or lead to deep personal insight.

Each one teaches you something different about yourself. For example, in one, you'll see why you go along with things that don't inspire you, and in another, you'll see how you are afraid to take action. In another, you'll see why you love surrender and are so good at it. Each one sheds light on different things.

Each one tends to evoke a particular erotic element. It may be a major theme or part of a full palette with which you play. It's also true that in either dynamic, the polarity between the two quadrants creates a charge, and that itself can be erotic.

Each one opens a certain kind of freedom. We all have aspects of ourselves that are confusing, hidden, or intimidating. They often have to do with the dynamics of the quadrants. There will be a certain kind of fear or shame about, for example, the impulse to reach over and feel someone up. Once we find what the quadrant actually is instead of what we were afraid it was, that aspect now makes sense and is no longer hidden in confusion, and we are able to play in it and express ourselves through it. This is a source of joy.

The quadrants have nothing to do with gender. Except this: how you experience your gender is one factor (of many) that can make finding any given quadrant difficult and liberating. A great many things affect how easy or difficult any quadrant is to find and what will challenge you, such as your culture and generation, your early experiences, and what you think your gender means about how you are supposed to feel and act. We talked about gender in chapter 6. There is no such thing as a "feminine" quadrant or a "masculine" quadrant. Whatever your sex and your gender, you need all four, and you deserve access to all four.

Each quadrant is both innate and necessary. We need all of them to realize the full potential of relationship, and we need all of them for a full expression of our natural and inherent eroticism. Because they are innate, if we haven't learned to access them, we still hunger for them on some level. They call to us in fantasy, erotic novels, and playing with power exchanges—thankfully!

It's fine to have favorites. Often one quadrant will be an erotic theme for you, and that's wonderful! Ideally you do want to be able to find a basic ease in all of them. If you can only find one, that doesn't make it your favorite; it makes it the only one you can find. Fear of chocolate does not constitute a preference for vanilla.

Each one has social and political implications. The same two dynamics inform relationships with friends, partners, business associates, and international relations.

Each quadrant has a "shadow." Each quadrant has ways it gets misused, overused, or distorted.

Each one evokes a spiritual principle. These can include gratitude, service, generosity, surrender, integrity, and more.

And as one student said, "All quadrants provide an equal opportunity to get pissed off. For not getting what you want, for not getting the appreciation you think you deserve, and of course for not having your mind read accurately."

THE CIRCLE

There is a circle around the whole thing. The dictionary defines consent as agreeing to something someone else wants, but we are giving it a larger meaning, which is our agreement. You ask me for what you want, or I ask you for what I want, and we agree to it. In the diagram, the circle represents our agreement. Ideally we want to be inside the circle, but it is possible to be outside the circle. Inside the circle, we have an agreement, and the agreement creates a gift from one to the other. This is what we have been describing so far.

Outside the circle. Outside the Circle, the same dynamic is happening but without consent. You have the action component but not the gift component. I call this the shadow of the quadrants. I am defining "shadow" loosely. This is not a psychoanalytic term; I mean when we act without consent or carry it too far. It's "the quadrants gone bad"—passivity, entitlement, manipulation, stealing, assault, and war. It is recognition that the same or similar dynamics can show up in ways that are not helpful, not a gift, not joyful. We talk about these in each quadrant.

No one is exempt from the shadows of the quadrants. Sometimes seeing the shadow of the quadrant is what makes the whole thing make sense. "Oh, now I get what you are talking about!" Sometimes seeing the shadow of a quadrant makes the whole quadrant frightening or confusing. "Oh, I'm not going anywhere near that quadrant!"

Playing with the Wheel over time, a couple of things about the shadows become clear. Until you can stand securely *in* the quadrant, that is, inside the circle, you will be engaging the shadow of it. It can't be avoided, because the dynamics are inherent to all of us. For example, if you can't stand solidly in Taking (which is receiving a gift), you become sneaky, coercive, or a bully, trying to get something without acknowledging it or taking something from someone without noticing you are (time, attention, resources, or access). Don't beat yourself up for this. These are adaptive behaviors for getting our needs met. We learned as children that it wasn't safe to ask for what we wanted, so we learned to sneak, manipulate, and more to meet our needs. That develops into unclear, ineffective, or abusive behaviors.

The second thing that becomes clear is that as you begin to experience the quadrant itself, the shadow cleans itself up. Being inside the circle requires that you learn how to be honest and vulnerable about what you want. That enables you to have your real needs met. When your real needs are met, you don't resort to stealing, passivity, or violence. This more than anything else is what inspires me about the whole process. It's why I wrote this book.

The muddy zone. There is a muddy zone at the edge of each quadrant—not quite inside the circle but not outside it either. Everybody's been here. You don't say no, but you don't say yes either. It's not a full-hearted gift, but neither do you object. It's going along because you can't be bothered to say no, you don't know how *not to* go along, you're trying to be nice, or you're overwhelmed.

Or you don't ask. You try something and see if it "works," or you put a little pressure on but not too much. "Awww, c'mon, are you sure?" You don't know how to ask, so you assume it's okay unless someone strongly objects. How strongly do they have to object before you notice?

Discussion of the muddy zone is controversial. On the one hand, you have responsibility for asking and for saying yes or no. On the other hand, there is the fact of overwhelm and freeze states and the influence of one person having more power in the situation. At the time of this writing, there is an explosion of calling to account various people (usually men) of power and the inevitable conflict between those who focus on the responsibilities of the perpetrators and those who focus on the responsibility of the potentially harmed to speak up and say no, suggesting that to say the harmed are helpless is to infantilize them. Then there is the mounting science about how the nervous system handles potential threat with the freeze response so the person *can't* respond. What is the situation in any given interaction? We can't know the exact situation in any interaction we are not part of. For that matter, we rarely apprehend the entire situation in any interaction that we *are* part of.

The lessons and labs describe a practice in which you learn to take an exquisite level of responsibility for your desires and limits. In the labs, you will mess up. For example, in Allowing, there will be times when you go along with something you don't feel good about. Because it's a lab, it's a practice in taking ever more responsibility, so I can in good conscience suggest that you forgive yourself, slow down, and practice not blaming your partner. Your responsibility for yourself grows.

That's in the labs. In real life, things are way more complex. In Take-Allow, for example, the Taker exerts some pressure or doesn't ask. The Allower assumes the Taker should know and doesn't say yes but doesn't say no either. How much pressure does the Taker exert? What kind? Are they aware of any imbalance of power? Probably not. Are they able to read signals of an Allower in freeze mode? How much responsibility did the Allower take for their limits? To what degree are they subject to overwhelm? Perhaps they felt fine about it at the time, maybe when they were sexually aroused, and later realized they didn't feel good about it. To the degree they assumed the Taker was supposed to know, they are likely to blame them for not knowing. It's a mess.

The muddy zone acknowledges that there are situations in which it's not clear. The muddy zones turn out to be important, because it's often where we blame ourselves or others, rightly or wrongly. What makes it muddy is that blame is not clear or even necessarily applicable: "But I thought we agreed!" Many people spend much of their time here. "I'm not really a yes, but I'm not a no either, so I guess we're going ahead" is a direct quote from a student. You will find that as you get better at discerning your full-hearted no and your full-hearted yes, that the mud doesn't grab your boots so tightly. My friend says, "I've learned to wait for an inner *Hell yes!* and until I hear that, it's a no."

In the labs, there is the opportunity to experiment with how much responsibility for yourself you can learn and how trustworthy you can become, both that you won't abandon yourself and that you will respect your partner's limits.

If you can't see the circle. I occasionally have people who dip their toe into a quadrant (most often with Taking) and are stopped in their tracks by overwhelming feelings of shame and fear as if the quadrant itself is horrible. I've had a few people simply refuse. "No, that is wrong, and I'm not going to do it."

I've come to see it like this. If you could stand in the center of the Wheel and look out toward the edge, you'd see inside the circle and outside it. If you can't see the circle—that is, if you don't understand consent, don't trust it, or don't have the skills to create it—you look out that direction, and all you see is the shadow. The whole quadrant looks dreadful. If you stand at the center of Taking and look out, the entire quadrant looks like abuse and assault. If you can't see the circle of consent, you can't see that inside the circle, there is a gift freely given to you. If you look out at Allowing and don't see the circle, all you see is victimhood, passivity, and dread. It all looks terrible. Who'd want to go there?

Another way of saying it is if you don't understand consent and trust yourself with it, you can't receive a gift or give one. The clearer you get about consent, the space outside the circle grows more abhorrent, and the space inside the circle becomes more joyful. More important, you get clearer on when you are stepping outside of it or dabbling in the muddy zone. This is where the Wheel becomes a spiritual path.

HOW DO YOU KNOW WHICH QUADRANT YOU ARE IN?

When I ask this in workshops, faces look puzzled. "Uh, intention? Well, I'm intending to give, doesn't that count?" I say, "Intention is meaningless without consent." Then they really look worried. It's not intention. It is possible to intend to give (either Allowing or Serving), which is where many of us are much of the time. Have you asked what your partner wants? If not, you can't give it. Perhaps you were hoping that your intention to give absolves you of the responsibility to communicate.

Likewise, it's not enjoyment. All four are enjoyable. What determines which quadrant you are in is which quadrant you agreed to be in. Who asked for what they wanted, and who agreed to give that? No agreement, no quadrants. Then there is the art of staying there. That is what the labs are about.

The fact that there is an inner experience of each quadrant creates an interesting glitch. Wherever you *feel* like you are, you will tend to assume your partner is in the opposite quadrant. For example, if you feel like you are in Serving, you will assume your partner is in Accepting, but they may not feel like they are. In fact, they can be in Accepting only if that's what you both agreed to. If you feel like you are in Allowing, you assume your partner is in Taking. They may or may not be; in fact, they are not likely to be, because most people can't find Taking to begin with.

What is happening? Giving is based on setting aside your Want-to list and moving to your Willing-to list. As soon as you move to your Willing-to list, you feel like you are giving. What happens if you forget how to value what you want and live in your Willing-to list all the time? Many of us do.

With heterosexual couples, it typically works like this. The man feels like he is Serving and is intending to Serve, because he's doing all the work. He assumes his partner is in Accepting. She feels like she is Allowing because she's going along with what he's doing. Apparently he likes doing it, so she thinks he is in Taking. Now you have him in Serving and her in Allowing. Who is receiving? Nobody. This can cause heartbreaking, long-term resentment. This is where both people end up saying, "But I thought you wanted that!"

This can happen the other direction too. You can feel like you are receiving (in either Taking or Accepting) but fail to notice that your "giver" is not as willing as you thought.

THE INSIGHTS OF THE WHEEL

The new insight of the Wheel is not that consent is a good thing. You already knew that. The contribution that the Wheel makes to the larger conversation about consent is that there are two factors to an agreement: what may or may not happen and who it's for. Recognizing the two factors creates some fundamental shifts in understanding human dynamics.

De-conflating. The first shift is that it de-conflates done-to = receive and do = give. This has multiple implications.

First is that when you think done-to = receive, whenever you are touched you have to fit it into the idea of it being for you even if it doesn't feel like it is. You will tend to think that you are supposed to like it even if you don't or at least appreciate it even if you don't. If you don't like it, you think the problem is you. After all, it's being done to you, so therefore it must be "for" you, so what's wrong with you, anyway?

I talk about this in depth in chapter 18 (The Receiving Half). If you don't like receiving, it may be that what you actually don't like is being done-to, because done-to in your experience means tolerating, enduring, going along with, and faking it.

Second is that conflating doing with giving likewise limits you. Every act of doing has to be for the other person. You have to take your natural desire to touch and force it into some frame that makes it about the other person, but there is still something you want, which you haven't admitted.

Third, when we de-conflate done-to = receive and do = give, each part is available to combine in the opposite pairing. Done-to can now combine with giving (creating the Allowing Quadrant), and doing can combine with receiving (creating the Taking Quadrant).

Perhaps the most important contribution of the quadrants is that they exist. It is possible to do for the other person or to do for yourself, and those are two different experiences.

The meaning of Receiving and Giving. When you de-conflate done-to = receive, receiving takes on a new meaning. If receiving is not done-to, what is it? We are using receiving to mean receiving *a gift*.

We said this in chapter 2 (Defining Receiving and Giving). The receiver puts their desires forward (moves to their Want-to list), and the giver sets their desires aside (moves to their Willing-to list). Receiving a gift means putting yourself and your desires first, requesting it, and having someone else set their desires aside to go with yours. Receiving this gift, with the tenderheartedness it often engenders, can be life changing.

Likewise, the meaning of giving shifts from "doing" to the act of putting your desires aside (while still respecting your limits). Putting your desires aside is the heart of giving a gift.

The difference between the two dynamics. Both dynamics are innate to humans and have a place in our lives. We have some cultural references to both of them, but they are incomplete. Confusing them creates internal dissonance and interactions that are unsatisfying or problematic.

When we can access both of the two dynamics, several things happen:

- We avoid confusion, frustration, and resentment.
- We open a new playing field; now that you know the dynamic exists, you can play in it, each one wonderful and liberating in its own right.

- We develop integrity; we are no longer pretending to be in one dynamic when what we really want is the other one.

That's how the Wheel works. In the chapters that follow, we look at each half of the Wheel and then at each quadrant. We explore what's challenging about the quadrants, where they take you, the shadows of them, and why we need them in the world. We start with the concept of directionality: the direction of the gift.

CHAPTER 15

The Direction of the Gift

*As he sang, tribesmen came and sat around us. I began to understand
that year about trading poems and songs. It involved giving, that
intangible, freeing human thing: giving something priceless,
even to a stranger, for nothing.*
—Susan Brind Morrow

Every Tuesday morning at nine, the phone rings. It's Teri, and she's there
to listen to me for half an hour. It doesn't matter what I talk about and
whether I cry or complain or work through something that's bugging
me or, as is often the case lately, think out loud through some chapter of
this book. It doesn't matter if it's interesting to her or not, because it's not
about her. It's about me. At the end of thirty minutes, I thank her, she
says, "You're welcome," and then I listen to her for thirty minutes. Now
it's about her—whatever is on her mind, whatever she needs to cry about,
rant about, or ponder.

This is a co-counseling session, and it can be short or long: two
minutes, twenty minutes, or an hour or two. It includes talking, crying,
laughing, or storming about something. A skilled listener can support
you into extraordinary depth. Besides getting a certain burden off your
shoulders, you come out of it with a new perspective and reevaluate your
situation, hence its other name, Re-evaluation Counseling. I learned
it forty years ago, and it built a foundation of emotional fluency I am
thankful to have.

The active ingredient is attention: undivided, welcoming, and non-judging attention, which is not always easy to absorb. At first, it felt awkward and contrived, and sometimes having that high-quality attention would bring up feelings of grief for all the times I had not had it.

Among other things, it taught me how to take turns. Taking turns is as natural to me now as breathing. It taught me a great deal about receiving and giving as well. When it's my turn, it really is my turn, and when it's your turn, it really is your turn. It taught me how to *have* a turn and how to make good use of it. I learned to use my listener's attention as an extra resource with which to feel, think, process and gain insight. Often I'd say, "Wow, I didn't know I felt that!"

It taught me that having a session is different than having a conversation. Sometimes I want the focused listening of a session; other times, I want a conversation where we explore together and see where it takes us. It taught me that neither of these two things, a session and a conversation, can replace the other, though most people, if they don't have the opportunity to have a session, will try to meet that need through conversation with minimal success. Either the conversation goes along and you're never able to pour your heart out, or you pour it all over the place without the consent of the listener. I've been on both sides of that, and I don't recommend either one. If you don't know how to take a turn and make good use of it, you won't be able to give a turn either.

When the Three Minute Game showed up, it was immediately obvious that it was about taking turns. I have found that many people are not used to the idea or are challenged by it, so this chapter is about how it works and why we need it.

DIRECTIONALITY

Directionality is the idea that when the receiver wants something and the giver is willing to give it and does so, it creates a directional flow, like a river, and that directionality has certain characteristics and benefits. The gift moves in only one direction, and because of that, the river is able to deliver certain gifts *that are possible no other way*. To experience the gift moving from one person to the other, you have to separate receiving and giving. You have to stand either on the receiving end or the giving end. You cannot do both at once, and *until you can take them apart, you can't experience either of them.* There are few things as satisfying and few things as challenging.

WHY PEOPLE RESIST TAKING THEM APART

When I played the Three Minute Game that first time, it felt completely natural, but I found that taking turns was far from natural for most people. A few said, "That sounds wonderful!" but a great many questioned it or offered some serious resistance, and a few flat-out refused. It took me some time to understand what was happening, but I've seen it enough now that I think I understand it. There are indeed some good reasons to resist.

First, we misunderstand what receiving and giving are. When we conflate receiving with done-to, we're back here again: if being done to feels like tolerating and enduring, then receive comes to mean the same thing. If you think, *Oh no, you mean I have to receive that?* this is where you are. Here are some examples of receiving meaning done-to:

"I don't like receiving massage, because they do things that I guess are supposed to feel good but don't."
"She wants to give me that. Aren't I supposed to be willing to receive it? If I don't receive it, I feel like I'm being ungrateful."
"I'm supposed to receive all this affection he wants to give me, but frankly, it's a burden."

On the giving side, to the degree you have not learned how to set a limit, giving is going to feel like a threat, a burden, or even a danger. If the thought of giving makes you feel worried or guarded, it's probably this. As one person said, "I felt I was expected to give more than I feel good about."

If you think receiving means tolerating and enduring, who would want more of that? If you think giving means having no choices or boundaries, who would want more of that either? You are resisting *something*, but it's not receiving or giving. You are resisting acquiescence, manipulation, or confusion, so it can seem wise to avoid the whole give-receive thing altogether.

Second, it doesn't sound romantic or enlightened. One person said, "We are beyond mere giving and receiving," as if that is the enlightened ideal. Or, "We love each other so giving and receiving are the same." So, gifts are only for those who don't love each other so very much?

The idea is that if we are in love enough, or enlightened, spiritual, attuned, or connected enough, giving and receiving cease to exist, melting together in a kind of mystical swirl. To be fair, there is a reason for this. When the body is deeply relaxed, the brain centers that enable us to make distinctions quiet down. The brain centers that create experiences of oneness and merging light up, and we call that spiritual, but it is possible to be in a oneness brain state in any quadrant or in no quadrant. Being in a oneness brain state means nothing except that you are in a oneness brain state.

Given this wonderful feeling, why would anyone want to mess it up by trying to take receiving and giving apart? This is a great question and one I have pondered. I think it's this: to learn to receive, you have to separate it from giving. It can be learned no other way. Learning to receive is vulnerable and develops integrity and allows you, when it's later your turn, to give selflessly. That is a spiritual path if ever there was one.

This objection could also be another confusion about the words. You may be using "receiving" to mean you feel good: *I'm in an altered state and it feels good, so I call that receiving.* Or *When I give to my partner, that makes me feel good about myself, so it feels like receiving.* Feeling good doesn't mean you are receiving. It just means you feel good.

I noticed that everyone who brought this up found receiving to be emotionally challenging, myself included, for all the reasons we've talked about elsewhere. There is nothing enlightened or romantic about not being able to receive. Learning to receive touches our vulnerability and much more. Anyway, it's a little arrogant: everyone needs help but you?

Third, receiving is inherently vulnerable. This is the reason that underlies all the rest. It's interesting that no one objects to their partner having a turn; it's their own turn they want to avoid. Receiving a gift is *inherently* vulnerable. When we reveal what we want and ask for it, we are subject to disappointment, embarrassment, shame, or guilt. We are also subject to feeling delighted, satisfied, loved, cherished, supported, comforted, turned on, affirmed, and blissed out, which can be even more challenging than feeling "bad."

When someone sets aside what they prefer and tends to what we want, giving us their full attention, it touches our heart, and hearts are vulnerable. There are a couple of time-honored ways to avoid that vulnerability. One is to always be the giver. Besides avoiding our vulnerability, we can claim the moral high ground. The other way is to play it safe by trying to do both at once. Either way, we dilute our discomfort. We are more insulated from our self-doubt. Our avoidance strategies are hard to argue with because they sound so virtuous! The only way to find out how open you are to receiving is to (temporarily) close the door of giving and see what's left. This is essentially what happens in the lessons and labs.

One person said, "Oh shit. When I'm in receiving, my fear and shame kick up. When I'm in giving, I feel good about myself, so giving is my way to feel good. No wonder I can't tell the difference. I don't care who it's for, and I can't even tell who it's for. I'm just going for what feels good to me, and what feels good to me is the giving side. So who the hell is *that* for?"

There is another reason too. We just don't know *how.* Our experiences of "receiving" have carried mixed messages. We've been told it was "for us," but it sure didn't feel like it, or we are so steeped in managing other people's experiences that we don't know how to tend to our own. Everything feels like it's for someone else. It's not that we resist taking our turn; we just don't know what it feels like to have something be genuinely for us.

For all these reasons, you are right to feel drawn to separating receiving and giving and right to feel resistant to it.

RECEIVING AND GIVING AS HUMAN NEEDS

To have the undivided attention of another human being in a way that is helpful, meaningful, and enjoyable for us, to have them set aside their own wants and tend to ours for that limited time, this is receiving. It is putting ourselves in the center. At other times, we set aside our wants and contribute to those of others. We step out of the center and allow others to be there. This is giving. Each is a fundamental need (for adults). When we understand receiving and giving as human needs, a few things become clear.

1) As is true of all human needs, they seek to be met in the simplest and most direct way possible. If we don't know how to do that, we will try to find some other way, which will be less effective or satisfying.

2) Neither of them can meet the need for the other. You cannot meet your need for receiving by more giving, no matter how pleasant it is. You cannot meet your need for giving by trying to get something back.

3) We can learn how to meet them more effectively. The principles may be natural, but our experience with them as children has been less than optimal, and we end up with misconceptions that don't work. But it can be learned, and it's not particularly mysterious. For most people, this means learning that when it's your turn, it really is for you, learning what that feels like and what to do with it.

4) Until we learn to meet our needs, they keep pulling at us. We may not understand it, and the messages from within may get garbled, but there remains something we long for. When the needs are not met, the hunger continues.

THE PHYSICS OF DIRECTIONALITY

I grew up around alfalfa fields that had to be irrigated. Watching the water flow through the pipes, it's hard to miss the basics of directional flow. The pipe carries the water from the acequia (canal) down the hill to the field. There's a valve at each end of the pipe. The valve at the top could be open, but if the valve at the bottom is closed or vice versa, no water. The water flows one direction only; you can't push it back up the hill. The size of the flow varies depending on how open the valves are. When they're both fully opened, a sizable flow of water goes through.

The field wants the water! We're not there to please the canal (except that time it rained so hard the canal overflowed). The farmer's job is to open the valves so enough water flows through without drowning the field or depleting the canal. It's pretty much the same with people.

Here's how to get a good directional flow going.

It is created by agreement. The flow does not happen by accident. Your agreement sets each of you on a different end of the pipe. This almost always has to be verbal. Without it, you will likely both think you are on the giving end. The act of choosing opens the valve; the more conscious the choice, the more the valve can open.

It is based on what the receiver wants and the giver is willing to give. Not the other way around. It's not what the receiver is willing to go along with and not what the giver "wants to give." What opens the receiver's valve is: *What do I want?* What opens the giver's valve is: *Am I okay with giving that?*

It is an active choice. There is nothing passive about either role, and it's a minute-by-minute choice. You have your hand on the valve.

You can't stand on both ends at once. Giving means you set aside what you want and move to your Willing-to list. Receiving means you put your desires first and move to your Want-to list. You cannot put your desires first and last at the same time.

Know which end you are on. If you don't know which end you are on, the water can't flow. Not because you are so enlightened that you are doing both but because you are doing neither.

The flow opens up. Once it's clear who it's for and you have verbally agreed, and both of you stand solidly on your end and stay there, the pipe opens. The clearer the flow, the larger the gift that can be delivered.

The moving of the gift feels good. It feels good at both ends in different ways. The clearer the agreement, the more flow there is and the better it feels to both of you. This is why people say, "I receive by giving," because it feels good to give. It feels good because you are standing in the current.

To get a really good directional flow going, stay on your end. It's easy to slip away to the other end. You start out asking to receive, but giving feels less vulnerable, suits your self-image better, or you forget where you are, so you start trying to give your giver a good experience. You have left the receiving end, so the flow stops. Or you agree to give but then try to get something back: a response you want to see or some approval you hope for. You have left the giving end, so the flow stops. It's like pretending to be on the giving end, but you secretly run a straw down the outside of the pipe and try to suck a little water back up again. Stay on your end (for the time and situation you have agreed on).

The larger the flow, the more it will challenge you. A puny, muddy, ambiguous trickle may be fine, and you can handle that, but a good strong flow of clear water will challenge you, because it delivers such a profound gift.

Do we ever get to 100 percent? Meaning are we ever able to be completely receiving or completely giving, without mixing it up with the other end? In real life, probably not, nor do we need to. This practice is an experiment: how close to 100 percent can you get? The closer you can get to 100 percent, the richer the power and discovery of it. The experiment is what changes you.

TWO FALLACIES ABOUT RECEIVING AND GIVING

"I receive by giving." Maybe you have said or heard this: "No, I don't need a turn to receive. I receive by giving!" This could be that you enjoy the doing role and are calling that giving. More likely it's one of these.

When I give, I experience some benefit, like enjoyment, validation, or connection. Here you are using "receive" to mean *Something in me feels good.* Because it feels good, you're calling that receiving.

Or this: *I feel thankful for the experience, and that feels like receiving.* Giving is satisfying, often fun. It's also true that in giving you experience the benefits of personal growth, tenderheartedness, humility, etc., or a good time. This is not a gift from your receiver; they have not set aside what they want in order to give you what you want. It's the nature of the situation. Feel thankful, and enjoy that feeling.

The problem is not that you experience some benefit; it's that when you use "giving" to get your "receiver" to provide you with the appreciation you desire, you're not really giving, so there's no directional flow, just a bunch of sloshing around. Your giving is not satisfying because it's not real. Your receiver is not satisfied either, because you are not actually giving.

"By receiving, I give my giver an opportunity to give." This often comes up in talking about receiving. "Oh right! Besides, this gives my partner an opportunity to give!" It's often said as if it's a relief. *Whew! It's okay to (sort of) receive, because I can frame it as giving!* There's an interesting twist of logic there: *It's okay to receive, because I'm not really receiving?*

When you ask for something, the other person does have an opportunity to give. It's up to them to choose that or not, but if you are trying to give (the opportunity), you have left the receiving end of the flow. Now there's no one there. The flow stops, and you have a conundrum. They want to give you a back rub. Great! You like a deep pressure, but they want to caress. Which one is it going to be? If it's for you, you're going to ask for deeper pressure, but if you're doing it for them, you allow a caress, which means it's no longer for you—which means they're not actually giving, and the flow stops.

Or it could be that if you tell yourself you are giving, you can dilute some of the emotional tenderness of receiving. You can pretend that it's not *really* for you because, you know, you're really doing it for them. Or it could be that you want them to have the experience of giving. This implies that you know what experience they need. That's a little presumptuous. The irony is that you are trying to let them give but are preventing them from actually giving.

WHAT SEPARATING RECEIVING AND GIVING DOES FOR YOU

Taking receiving and giving apart affects us in two main ways: first is the experience itself, and second is what we learn from it.

The experience itself. To be touched, listened to, or served in ways that are meaningful, useful, and enjoyable for you, when there is nothing to give back and no one else to tend to, allows you experiences that are available no other way. They can be challenging and also luscious, nourishing, affirming, sexy, healing, mind blowing, and liberating.

First, there is the touch itself, the listening, the holding, the scratch right there. Then there is the fact of that person's care, that they have set aside what they would have preferred for you. That can be its own challenge and its own healing salve. In the experience, these two intertwine. We mentioned this in the lessons.

What you learn from it. As you experience receiving and giving one at a time, you learn to tell the difference, and that shows you what they are. It lets you learn how to use each of them wisely and with integrity, and lets each of them feed you in the way it is meant to. You appreciate the joy and power of each of them, and you no longer have to avoid either of them. This gives you freedom and opens the door to real play. There is a kind of relief, healing, and a lot more fun. The truly amazing thing about receiving and giving is that they exist.

You learn to receive with grace, ease, gratitude, and heart and to give with generosity, confidence, and effectiveness. You clear up the directional flow so the river is clear and strong and quenches your thirst. When you acknowledge that someone is giving up something for you, it tends to be humbling, and it feeds your heart in a certain way. It makes you notice that they have limits to what they are willing to give you. This engenders respect, and the world needs this kind of respect.

When you learn to acknowledge that there are things you want and take responsibility for that, it creates integrity. You no longer have to pretend that there is nothing you want or use "giving" to get it. You notice others have the same kinds of needs. This is compassion, and the world needs more of it too.

Learning to take receiving and giving apart always starts with learning to receive. We learn how to receive, then we learn how to give, and then the difference becomes clear.

THE THIRD MODE

There is a third mode: a place that is neither receiving nor giving but is hanging out in the middle. This is the conversation as opposed to the listening session I talked about at the beginning of this chapter. Neither of you are setting aside what you want; both of you are bringing your desires forward. This is where play happens as you saw in Lab 3.

This is where most people seem to think they are or want to be, but *until you can occupy the quadrants, you can't actually get to the middle.* Imagine a square room. Attached to each corner is a cord, each cord comes to the center, and together they hold up a lantern. As long as each cord is the same length, the lantern hangs in the center; if one cord shortens, the lantern sways to the side. If you want to hang out in the middle of the Wheel where there is no receiving or giving, you have to have all the cords supporting the lantern. You have to have access to every quadrant. As long as you have one, two, or three quadrants that are not accessible to you or that you are avoiding, your lantern can't hang in the center, and neither can you.

The quadrant(s) you are avoiding are almost always the Receiving Quadrants. In order to play, you need your desires, and the Receiving Quadrants teach you how to bring your desires forward with integrity. Trying to stay in giving isn't play—it's outcome management. It may seem ironic that learning to take them apart allows you to play in the middle.

We need all three modes. We need times to receive and times to give and times when we are doing neither. Without receiving and giving, there is not much depth in the relationship. Without time to hang out, there's not much space to have a friendship. Receiving and giving make the third mode possible.

CHAPTER 16

The Doing Half

What you gonna do to me, what I'm gonna do to you,
I bet you'll like it.
—Trombone Shorty

T he Doing Half includes the Taking and Serving Quadrants.

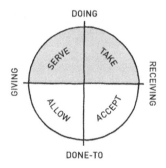

Whether in touch or in life, taking action is part of an empowered, expressive, rich, and meaningful life, and getting clear about who it's for is essential.

STRATEGY AND EXPRESSION

The underlying principle affecting the Doing Half is the difference between strategy and expression. Strategy is doing to create a feeling you *want* to have. Expression is doing to express a feeling you *already* have.

With strategy, you do something for the purpose of creating a result. You do this thing *so that* this other thing. You stroke here so that (hopefully) it creates a feeling in the person you are stroking.

With expression, an inner impulse arises and you let it out: the impulse to move, reach and explore, to laugh, cry or sing. There is no "so that" in this equation. Expression is *inherently* satisfying (assuming it is not harmful to another person). The satisfaction is in letting it out. No result is needed. Children are naturally good at this but adults rarely so.

Strategy is essential to an effective life. We need it for surgery, designing a bridge, or negotiating a peace accord. Your intention is on the goal, and you alter what you do in order to meet the goal. As Dr. Martin Luther King, Jr. said, "Keep your eyes on the prize." Sadly, strategy is a common approach to touch and sex. Nowhere is this more apparent than the magazine aisle: "Drive your man wild!" or "Give her six orgasms tonight!" Strategy brings your focus to the future with a kind of calculation: *What is going to work?*

In our culture, expression is suspicious, conjuring images of screaming women, shouting men, and hippies dancing in the park. Those are expressive, true, but enlarge the concept. Expression means that what's inside comes out. We stretch, dance, moan, or cry. We hold or caress. This is a basic need for all mammals including ourselves. Expression is risky, no question about it. We are exposed, especially with joyful, sensual, or erotic expression. It's suspect or the purview of only certain people like dancers or artists. It easily taps into the primal, which can feel intimidating. When was the last time you danced for joy in a public park?

Touch as a strategy. In a culture where expression is suspect (and often inaccessible) and touch and sex are conflated, it's extremely easy for all touch to become strategic. You touch so that you can get to sex; you do sex so that you can get to orgasm.

Your strategy will work or it won't. That's an interesting phrase: "It works." It means it produced the result you were hoping it would. If you hear yourself say "It worked" or "It didn't work," you'll know you are in strategy, and if it didn't work, you feel disappointed, frustrated, and cheated. After all, you did the thing, didn't you? Another way to tell if you are in strategy is asking yourself *Does it feel like work?* If it does, it probably is.

The problem is that we don't know how else to get there. We try some other stroke or buy another video with even newer ancient secrets. The more determined you are to get the result, the less play it is and the more work. This is a terrible loss of potential joy. However, it does sell a lot of videos.

It's natural to want some instruction on what to do. The problem is that nowhere do we get to learn how to express what is inside. Strategy and technique are easy to teach and to learn. There is a script to follow, and because it is less revealing of who we are and how we feel, it feels safer. All we have to do is get the right stroke.

Expression is *much* harder to learn. It is difficult because we may have been shamed as children for shouting, reaching, crying, or moving. It's difficult because we don't know how to trust ourselves, or we fear to show who we really are and what we really feel. Expression is not learned so much as recovered. What you do learn is the skills that allow you to access your self-expression and do so with respect, and that lets you trust yourself enough to cut loose.

Touch as a sexual strategy can feel safer and more predictable, but eventually it will get tense, boring, or both. It requires an outcome, but it cannot satisfy the heart. When self-expression is recovered, improvisation is a joy. It spreads to other areas of life, opening up a deep sense of creativity and play.

Why might we get stuck in strategy? It feels safer. We don't risk self-exposure, getting beyond our skill level, or doing the wrong thing, which we fear could cause us to lose connection. We resort to strategy because there is some feeling we want (self-worth, connection, power, entertainment, self-image), we want to avoid the shame and guilt that come with desire and expression, or we just don't know *how*. (We'll come back shortly and talk about how to recover it.)

THE CHALLENGES OF THE DOING HALF

The Doing Half may feel natural, or it may feel intimidating. You may be worried about getting it wrong or don't know how to access spontaneity. I've had more than one person freeze here and say, "I don't know what to do!" Or you may feel stuck. You may feel like it's what you are supposed to be doing or fits your self-image as the "giver." It may feel like the safer of the two options if the Done-to Half feels too vulnerable. Maybe you don't know how not to be here. Or you may feel stuck in the Serving Quadrant: *I'm the one doing all the work!* You may be unsure how to talk about it, how to find out what your partner wants or what they are okay with, or what the difference is. Maybe the conversation itself feels intimidating, so you avoid the whole thing.

WHAT WE WANT IN THE DOING HALF

- We want our doing to be genuine, real, and expressive of who we are and what we feel.
- We want our doing to be respectful and caring, so we are not using anyone.
- We want our doing to lead to connection.
- We want some confidence that what we are doing is welcome and enjoyable.
- We want to convey our affection and care and, when applicable, our love and desire.
- We want to enjoy the feel of their skin in our hands, their shape, texture, and warmth.
- We want to feel that what we do matters, that we can contribute to another person's joy and pleasure.
- Sometimes we want to exert the utmost care for our partner and be attentive to their desires.
- Sometimes we want to cut loose and play with wild abandon.
- We want to access different moods—tender, rowdy, playful, passionate, nurturing—instead of being stuck in only one mode.
- We want to be clear about who it's for.

THE SECRET TO EASE AND JOY IN THE DOING HALF

The secret to ease and joy in the Doing Half is learning the Taking Quadrant. Taking teaches you that you are welcome here even without technique. It opens the inflow, relaxes your hands, and improves the quality of your touch. Taking teaches you how to notice and follow your impulses and, at the same time, respect your partner's limits, which makes you trustworthy and opens confidence and the ability to play. Perhaps most important is that Taking teaches you the difference between Taking and Serving, which is the crux of the Doing Half. Until you can tell the difference, you can't do either of them.

WHAT YOU ARE RESPONSIBLE FOR

In the Doing Half, you are responsible for knowing whether you are intending to Serve or to Take and communicating that. Everything else follows from there. There is more responsibility in the Doing Half, because the person being done to will tend to follow your lead even if you don't think you are leading. As we said earlier, intention is not enough. You may feel like you're always giving. What matters is the agreement. Did you make a request? ("May I...?") You created the Take-Allow dynamic. Did you ask what your partner wanted? You created the Serve-Accept dynamic. Then your responsibility is to stay in the quadrant you agreed to. If you slide into the other one, your partner will be left high and dry with no one on the other end to play with.

DEVELOPING YOUR CAPACITY FOR SELF-EXPRESSION

There is nothing more human than the impulse to move—to reach, run, stretch, dance, shake, curl up, and climb. Our bodies express our desire, our joy, grief, curiosity, excitement, playfulness, and sexual turn-on, yet few things are more emotionally challenging.

236

Children are naturally good at this—it's one reason we find them so charming. As small children, expression is pretty much all we do, and it takes a certain amount of brain development to learn strategy. As adults, we learn to curtail our impulses and have to learn all over again how to move in ways that are not calculated. You might think that all you need to do is decide to do so. I have not found that to be true. We have a certain amount of repression; we don't know how to find the inner impulse and let it out. Saying "I don't know what to do!" is testament to this.

To relearn how to move, we need to learn that it is safe to do so. First, we need to feel confident that what we are doing is not unpleasant, annoying, or harmful. These are not touch skills; they are noticing and consent skills. (We talked about that in the Taking lab.) Second, we need inner permission. You may have one and lack the other, but you need both. Let's look at those.

1) Consent and noticing skills. To have confidence you won't harm anyone or that what you are doing is not unpleasant, you need consent skills, which includes the ability to notice your partner's state and how it changes moment by moment. It's also the same principle as Play (Lab 3). If you don't have a script, you have to rely on yourself, and to do that, you need to be able to notice at least as fast as you are doing. When your doing gets ahead of your noticing, you risk harming someone.

For example, your hand is gliding down your partner's side, over that nice curve in the hip there, and suddenly their muscles tense, and they hold their breath. Are you able to notice that? If you are determined to get the technique right, that's where your attention is, and you keep going, right over the moment. I have seen that happen where one person, trying to learn erotic massage, didn't notice that their receiver, who was lying face down, was holding their breath and hunched over in a protective stance. How could anyone *not* notice that? But they didn't.

2) Inner permission. Suppose you have enthusiastic consent, but when you start to reach, you freeze. This one is more difficult. We talked about how our impulse to express ourselves can be shamed out of us as children. It's not easy or natural for a child to stop moving. Not moving creates bodily and emotional tension and shame. When you start moving again, those feelings arise. It is well known in somatic psychotherapy that when you move your body in certain ways—expand your rib cage, extend your arms, or open your jaw, for example—you will access feeling states, memories, and insights that are not accessible though talking and thinking. This takes emotional courage and self-compassion. It is a lifelong process.

For many with restricted movement, when you increase the movement, feelings come up. Ken was in my studio to have some experiences with more freedom than he was experiencing at home. He was convinced that the problem was that his wife was repressed. At one point I had him stand up and move: a simple experience of breathing and shaking, then moving his pelvis back and forward (clothed). He stopped with a look of fear and shame. "This is hard!" he said. "This is like therapy! I guess it's not my wife after all."

My friend, a trained surrogate partner, said this about working with men who are intimidated by sexual activity: "Every one of these guys was unable to move their pelvis forward. In order to thrust, they have to move their whole body. They could not move their pelvis."

The opposite can also be true. Slow down, and feelings come up. My movement therapist friend describes this exercise: Sit or stand, and reach forward with your hand very slowly, so slow it's barely noticeable. What comes up is similar to feeling the object in Waking Up the Hands: self-doubt about wanting, about moving toward something. It can be seriously emotionally challenging. In teaching the lesson on Take-Allow, I remind people to slow their hands down, and they almost always speed up again. The slowing down lets the sensations come forward, Taking clicks, and then the feelings come up.

In the Taking Quadrant, as you learn consent skills and noticing skills and develop your inner permission, the ways you move and express yourself become less predictable and arise naturally out of the moment. Erotic play becomes a full-body event. It starts to look like this: stretching out, curling up, reaching, rolling, humping, biting, laughing, crying, looking, panting, arching, and climbing. Letting yourself show tenderness, lust, grief, joy, silliness, and gratitude. Letting the sounds out: sighs, moans, whispers, roars, sobs, giggles, and guffaws. These take a lot of inner permission. Start with the Taking Quadrant.

EXAMPLE: TOUCH ME WITH PRESENCE

James and Mandy were a couple who had been together a few years. The sex had been wonderful at first, but something wasn't clicking anymore. We spent a few sessions with Waking Up the Hands and then Take-Allow and Serve-Accept. They were experimenting at home. After several sessions, they asked to learn how to give each other a sensual massage.

I asked who wanted to receive first, and she did. She wanted to experiment with some new ways to touch, so we did that. Halfway through, she was on her back, and I noticed that he seemed to be carefully avoiding her breasts. His hands were everywhere but there. I asked him about it.

James: Yeah, I am avoiding them. I know that she is particular there, and I don't want to mess it up.

Mandy: I want him to touch me with presence.

Me (to James): Do you know what she means when she says "presence"?

James: Uh no, I never have.

(I ask her if it is okay to switch gears and do an experiment, and she says yes.)

Me: Remember when we were doing the other dynamic, the one where you feel her up instead of trying to give to her?

James: Yes.

Me: Ask her if it's okay if we do that for a while.

He does, and she agrees.

Me: Stop trying to give her the right stroke. Just move your hand slowly and feel her breast and all around it. Feel the shape, feel the softness, the skin, the warmth.

(He does so, slowing down. His hands are no longer tentative; they are relaxed and curious).

James: I can't believe I get to do this. It's what I've always wanted. I love her breasts, I just want to touch them.

Me (I wanted to confirm that we were in the Taking Quadrant): Do you notice that she is giving you this gift?

James: Yes, I do. (tears begin to form in his eyes)

James (to Mandy): Thank you.

Mandy: You're welcome.

(We stayed there, and he continued to explore. It was a tender moment. My eyes moistened too. I love my job!)

Mandy (after a few minutes): That's it! This is presence! This is what I was looking for and didn't know what it meant! It feels so wonderful! Thank you!

(After a while, we switched back to Serve-Accept. I reminded him that even though he was now doing what she was asking, he could bring the same kind of attention to sensation into his Serving).

Presence is one of those qualities that is impossible to describe but easy to feel in hands that are on your skin. You cannot manufacture it however hard you try. In fact, the more you try, the less you have it. Presence is a hand that is fully here in this moment, not "on a mission," not in the future, not on a strategy. It relaxes. It tends to drape and move slowly and gently because it's curious.

I empathized with both of them. On her end, hands that were tentative, worried, or determined were unpleasant, though most people have no idea what is missing or how to describe it. On his end, he knew something was missing but likewise had no idea how to find it. Lord knows he was doing his best, trying so hard to get it right. All he needed was a context for not performing but to attend to his sensation. Take-Allow was that context.

WHAT IS POSSIBLE IN THE DOING HALF

In Taking, it is possible to express how you feel, to roll, reach, play, laugh, and cry. It is possible to experience your partner in a direct way, to stop planning and strategizing and show up in the present moment. It is possible to bring your own desires forward and not feel stuck in give-give-give. In Serving, it is possible that when your partner asks for something or you are inspired to offer it, you are able to show up for them with all your attention and touch them in ways they love. It is possible to create spaciousness for them to feel safe enough to ask for what they want and experience whatever they do.

When the difference between Taking and Serving becomes clear, the Doing Half becomes rich, expressive, and deeply satisfying.

SUMMARY: THE DOING HALF

The Doing Half includes the Taking and Serving Quadrants.

Taking. Taking combines Doing and Receiving. It's for you. The gift you are receiving is the gift of access. You are doing what you want (within their limits).

Serving. Serving combines Doing and Giving. It's for the other person. The gift you are giving is your action. You are doing what they want (within your limits).

In Taking, the question you ask yourself is, *What is it that I want?* The question you ask your partner is, "May I...?"

In Serving, the question you ask your partner is, "What would you like?" The question you ask yourself is, *Is this something I can give with a full heart?*

We need both. Neither quadrant can meet the need for the other. You cannot meet your need for Taking by Serving more; you cannot meet your need for Serving by Taking more.

Your first responsibility is to know which one you are intending to be in and communicate accordingly.

Trustworthy. In Taking, you become trustworthy that you will not overstep the limits of the Allower. In Serving, you become trustworthy that you will not overstep your own limits.

Strategy and expression. Strategy means you do something to produce a feeling you want to have. Expression means you express a feeling you already have. Strategy is satisfying when it produces the desired result. Expression is inherently satisfying, so no result is needed.

In both quadrants, you care about their experience. You keep the inflow open and notice what is changing. In Serving, you add generosity. In Taking, you add your own desire.

The key to the Doing Half is learning Taking. Learning Taking is what opens the inflow, allows you to relax, and clarifies the difference between Serving and Taking.

If the Doing Half is particularly challenging. If you have no idea where to start or have no confidence, start with Taking. Taking is where you learn you are welcome here as you are, without technique, and that your curiosity is welcome too.

CHAPTER 17

The Done-To Half

All I want is to be in the arms of someone who believes in me.
—Michael Franti

He may be "vanilla" but he actually begged me not to have to give back during sex. "I know this sounds bad but I really don't want to. I just never get the chance to be the one who lies back. Please don't make me lead. It's why I come to you, because I know you will lead."
—Artemisia

The Done-to Half includes the Accepting and Allowing Quadrants. The difference between the two is the question *Who is this for?* In Accepting, it's for you. In Allowing, it's for the other person.

Your level of comfort with the Done-to Half depends on how well you know you have a choice about whether and how you are touched and have the skills to exercise that choice.

The Done-to Half offers some exquisite experiences, and there is a far wider range of options than most people have thought of. It can be nourishing, comforting, sensual, erotic, fun, and affirming, and it's challenging for lots of good reasons. You are right to both crave it and fear it, and wherever you are with it is fine.

ADAPTING OURSELVES TO WHAT IS HAPPENING

The underlying principle of the Done-to Half is our tendency to accommodate whatever is happening (or about to happen). We looked at this principle in depth in the Allowing lab. Because we have all been touched in ways we did not want and were powerless to prevent, before we could talk, to some degree this feels normal. We start to believe that whatever is happening is right, and our job is to change how we feel about it. When you understand this principle, everything else in the Done-to Half makes sense.

When your partner asks you how you would *like* to be touched, and you answer with how you *don't mind* being touched, this is what is happening. When you are being touched in some way you don't like but you think you are supposed to like so you try to like it, this is what is happening.

This assumption—that our job is to adapt ourselves to whatever is happening—creates a couple of myths. One is that there is something you are supposed to want or like, or at least be okay with, and its extension, that you are supposed to be okay with everything! If only you weren't such a bore. And if you're not enjoying it, something must be wrong with you, so fake it till you make it. This is terrible advice! It is advice to ignore yourself. I don't know anyone who needs more practice at that. There are some things you like and some you don't and some you are fine allowing and some you aren't. They change over time and depending on who you are with; they change in a few minutes or in a micro-moment. This is a good thing.

Another myth is that you should trust your "giver" (by which people usually mean your do-er) to do the right thing. That assumes you should, again, be okay with or appreciate whatever they are doing. The Accepting and Allowing Quadrants teach you to reverse this myth. Rather than changing yourself to suit the activity, your job is to change the activity to suit yourself, to notice what you want (Accepting Quadrant) or what you are genuinely okay with (Allowing Quadrant). That is a lifelong journey. I'm still on it.

THE CHALLENGES OF THE DONE-TO HALF

Some people are comfortable with Accepting but not Allowing, some with Allowing but not Accepting, and some people are uncomfortable with this entire half. There are lots of reasons for that, and they are perfectly natural. First, your body and your desires are exposed. Your pleasure may be visible in either quadrant. You are the focus of attention, so self-doubt and shame can come up. You no longer have the safety of hiding. Second, you may bump into your gender role, which tells you who is supposed to be doing what. It can profoundly shake up your self-image. *But I'm the Giver!*

Third, you may not like being "not in control." This is a fallacy. When in Accepting, even though you are not the one doing, you are the one choosing what happens. Still, the fear can be real and is common, especially in men, who have been taught it's their job to be in control at all times. Shaking that up can be confusing and frightening.

A variation of this is that you may worry that more is going to happen than you are comfortable with. It probably will. This happens in different ways. In Allowing, "more is going to happen" may mean more action than you are okay with. Maybe you have not yet learned what your limits are or how to speak them, or you worry they won't be respected. In Accepting, "more is going to happen" may mean you will experience more pleasure than you are accustomed to, and shame or unworthiness can come up. That can happen in Allowing too.

So the Done-to Half is often challenging. On the other hand, you might feel stuck here. You may be avoiding the Doing Half for the reasons discussed there: fear of hurting people, lack of confidence, or you haven't had much opportunity.

WHAT WE WANT IN THE DONE-TO HALF

- We want to be touched in ways that are meaningful and enjoyable to us.
- We want to have a choice about how we are touched.
- We want our limits to matter and our desires to matter.
- We want to know the difference between what we want and what we are okay with.
- We want sometimes to be touched in exactly the ways we want and at other times to surrender, be surprised, and not be in charge.
- We want to be wanted, desired, and enjoyed in ways that are real for our partners and respect our autonomy.
- We want both autonomy and connection. We want to not give up our choices in order to maintain connection and not have to give up connection in order to respect our choices.
- We want to relax and be more confident and more flexible.
- We want to expand our capacity for pleasure.

THE SECRET TO EASE AND JOY IN THE DONE-TO HALF

The secret to ease and joy in the Done-to Half is being certain, beyond a shadow of a doubt, that you have a choice about whether and how you are touched. Without knowing this, the Done-to Half is risky and potentially frightening. It's a direct correlation. The more confident you are in having a choice, the more enjoyable this half is. This confidence comes from gaining the skills to notice your limits and desires and to speak them. If you feel tense, guarded, or even a little reticent, this is where to look. To really sail in this half, learn the difference between the two quadrants. When that is crystal clear, the difference is spectacular!

EXAMPLE: FROM ALLOW TO ACCEPT

Some years ago, I had the good fortune to have a neighbor start massage school. A couple times a week, I walked next door and stretched out on her practice table. At first, it was about her learning, with some new body part each week. When she was learning shoulders, I would lend her mine. She would move it this way and that, feeling the tendons, figuring out how it worked. I, of course, was so very generous and patient. I was a single mom and glad for any friendly touch I could get, so I relaxed and enjoyed whatever she needed to do. Later, she was learning new techniques and asked for feedback. This was more give and take. In this way, she got very good at her craft, so that the following year, I went to her studio and paid her for massages. Now it was different still. Her attention was on my well-being, and so was mine. We started our touch relationship in Take-Allow, and later it changed to Serve-Accept. All of it was wonderful.

SUMMARY: THE DONE-TO HALF

The Done-to Half includes the Accepting and Allowing Quadrants.

Accepting: Accepting combines Done-to and Receiving. It's for you. The gift you are receiving is your partner's action. They are doing what you want (within their limits).

Allowing: Allowing combines Done-to and Giving. It's for the other person. The gift you are giving is access to yourself. They are doing what they want (within your limits).

In Accepting, the question to ask yourself is, *What do I want? What sounds wonderful right now?* The question you ask your partner is "Will you...?"

In Allowing, the question to ask yourself is, *Is this within the limits of what I am okay with? Is this something I can give with a full heart?*

We need both. Neither quadrant can meet the need for the other. You cannot meet your need for Accepting by Allowing more; you cannot meet your need for Allowing by Accepting more.

The key to enjoying anything in the Done-to Half is knowing you have a choice about whether and how you are touched, having the skill to exercise that choice, and knowing the difference between Accept and Allow.

Trustworthy. In Accepting, trustworthy means knowing that you will tend to and honor your desires and will not overstep the limits of your giver (Server). In Allowing, trustworthy means that you will not overstep your own limits.

Main principle. The main principle of the Done-to Half is Adapting Ourselves. We have all been touched against our will and tend to act as if the touch, or action, is more important than how we feel about it, so we try to change how we feel about it. You need to reverse that. Instead of trying to change yourself, you need to change the activity.

First responsibility. Self-care. There is a direct correlation: the more self-responsibility for your choices, the more enjoyment.

If the Done-to Half is particularly challenging. If it is intimidating, frightening, or suspicious, start with Accepting, so you learn how to be completely in charge of whether and how you are touched. As that becomes more natural to you, Allowing will also become easy.

DOING, DONE-TO, AND GENDER

Maybe you've heard, "It's the nature of men to take action and the nature of women to be acted upon!" Not true. This is the source of untold disappointment and lost wonderfulness. Still, it can help to notice that the training we get growing up as boys or girls has an effect on how we experience doing and done-to.

It's common for men to feel stuck in the Doing Half or feel like they are doing all the work. They tend to have the most fear about Taking and feel stuck in Serving. It's common for them to be afraid of the Done-to Half, thinking it implies vulnerability. On the other hand, men make up the vast majority of erotic massage clients. The quote at the top of this chapter is from a man who was visiting a sex worker and longed to not be in charge, which is quite common.

It's common for women to be taught our place is in the Done-to Half. A big factor for women is the tendency to go along with and settle for whatever crumbs we can pick up along the way. Men can experience this as well, but for women, it's endemic and tends to be invisible to us. Many women are accustomed to being touched but have no idea that it's possible to be touched the way they want. On the other hand, you may feel that as a woman, it's your prerogative to be done-to. Also not true.

I once had a woman say she wanted to awaken the divine feminine in herself and become more receptive. I asked what she meant, and she said she wanted to learn to surrender more, to try to not be in charge. Oh dear. My question was "Does that mean you want to get better at going along with whatever is done to you? Why do you call that feminine?" Of course there is a reason we call that feminine. It's because that is the societal role of women in our culture. This person needed to learn how to notice what she actually wanted. Then surrender becomes possible. (We talked about surrender in the Allowing lab.)

Every person, regardless of gender, needs opportunities to be in the Doing Half and in the Done-to Half, and every person can learn them.

CHAPTER 18

The Receiving Half

In folk tales the gift is often something
seemingly worthless—ashes or coals or leaves
or straw—but when the puzzled recipient
carries it to his doorstep, he finds it has
turned to gold. Such tales declare that the
motion of the gift from the world of
the donor to the doorsill of the recipient
is sufficient to transmute it
from dross to gold.
—Lewis Hyde

Receiving is vulnerable. It's not because there is something wrong with you. It is *inherently* vulnerable. I can leave you a wonderful gift on your front porch, but if you want to bring it in, you have to open the door, and as soon as the door is open, goblins and snowstorms can get in. Receiving is what happens when the gift on the porch is something you want, so you open the door. Now you are vulnerable because you risk being denied or ridiculed by others, feeling shame, embarrassment, or disappointment. You risk getting what you want and experiencing pleasure and gratitude. Sometimes you might prefer to keep the door closed. Fortunately, there are some things that make receiving easier. We'll come back to all this shortly, but first we're going to clarify what we are talking about. Much about the Receiving Half we have talked about elsewhere in parts. Here we put it together.

In Receiving, we are talking about this half:

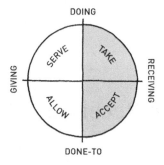

Not this half:

When receiving and done-to are de-conflated, the nature of receiving becomes clear. There are times when someone we care about needs or wants something, and we set aside what we prefer so that we can go with what they want. That is giving. There are other times when we need help or want something, and we hope the other person is willing to set aside what they prefer. We ask for that, and they agree. That is receiving.

At the heart of receiving is noticing what you want. Everything else flows from that. When you grasp that, you stop confusing your Want-to list with your Willing-to list. Indeed, sometimes the hardest part of the Receiving Half is the noticing what you want.

As well as being inherently vulnerable, receiving is also inherently wonderful. If it's not wonderful, it's not because you are not a "good receiver," it's because it's not the thing you want (or it is more of it than you want). If it is what you want, the enjoyment of it is automatic. The question to ask yourself is not, *Why don't I like this?* It's, *What is it that I actually want?* That is a very different question.

There is something healing and affirming about receiving, about having a turn to tend to your desires and learning to trust and value them. An experience of real receiving tells you *You matter. What you know about yourself matters, and what you desire matters.* We don't always get what we want, of course, but it matters.

Receiving is a fundamental human need, a need to experience having someone else set aside what they might prefer and put us first. We need to do this in a way that respects the other person's limits and boundaries. In other words, the need to receive is not a need to steal. It is a mature capacity to take in focused attention and care and to nourish ourselves with it and enjoy it.

Receiving and giving are distinct human needs; neither one can meet the need for the other. You can't meet your need to receive by giving more, no matter how much you enjoy giving, and in my work with people, it seems that most people tend to automatically try to give at the first opportunity. It's less vulnerable.

WHAT IT ISN'T

Receiving is not going along with something you think you are supposed to like or want. It's not making yourself appreciate whatever happens. It's not assuming that someone owes you something so you take it without their giving it. Gratitude happens with receiving, but gratitude is not the sign of receiving because gratitude can happen in any situation or dynamic. Same with pleasure. Pleasure can happen in any quadrant or no quadrant, so the experience of pleasure does not mean you are receiving.

WHAT IT IS

Two quadrants. The Receiving Half includes two quadrants: Accepting and Taking. In Accepting, you receive the gift of the other person's action. In Taking, you receive the gift of access to the other person's body or belongings.

Two things at once. In the Receiving Half, you are doing two things at once: 1) putting your own desires first, and 2) respecting the limits of your giver. Neither one alone is enough.

The agreement. The dynamic begins when you request and they agree. When you ask, "May I…" you create the Take-Allow dynamic (and you are in Taking). When you ask, "Will you…" you create the Serve-Accept dynamic (and you are in Accepting). Or they offer something and you say, "Yes, please!" The agreement is temporary, specific, and by choice. You open the porch door and bring the package in.

Two components. We talked about this in the lessons and labs. One component is the gift itself: the back rub or the truck they let you borrow. The other component is the dynamic: that they set aside what they preferred to go with what you want. Both of these are happening, and sometimes one is more meaningful, sometimes the other. The gift may be pleasant but not earthshaking, but knowing your partner is setting aside their desires in favor of yours may be profound. This is why the simplest gift can surprise us with its emotional potency. This is one of the meanings I hear in the quote above about "dross to gold."

Your responsibility. You might think that your responsibility in receiving is to be appreciative. It isn't (though that will also tend to happen). It is to be honest about what it is you want and to respect the limits of your giver.

WHY WE NEED IT

We need to receive affection and attention from others in ways that are useful and meaningful to us. We can meet it directly, or we can look around for crumbs in some way that doesn't fill us. Receiving (both quadrants) brings joy, satisfaction, and freedom and connects us with others. It brings us out of hiding. It contributes to our awareness of vulnerability, so we develop more compassion for ourselves and others. It elicits emotional tenderness and a sense of self-acceptance, often gratitude. It says we are valuable and our wants and needs matter. We experience nourishment, pleasure, healing, affirmation, insight, and growth. This is why we both crave it and fear it.

As we come back to this dynamic again and again, it does its magic and, like a sacred elixir, mends our hearts and sets us back on our feet. It allows us to clean up our giving so we can help each other. And the world needs people who are both nourished and available to give.

THE SECRET TO EASE AND JOY IN RECEIVING

Receiving is inherently enjoyable, satisfying, and affirming. If it is not those things, it is not because you need a better attitude. It's because it's not the thing you want. When it is what you want, enjoying it is automatic, so finding the ease and joy starts with taking the time to notice what you want. In order to receive, you also have to set your heart at ease, knowing you are not taking advantage of your Giver, which requires consent skills.

WHY RECEIVING BRINGS UP SO MANY FEELINGS

Everything we liked or wanted or felt joy in had to be hidden or suppressed. I'm sad to say that this method works. If you don't give as much credence or value to whatever it is that you love, it hurts less when it is inevitably taken from you.
—Alan Cumming

Receiving is vulnerable. Our desire, pleasure, tenderness, gratitude, and shame are exposed. Receiving brings us face to face with the fact that we need each other. As difficult as that can be to acknowledge, it is also what heals us.

We all have a comfort limit, or ceiling on receiving. First, for what *kind* of gifts we can receive. Some will be easier than others. We may be comfortable getting help when we're sick but not with asking for pleasure, or the opposite. It may be easy to ask for sexual pleasure but not for comfort, or the opposite. Taking may be easier than Accepting or vice versa. Sometimes both of them are difficult. Second, we have a comfort limit to how *large* a gift we can receive. It may be a teaspoon, a cupful, a bucket, or an ocean, but when the gift is big enough or the right kind, we hit our self-doubt. The question is not whether you will become uncomfortable with receiving a gift but what kind and how large of a gift it takes before you hit your ceiling. What does it take for you to notice it's for you?

In addition, receiving can be suspect. You don't trust their yes or fear it will be used against you, or you fear there's something they want back that they're not saying. Sometimes those things are true. We have all been used, confused, and hurt, and we carry a host of fears because of that.

But mainly receiving is hard because feelings arise when we notice that someone cares about us, and feelings arise with enjoyment. It is important to note that it's not the receiving that's hard but the feelings that are hard: the shame, fear, and self-doubt. Let's talk about those feelings. Why are they so universal and so deep?

Needing help. We start our lives completely dependent and helpless. That you are reading this attests to the fact that someone fed you. Along with the help itself you got a message about what needing help means about you. For example, you may have learned that it's natural to want and we take turns helping each other, or you may have learned that it's dangerous to reveal your needs or to express any wants at all. Maybe you learned that it's shameful to want something and it implies lack of power. That people who need anything are sissies or deserving of pity. That you get loved and appreciated only when you don't have any wants. That the only way to get it is to be nice and quiet, or the only way to get it is to be demanding and loud, or that there's not enough to go around so it doesn't matter anyway. That you're going to pay for it later, that it's subject to someone else's whim, or that as soon as you want something, it automatically means someone else is going to suffer. Now you're an adult, and as soon as you want something, these beliefs come up, and you feel shameful, weak, unworthy, or all the rest. You create a self-image about who you are in relation to receiving help. If you hear yourself say, "But I'm a giver!" this is part of the reason why.

Fear of selfishness. A variation on this theme is the fear of selfishness. When teaching people the Taking Quadrant, to help them stop trying to give and get them to attend to their pleasure, I would sometimes say, "Be selfish." It often worked. "Oh, I get it!" For others, the meaning of "selfish" was so abhorrent they couldn't imagine why I would say it. I came to see that word had two meanings. In my mind, it was the ability to put yourself first when appropriate. The other meaning (and the one in the dictionary) means without regard or consideration for the other person. The first meaning applies here, not the second. Perhaps a better word would be "self-focused." Regardless, I came to see that for some people, the fear of feeling selfish or being thought of as selfish was nearly paralyzing.

There can be numerous factors here. One person said that in his youth, he was selfish in using women and disregarding their experiences, and that eventually felt so awful that he couldn't stomach it now. Or there can be shame about wanting or needing, for the reasons above, especially about believing that wanting anything automatically harms others.

I saw this mostly in people trying to learn Taking. The fear was not that they would harm someone (their Allower) but that the very fact of wanting was shameful. They were afraid and ashamed to put themselves first. Over the years, I came to see another angle. The determination to stay out of either Receiving Quadrant and keep your partner there means putting them in the more vulnerable place so that you can avoid it. This is a kind of selfishness much more subtle and cowardly.

The principle of contradiction. A principle used in counseling works like this. When we have distressing experiences, we carry them in our psyche, and one thing that will shake them up (in a useful way) is noticing they are no longer true. A contradiction is a completely different experience that helps us notice that the distressing event is no longer present. Here is the key: because it is now safe, the old doubts and feelings that have been waiting under the surface sometimes arise, and they arise in a way that is not distressing but is a relief. A contradiction, because it's good, brings up old feelings in a gentle way.

When we have been touched against our will, the experience of having a choice about it will contradict that. When we have lacked the touch we needed, being touched with care will contradict that. When we have had our desires shamed or ridiculed, having them respected and welcomed will contradict that. When we have been pushed into something, having the time to notice what we want will contradict that. When we have had the experience that our wants don't matter, having room to notice that they do will contradict that.

In the labs, the degree of spaciousness, respect, and care, and the opportunity to notice and choose what you desire, is bound to contradict something, and you will have feelings arise. If you are able to accept the feelings, you'll notice that it is a relief to acknowledge them. *Oh, finally!* There may be tears that you have been holding back for decades, and the insights will follow. What allows the old feelings to arise in a useful way is nonjudgmental attention to whatever contradicts the old beliefs and keeping enough attention on the present that you don't get swamped in the past—and a generous amount of acceptance and compassion.

So, three big factors that bring up the feelings: 1) the belief from childhood that wanting something means you are shameful or hopeless, 2) the fear of feeling selfish, and 3) the principle of contradiction. To the degree that you don't know what to do with the feelings as they arise, you have to avoid the whole thing.

Wait, there's more. The pleasure.

The pleasure. One kind of vulnerability is the risk of having your desires met. You risk feeling satisfied, loved, supported, comforted, turned on, affirmed, and blissed out, all of which are going to contradict something. Then there is the experience of pleasure: that it's okay to feel, that it's a good thing to do, that you are worthy of it, and that you get to have it. The experience of pleasure will bring you to your self-doubt. There is some way we instinctively know this, which may be why we avoid it even when alone.

The combination of experiencing pleasure and receiving a gift is particularly potent. Either one can tenderize us; both of them together can crack our hearts right open. Again, it's not pleasure or receiving that we avoid but the feelings we know will arise when we do.

That's about *experiencing* pleasure, and then there is *expressing* pleasure. You have exposed yourself in another way, which may feel even scarier. You are vulnerable to the other person's judgments about your pleasure, although they are less likely to make them about you than you are. How much pleasure you allow someone else to see you in may be considerably less than you are comfortable experiencing alone. At other times, support from our partners gives us the added courage to access more emotional vulnerability than we might alone. To be witnessed, supported, and affirmed in our desire and pleasure is profoundly healing.

Gratitude. In case that is not enough, there is the gratitude. Maybe it's for the gift itself or for the fact that your partner cares. Maybe it's for the minuscule chance that you were born as you in a body that is capable of these sensations. Maybe it's for God or the Universe or Aphrodite. Whatever it is for, the trouble with gratitude is that when there is enough of it, you will cry. That is the nature of it, the operative word being *enough*.

It is possible to feel gratitude when you are not in the Receiving Half. I hope you do often. You can feel gratitude for the opportunity to give, for sunshine, for adversity, for changes in your community. A common confusion about gratitude is that if you feel grateful, it means you are receiving. Not true. It is possible to feel gratitude in any quadrant or no quadrant. What constitutes Receiving is that you are putting your desires first, have made an agreement, and are respecting the limits of your giver. Gratitude is one of the signs but is not the indicator that you are receiving.

When receiving, there will tend to be tenderheartedness and sometimes tears of relief and gratitude. If you want to avoid that, stay out of the Receiving Half. Now we are back where we started. Perhaps the most fundamental thing of all is that in receiving a gift, we have to come to terms with the fact that we humans need each other, and because of that, we are vulnerable.

What to do with the feelings. In the Accepting lab, we talked about following the pleasure, and that applies here. Sometimes the opportunity to feel what you feel is a relief. At other times, it may be more than you have the resources for at the moment. It helps to know that you get to choose how much discomfort you want to feel today and go only that far.

It may be that today you want something familiar and not too challenging, or today you want to slow down, make eye contact, and really notice the gift. Maybe you want to ask for something that feels big for you and, when feelings arise, keep going, or you want to be comforted. When the feelings arise, you'll decide then what sounds wonderful next, *because it's for you.*

On the one hand, it's hard to find real receiving because we think there is something we are *supposed to* want, and we try to do that instead of what we *actually* want. Then somehow we learn to notice what we want and then have to feel the self-doubt, shame, or fear of what it might mean about who we are. Then we have to choose how much to risk by revealing what we want. If, by some miracle, our request is granted and we enjoy ourselves, we have more feelings that arise by being in pleasure and being seen in pleasure. And then some other feeling arises from nowhere that is confusing and stops us in our tracks. It's a wonder any of us ask for anything beyond "Please pass the butter."

- What will bring so much relief and gratitude that it brings me to tears?
- What do I do to avoid the possibility of feeling that?
- What do I think I am supposed to want? Where did I get that idea?
- What sounds wonderful right now?

HOW TO LEARN

It is possible to have all manner of fabulous, exotic, and sexy things done to your body and get nothing out of it. It doesn't reach you somehow. It is also possible to receive one small caress and have it pierce your heart with joy. What is the difference?

The richness of it depends on your attention. It's like sitting at a luscious banquet. What matters is not how fancy the food is or how much there is. If you know how to be attentive, the simplest bowl of broth is exquisite. The limiting factor is not the food but your ability to notice that it is here and take that into your heart.

In a session with me, Penn thought they should learn to receive, but it doesn't work that way. Only when they turned it around to wanting could we start.

Penn: I should learn to receive.

Me: Really? Why?

Penn: Isn't that what you are telling me?

Me: No. I don't care. I don't live with you. Do *you* want to?

Penn: I'm not sure.

Me: Okay. What would be helpful right now? What would you like me to ask you?

Penn: Ask me why.

Me: You mean, why you want to learn how to receive?

Penn: Yes.

Me: Why do you want to learn how to receive?

Penn (their eyes become moist): Because I'm exhausted.

Me: Yeah, there's a limit to how long you can give-give-give.

Penn: I do want to learn. I just don't know *how*.

Me: Would you like some help with that?

Penn: Yes.

Me: Okay, look me in the eyes and say, "Will you help me learn how to receive?"

Penn (it takes a while for them to gather the courage, and they do so with tears in their eyes): Will you help me learn to receive?

Me: Yes, I will. (I hold eye contact so they notice and can't ignore what is happening.) You have already started by asking for what you want. I'm going to stay right here with you while you feel whatever you feel, as long as you want. The first step is noticing what you want right now, like some touch, some listening, or something you want me to do like bring a glass of water. It doesn't matter how long it takes. We're going to wait for it. It's in there.

So if it calls to you, here is what it takes:

1) You have to take receiving and giving apart. You cannot learn to receive by combining them. In giving, you set aside what you prefer, and in receiving, you bring it forward. You can't set your desires aside and bring them forward at the same time. Taking them apart means doing only one of them at a time. If you want to experience receiving, you have to stop giving (temporarily).

2) You have to de-conflate receiving and being done to. Because done-to so often means tolerate and go along with, if you conflate them,

THE ART OF RECEIVING AND GIVING

receiving comes to mean the same kind of tolerating. You try to change your attitude so you can tolerate better. When receiving includes doing (as it does in the Taking Quadrant), it becomes clear what it actually is: putting your desires first while respecting the limits of your giver.

3) You need a physical experience of it. Until that point, it remains a theory. Touch is not the only way to feel this but is a profound way, because the sense of touch is wired into our self-concept and our emotions. The physical experience makes it real, so you know beyond a shadow of a doubt it exists.

4) It requires another person. It is possible to receive the gifts of nature or the universe/god/goddess, and I hope you do. Animals are great, too, as they don't judge us. But yeah, humans.

5) You must make a request. You cannot learn to receive by having someone choose for you, no matter how tuned in they are or how good it feels. This is especially true in Accepting, but it also holds in Taking. As soon as someone else chooses, you are in the position of going along. It doesn't matter how small the request, usually the smaller the better, but it must be what you want, not what someone else wants to "give" you or thinks would be good for you. The request will be, "Will you…?" or "May I…?"

6) You need to set your heart at ease that you will not take advantage of someone. This is to say that you need consent skills. You need the skill to request clearly so they know what they are agreeing to, you need to notice their yes and, if you feel the need, ask again to be sure and let that yes sink into your heart. You have to get it that it's for you; then you need to respect their limits. This is often the key that makes receiving accessible.

7) You need to never push yourself. This is another manifestation of the tendency to adapt to what is happening (or you think is supposed to happen). If you push yourself to go for something too big or intense, it overwhelms your capacity to take it in, so you adapt yourself and endure. Start with something that you already know how to receive, that brings a sigh of relief. You are either receiving something you want or adapting to what is happening; you cannot do both at once.

8) You need compassion for yourself. There are reasons why it's challenging; you didn't make the whole thing up. Feelings are going to arise, so have compassion for yourself. There is nothing broken, so there is nothing to fix.

9) The structure helps. In real life, we often accept gifts we didn't ask for and gladly so. It would be a sad world if we never surprised each other. Also in life, we adapt to things that happen; it's part of growing up. In the practice of the labs, this is different. Until you request something, *nothing happens*, and it's not going to lead to anything else. This practice sets you up in a somatic experience in which you are able to experience receiving, because we are interrupting all the habits that get in the way.

NOTES ON ASKING FOR WHAT YOU WANT

Desire Smuggling: Hiding what you really want from yourself and/ or a loved one, then finding covert strategies to get (at least pieces of) what you want.

—Marcia Baczynski

Manipulation never works to get the result desired, but it always seems like it's just about to work. When you get what you said you wanted by manipulation, it is never enough. When you tell the truth and get what you want, getting what you want is like gravy—it feels like you are getting more than you ever hoped for, rather than just okay but not quite good enough.

—Brad Blanton

Asking for what we want is easy and natural; it's the only thing we know how to do at birth. It's hard because along the way we had bad experiences with it, so we stopped. We had to make up some convoluted way to get what we needed: hint, manipulate, steal, or pretend to offer. When you recover asking, it's a huge relief for you and everyone around you.

In our regular life, there is a range in whether and how we ask. That's natural. This book describes a practice in which we get very specific and direct. I learned early on that when I brought people back to the simplest, most direct forms of asking ("Will you…?" and "May I…?"), it helped people notice that they were in fact asking for something, and that brought vulnerability and tenderheartedness. I began to see that we were oiling the gears at the center of the mechanism and that once those gears were moving, you can add all the flourishes you like. First you have to oil those central gears by starting with the simplest, most direct questions. That is what we are doing in this practice and why it is so challenging and so liberating.

Part of the process is getting emotionally comfortable with the fact of wanting. Wanting can be a tender place. It is easy to filter things out before we even notice them. What we can want is limited by what we believe is possible and acceptable. *Does it even exist? Will this fit my idea of who I am?* This is not particularly conscious, though sometimes it is. Asking for what we want makes us face our desires and acknowledge them.

We said in the lessons that the words make a difference. They reveal what you are thinking and set you up for what you can think and therefore experience. The language of putting your wants first is: "Will you..?" and "May I...?" and "Yes, please!" The language of putting your wants aside and following someone else's desire is: "Okay, sure, I guess so, you can, maybe, fine," Which essentially mean "I don't mind terribly much."

We often don't notice what we say. In a workshop, Kay was asking for what she wanted—or thought she was.

Kay: Maybe you could rub my neck.
Me: It's true, maybe he could, but what is it you would like?
Kay: Oh, yeah. I guess I would like that.
Me: You guess you would, or you would?
Kay: Uhhh, yes, I would like that.
Me: Okay, go ahead and ask like this: Will you rub my neck?
Kay: Okay. Wow, that's hard! I can hardly say it. Will you rub my neck?
Her partner: Yes, I will.
Kay (a minute later): Maybe go down to my shoulders too? (another couple minutes) And maybe a little harder there?
Me: Maybe?
Kay: Did I say maybe again?
Me: Yes.
Kay: I didn't even hear it. God, I can't believe this is so hard! Would you go harder on my shoulder there?

WHAT WE WANT IN THE RECEIVING HALF

- We want to know that what we want matters, though we don't need to always have it.
- We want to know that others care about us enough to set aside what they might prefer.
- We want to not take advantage of others.
- We want to be honest about what we need and want.
- Sometimes we want others to do things, and sometimes we want to be the ones doing.
- We want to know our givers are honest with us about what they are willing to do.
- We want to trust that our giver is not using us to avoid their own receiving.
- We want to be respected. Just because we want something or need help does not make us worthless or shameful.
- We want to distinguish between what we want and what we have been told we should want.
- Sometimes we want others to make a sacrifice for us, and sometimes we want them to give to us only if it's easy for them.
- Sometimes we want to be surprised, and sometimes we want to give directions and have them followed exactly.
- We want to change our minds any time.
- We want to express our appreciation in whatever way fits for us.

THE SHADOW OF THE RECEIVING HALF

Entitlement. The shadow differs a little by whether it's the Taking or Accepting Quadrant, but the underlying dynamic is entitlement. You act as if it already belongs to you, something you have access to, control over, or expect some benefit from. Usually we don't notice the benefit until it is taken away or not given. We don't notice that someone else is giving up something for our benefit and not necessarily voluntarily. There is no gratitude; it doesn't touch our hearts.

If you don't get what you want, it's natural to be disappointed. If you are incensed or indignant, it's probably because you thought you are owed it. Many men feel incensed if a woman declines to interact with them, switching from compliments to name calling or even death threats. White people assume they can reach over and feel the hair of Black people. Cisgender people ask about the genitals of transgender people. Why on earth would we think we have those rights? That's entitlement.

Privilege. A cousin of entitlement is privilege, which is an unearned advantage, usually by virtue of race, age, class, gender, etc. The first privilege of privilege is that you don't have to notice that you have it, because unlike those who don't have it, your life does not depend on understanding it. It feels like the natural state of affairs, so you don't notice it. Wiser people than I have developed this theme. See the online resources.

Exploitation. Another shadow of the Receiving Half is exploitation: taking advantage of someone who cannot say stop. Or they said it but we walk right over it—because we can. As a nation, we're good at this. Our nation was built on stolen land, labor, and lives. Now we use covert manipulation for access to oil and cheap labor. More on this later.

What keeps us in the shadow is not being able to be in the quadrant itself (in this case, the Taking and Accepting Quadrants), and we can't be in the quadrant itself because we have not learned to ask and create the agreement. Until you learn how to access the quadrant, you will be in the shadow of it. You will use it without consent and without realizing it.

WHEN RECEIVING IS HARD

When the Receiving side is hard, we avoid it. Some of the time-honored ways to do this are never asking for what we want, settling for whatever crumbs fall our way, staying on the Giving side, or diluting it by trying to receive and give at the same time. Or we may turn it around: "I receive by giving!"

In the Wheel, you slip from Taking into Serving and slip from Accepting into Allowing or tolerating. In bed, you become lonely, starved, bored (and boring), and resentful. You wonder why you are not inspired but have no idea what the missing piece is. Often both people will assume they are giving or may battle for the Serving role. In life, it's pretty much the same: lonely, resentful, always giving.

When receiving is hard for us, we blame others for not reading our minds, think someone different will read our minds better, or give up altogether. We blame others for wanting something, or we resent their clarity. If we confuse receiving with the selfish disregard of others or with weakness, we see it as a pathetic state that no one would allow themselves to be in if they had any other choice.

When receiving is hard, we may try to use giving as a way to get things like appreciation, acceptance, self-worth, recognition, access, or sex. This is not giving at all—it's manipulating. It's using your "receiver" as a means to make yourself feel better. We can also use giving to connect. It's the only way we know *how* to connect. At least we're in the same room where receiving is happening.

Eventually we starve. When we are starving, we do all kinds of crazy things—repetitive, nonproductive behaviors that look right but don't satisfy. Instead our behavior keeps us farther away and becomes compulsive (much of people's sexual experience is this). We can become demanding, pushy, or even violent. This is not actually receiving. It's a result of being really hungry.

Someone unable to receive is just as hard to live with as someone unable to give, but it's more confusing. It seems like we should appreciate their generosity, but the engagement can only go so deep. It's as if they are walking around with their arm held up in a STOP gesture. Ultimately, without taking responsibility for our desires, the only option is to manipulate, and the guaranteed outcome is resentment.

Stuck in receiving. Being stuck in the Receiving Half is theoretical; I've never known anyone there. It may look like being demanding, but when that is the case, it's because they have not learned to take a gift into their hearts, so they are hungry. We keep repeating ourselves until we feel heard. We keep stuffing ourselves until we feel nourished. We keep demanding attention until we feel accepted and affirmed.

WHEN RECEIVING IS EASY

You might worry that if you get too good at receiving, you'll become selfish. What actually happens is that you become respectful of others' limits. You get good at asking what those limits are and are gracious in abiding by them. You get good at drinking in the gifts you are given, taking them into your heart.

In the Wheel, you drop into your experience, enjoy it, and let it take you where it does. You equally enjoy your Giving and Receiving roles. In bed, you are nourished and self-expressed, you respect others' limits, and you value clarity and consent. Your requests are clear but not pushy. You trust other people's giving and have compassion for yourself and others. Your giving becomes clear, clean, and generous. You flow easily from receiving to giving and back again.

In life, you appreciate others' flexibility and find that people are, for the most part, generous. Your heart is nourished. You accept the gifts you receive with confidence, gratitude, and a certain humility. You feel appreciated and connected, and on occasions when you do feel lonely, you ask yourself, *What do I want to receive that am I not asking for?* You then ask for it. You take the experience into less tangible realms, receiving the gift of sunshine, of beauty, of life.

THE SPIRITUAL PATH OF RECEIVING

Wear gratitude like a cloak and it will feed every corner of your life.
—*Rumi*

Receiving cracks open the heart, which is to say it engages the emotional system in ways that evoke compassion for yourself and others and contributes to your awareness of your vulnerability. This heals self-doubt, connects us to each other, opens new perspectives, and nourishes the hungry soul. It teaches us that we need each other. This may be the hardest part. It's not great for keeping us insulated from our vulnerability, but it is great for cracking our hearts open.

Physical experience takes you where theory and belief cannot. Feeling accepted and affirmed remains theory until you experience it in the body. Feeling abandoned on the shore of existence? A deep state of pleasure with a thankful heart will cure that immediately.

Integrity. Receiving builds integrity. When you learn to acknowledge that there is something you want, you stop using "giving" to hide it. You stop using Allowing to make it okay to get any touch at all, and you stop using Serving as an excuse to get your hands on someone. It has not been easy, but I have come to believe that *if there is something you want that involves another person, the only thing that has integrity is to ask for it.*

Worthiness. It is easy to receive a paycheck. You earned it, therefore you deserve it, so earned = deserving = okay to receive. But there is a glitch in this formula. If we believe that the only way to deserve it is to earn it, then we believe our nature, in and of itself, is not enough. That is a spiritual question. It is your nature as a human being to deserve love. You may not have received all the love you deserve or experienced the optimal expression of the love that others have felt for you, but it's not because you did not deserve it. It's because none of us have perfected the art of loving. If you want to learn to trust in the worthiness of your existence, learn to receive from a person, in a tangible way, with your body.

Vulnerability. There is nothing enlightened about not being able to receive. Learning to receive brings you face to face with your vulnerability and much more, and that is a spiritual path if ever there was one.

SOCIAL IMPLICATIONS

The Accepting and Taking Quadrants differ, but the implications of receiving in the world are countless. We receive in ways we are aware of and ways we are not, which creates entitlement and privilege.

I have had some extraordinary experiences of receiving gifts I neither deserved nor earned, and as a result, I have seen my compassion grow. I know how it changes us, and I hope that for you. There is another reason: when we learn to receive, we become respectful of other people's limits. We take more responsibility for the fact that there are things we want. We stop stealing other people's time and resources, the minerals in their land, and crops they have relied on for centuries. Humility, compassion, integrity, because that is the kind of world I want to live in.

SUMMARY: THE RECEIVING HALF

De-conflate. To experience receiving, de-conflate it from done-to. You are in the Receiving Half when you want something for its own sake, not because it makes the other person happy. You have requested it, and the giver says "Yes."

The Receiving Half includes two quadrants:

- **Accept:** Accepting combines Done-to and Receiving; the gift you receive is your partner's action.
- **Take:** Taking combines Doing and Receiving; the gift you receive is access to your partner's body.

The agreement creates the dynamic. "Will you..." creates Serve-Accept. "May I..." creates Take-Allow. You are in your Want-to list.

Receiving and giving are different needs. You cannot meet your need to receive by giving more. Receiving can be experienced only when you stop giving (for that agreed-on period of time).

The crux of the Receiving Half. The crux is getting clear on the difference between Want-to and Willing-to. Everything else grows from that.

You must request. You cannot learn receiving by having someone else choose for you.

Receiving is inherently enjoyable. If it's not enjoyable, it's not because there is something wrong with you. It's because it's not what you actually want.

Receiving is inherently vulnerable. You get to choose how vulnerable you want to be at any given moment and whether to back up or slow down when you want to.

You are doing two things at once. 1) Putting your desires first, and 2) respecting the limits of your giver. Neither one alone is enough.

Your responsibility. Your responsibility is not to appreciate anything that happens but to be honest about what you want.

Getting good at receiving. You might think this means you reach out and take more than what is given. What actually happens is that you get good at respecting limits.

Shadow. Entitlement is acting as if you already own or deserve something. We usually don't notice this until we don't get what we want.

Myths about receiving. 1) There is something you are supposed to want or like. 2) If it's not wonderful, you should surrender and let it in more. 3) Your job is to receive anything anyone wants to give you. 4) If you give enough, you won't need to receive.

CHAPTER 19

The Giving Half

"Which," said Ilka, continuing to address the child,
"is another mystery. Good people don't think they are being good
when they like doing the good thing. If they did it with gritted teeth
then they would think that it is good. Isn't that funny of them?"
—Lore Segal

Giving is just as real a need in our lives as is receiving. We need to know we can be of use to others and are able to contribute to their happiness in ways that are meaningful to them. That makes it meaningful to us. Giving is rich, satisfying, and brings meaning and depth to our relationships. When you give, you set aside your preference in order to go with what the other person wants, and you do so temporarily and within limits that are okay with you. Like the previous chapter, much of what we talk about here we've talked about elsewhere in parts. Here we put it together.

We're talking about this half.

The important thing to know about giving is that you can't give something you don't own. You have the right to say no and the skill to say no. You have a limit to what you are willing and able to give, and that is a good thing. Only to the degree you take responsibility for those limits can you give a gift, and as you do take responsibility for your limits, you relax and become generous within those limits. Your giving becomes a real joy. If your giving is not a joy, it's a signal that there is some limit that you are ignoring, haven't noticed, or don't have the skill to speak. There is a direct correlation between the responsibility you take for your limits and the ease and joy you feel in your experience of giving.

WHAT IT'S NOT

Giving is not the failure to have a boundary. It is not acquiescing, placating, or tolerating. It is not going along with something because you don't know how not to. It is not a begrudging assumption that there is no other choice. It is not "getting a better attitude" about something that is happening. Are there times in life when we do need to placate or tolerate? Apparently so, but I don't consider those giving. Giving is wonderful and empowering—unless you can't do anything else. Give from your heart, not your compulsion.

Giving is not all or nothing. You get to choose how much you give. It's not doing something so that you get a response you want to see or a feeling you want someone else to have. That is not giving; it's strategy. Giving is not an investment in a future result (even if the future is thirty seconds from now). It is not the only way to connect, a way to impress the other person so they like you, a way to make them feel indebted to you, a way to make yourself feel worthwhile, or a way to avoid the vulnerability of receiving. Giving is not always pleasurable for you, but it is naturally satisfying.

WHAT IT IS

Two quadrants. Giving includes two quadrants: Serve and Allow. In Serving, you give your action. In Allowing, you give access to yourself, your attention, or your possessions.

Two things at once. Giving requires doing two things at once: 1) setting aside what we prefer in favor of what our partner wants, and 2) keeping responsibility for our limits. Neither one alone is enough.

Setting aside what you prefer. Setting aside what you prefer can be easy to see in the practice. In Serving, you'd like to run your hands along their back, but they want your hands on their legs, so you go with the legs. In Allowing, you'd rather have a good scalp massage, but they want to play with your hair. You set aside the scalp massage for now and go with the hair. But you have other preferences you may not notice: what you want to "give" or how you hope they respond. We don't usually notice we have these preferences until they are not met. If you find yourself disappointed or working hard, it's probably this.

Your Willing-to list. In Giving, you move from your Want-to list to your Willing-to list, which could be said to be the real gift. This creates a small glitch. When you set aside your preferences for some other reason (you don't know how not to or don't value your own wants), it *feels* like giving, but it's not.

The flow of directionality. When you have an agreement, you create a directional flow. In chapter 15, I used the metaphor of an irrigation pipe. I said that when there is something one person wants and the other person agrees to give, there is a directional flow from the giver to the receiver. People often say, "I feel good, so I'm receiving," but it is the flow *itself* that feels good. You are standing in it. Your job as the giver is to tend the directionality so that it is as clear and clean as you can make it. The clearer it is, the more flow and the more of a gift can be delivered, and the more satisfying it is for both of you.

The challenges of giving. The challenges of giving vary by whether you are Serving or Allowing. What they have in common is how hard it can be to respect our own limits. When we struggle with our own limits, we tend to feel worried or afraid to give anything at all. Another challenge is the tendency to feel that what they want or how they respond says something about us. In reality, the receiver's experience belongs to them.

LIMITS AND GENEROSITY

We talked about this in the Allowing and Serving Labs. The common misconception about generosity is that being generous means you are willing to give pretty much anything and that you somehow *should* be able to give almost anything. Neither of those are true. The secret to feeling generous is to take full responsibility for your limits, then within those limits, you relax and become generous. It's fairly automatic.

Limits mean what you are willing or not willing to do in any given interaction. They change, and this is a good thing. There are some things you will not do with anyone due to ethical, health, or safety reasons and many other things you do with people depending on who they are, what your relationship is, what sparks your fancy at the moment, or how tired you are. Having a limit says, *I am not available for this.* Having a limit is the difference between your Willing-to list and your Not-Willing-to list. Sometimes the limit is a "No." Sometimes it's "Not that but something different" or "Yes, up to here" or "Yes, for about ten minutes" or "Yes, next Friday." So it's limits first, then comes the generosity.

Taking responsibility for your limits means that you finally and blessedly admit that no one but you can know what they are. Sometimes even you don't know what they are. It means you don't expect others to guess correctly, and you stop blaming them for not being able to do that. There are situations in which it may be easy to speak a limit and other situations in which it's harder. This is natural. The practice gradually enlarges the situations in which you can easily notice and communicate your limits. It teaches you how to do that, and you can then take that skill into the rest of your life.

A thought experiment. Imagine you are going to walk into a room of people, and you are not allowed to say no to anyone there. They can ask you to do things and can do things to you, but you can't say no. Would you enter the room? Of course not. You can't afford the risk of having anyone ask you for anything. Suppose you did enter—what are the options now? Constant tension and worry. You could try to suss out who is "safe." You could hide in the corner and hope no one sees you. You could walk in with a bluster and roar, hoping everyone will be sufficiently intimated to not ask for anything. You could acquiesce to every request, hoping everyone will like you for it. You could look pitiful and hope that someone will rescue you or take you under their wing. You could do what is asked but with such a bad attitude that they regret it and don't ask for more. You could get buffeted around and feel hopeless. You could even criticize yourself for not being okay with all of it. Any of those sound familiar?

(On the other side, imagine you are in the room and in come the people who aren't allowed to say no. Now you have to figure out what they are okay with before you ask them. You could ask for nothing at all for fear of making a mistake. You could be hypervigilant for signs of discomfort. You could make a mistake and feel awful about it. Or you could take advantage of the situation and do whatever you want.)

This is why the ability to say no is required for intimacy. Without the ability to say no, you can't afford to be in the same room with anyone. When you can say no, your yes can be trusted.

In the Allowing Lab, I described playing with this in workshops by drawing a big circle on the floor. Put everything inside the circle that you are happy to give and outside of it the things you are not willing to give. Your job is not to try to move everything into the circle. Of course there are things outside the circle. There have to be. Your job is to notice that there is a circle, what's inside it, and what's outside it and to be as clear about that as you can. When that is clear, you feel confident about the circle. You don't apologize for something being outside it, and with what is inside it, you become joyful and generous in giving.

Becoming trustworthy. Another effect of taking responsibility for your limits is that you become trustworthy to yourself, trustworthy to not abandon yourself. Then you naturally become curious about new things and are able to handle new experiments. Some things remain outside the circle of what you are willing to give because they belong there. Other things begin to look interesting *because you trust yourself.* If you are interested in enlarging the circle of what you are comfortable giving, the key is not to push yourself but to listen carefully to your inner no and abide by it.

Why it's so hard to set limits. When my grandson was about three, we stood in line at the zoo, waiting for tickets. He was a forward little guy, assuming that everyone in the world welcomed him. Up rolled a little girl about his size in a stroller, and he walked over to her and was about to climb into the stroller with her. She held up her hand in a stop signal and said, "No!" Smart move. But then her mother said to her, "Oh honey, it's not nice to say no!" I didn't have the presence of mind to say to the mother, "Oh honey, in about ten years, you are going to be hoping she can say no!" I told my grandson, in a voice I hoped the mother could hear, "No means no. She doesn't want you in her stroller" and walked him a little farther away.

It's hard to say no for the same reason it's hard to ask for what we want. It is trained out of us and becomes heaped with shame, fear, and self-doubt. Shame because it's "selfish" to set a limit. Fear because we fear being shunned, punished, or abandoned. Self-doubt because we wonder what it means about us. *Am I not generous enough? Enlightened enough? Good enough? Do I really know myself?* To ignore our inner no or overrule it, we had to shut down our way of knowing what we felt. We get trained out of trusting our inner signals, so now when we need them, we can't hear them.

Here's a testament to how difficult it is for grown-ups when children say no. At about two years old, we develop enough brain cells to notice we are a separate being, and we learn to say no. What do we call this crucial developmental landmark? The "terrible twos." Do you know any parents who say to their kids, "Susie, you do such a great job saying no! I'm so proud of you!" Hardly. The message to the child in the stroller was *The other person's wants are more important than your limits.* Or *What you know about yourself doesn't matter.*

We go along with things because we are afraid of losing the connection. We're afraid they might leave, emotionally or literally. Sometimes this gets disguised as *I don't want to hurt their feelings.* Kindness is good, but the problem is that if we hurt someone's feelings, what does that mean about us? It's our own feelings we are avoiding. This is often really about our self-image as a giver. We can be kind to others because it is our nature, because it is our practice, because it is what is real for us, or because it serves us in some other way. When we avoid saying no because we don't want to deal with the consequences, that is a very different story.

We go along because it feels like the safest thing to do. It avoids conflict. If we are afraid of outer conflict (someone might be disappointed, grumpy, even violent), we bring the conflict inside, saying, *Should I…?*

or *Can I...?* This feels safer than confronting it. Sometimes it is, and sometimes it isn't. We go along because we don't know how not to. We go along because it feels normal. The fear of what will happen if we *do* say no is greater than the fear of what will happen if we *don't*.

Sometimes our go-along-with behavior is a minor bump that is easily overlooked (for a while, anyway). Sometimes it's a major breach, and sometimes we don't notice it until much later. When we set aside our responsibility for our limits, we build up resentment. Then we either dry up or blow up. Or maybe we did try to speak our limits, but they were not respected. We start thinking our limits don't matter, so they stop mattering to us. We think they're wrong. We forget how to communicate our limits, how to say no or "Only to here." Ultimately we forget how to *have* limits.

Sometimes, when the Intensity Factor kicks in, we are overwhelmed and freeze. Science is starting to understand this as a neurological event that we have no control over. It helps to understand this so you can stop blaming yourself for not speaking up. This is one reason why I encourage you in the labs to go slowly, pause, and wait for the inner *Hell, yes!*

We need to know that we can say no to a request and still stay connected to the person. It takes having experiences in which it's true and slowing down enough to notice it's true. These happen in the lessons and labs.

THE SECRET TO EASE AND JOY IN GIVING

The first secret is learning to receive, because when you learn to receive, you no longer have to use giving to avoid it. Tending to your limits and allowing yourself to have a full-hearted no creates ease and joy. That allows you to have a full-hearted yes. If there is no joy in it, you are adapting yourself in some way to what you think is supposed to happen. There is also freedom in letting go of the outcome and letting your receiver have their own experience.

HOW TO LEARN TO GIVE

We don't want to create this false separation between self-care and service. You fill your heart up and then from that overflowing heart you are able to pour out that love to others.

—*Mark Silver*

The single most important factor in learning to give well is learning to receive. Your ability to give what is real and effective is directly proportional to your ability to receive what is real and meaningful to you.

First, so you can tell the difference. As you learn to trust your desires and put them first, you learn what that feels like, so you can learn how to put your desires last. Second, you stop trying to avoid receiving. As you learn what receiving is, you fall in love with it. You no longer have to avoid it, so giving stops being a way to avoid receiving. Third, you stop using "giving" to get something back: reassurance, affirmation, love, respect, appreciation, or a feeling of connection. For example, if you don't feel loved, you can try to earn love by "giving." Receiving teaches you that you are already loved. This is why until you learn to receive, your giving cannot be trusted, because you will be using it to avoid something or get something. A student of mine says, "When I can see your selfishness, I can trust your generosity."

Finally, you need to learn to receive so your needs are met and you have something to give. When you are well nourished and rested, you have more attention and compassion. True physically, true emotionally. When your hands have met their desire for exploring, which happens in Taking, they are not starved for it or afraid of it. Then when you are Serving, you can show up with flexibility and generosity. Likewise, when you have been touched exactly the way you want, which happens in Accepting, your skin is happy and your emotional tank is full, so you become more generous in Allowing.

Learning to give requires learning to say no. The easiest way is to slow down. Take the twenty-second pause that is built into the labs, and take longer if you need it. We also talked about this in the labs: If you feel any hesitancy, it will be one of three things: 1) you need more information,

2) there is some limit you need to set, or 3) it's an inner no waiting for you to hear it. You might need more time. Add this to your repertoire: "I'm not sure yet. I'm going to take a little time to consider that."

Then wait for the inner resounding *Yes!* Commit to *doing nothing* until you hear your inner yes. In other words, your current default is: *I'm not hearing a Hell no, so I guess it's a yes.* Switch to: *I'm not hearing a Hell yes, so it's a no.* That puts both of you at ease. You stop worrying about giving too much, and your receiver stops worrying about taking advantage of you.

The question to ask yourself is not, *Why aren't I okay with this?* It's, *What am I okay with and happy to give? What needs to change in order for me to give a full-hearted yes?* Again, this is not about changing your attitude but changing the request.

A couple more things about saying no: "No" is a complete sentence. It needs no reason or explanation. In real life, it can be considerate (and helps maintain the connection) to give context or more information (without apologizing for having a limit). In the practice, experiment with saying no and leaving it at that, and see what you notice about yourself.

No is a yes to something else. If you are in the mood to stay home with a good book and your friend invites you out, if you can't say no to them, you are saying no to yourself. By saying no to going out, you are saying yes to staying in. Getting clear on your yes and what you want makes it easier to notice your no.

The other person deserves the truth from us. The kindest thing we can do is give them accurate information so they can navigate their world successfully and make choices that work for them. Neglecting our no is essentially a lie.

There are times when we are going to say no but we want to still keep the connection with the person. The other person still wants to be seen and heard and to have their desires acknowledged. You can acknowledge that you hear and respect them: "That sounds good" (if it's true) or "That sounds interesting. I see how you might like that." Then set your limits with a no or a negotiation: "I can't do that this month" or "That doesn't work for me" or "I'm not up for that, but how about this instead?" If applicable, ask for what you want: "Please ask me again next month" or "Are you open to this other thing, and would that meet your need just as well?"

The art of giving is creating spaciousness. We talked about this in the Serving Lab, but I want to mention it here, because it also applies to Allowing. You know that it's hard for the receiver to ask for what they want. Creating spaciousness means to make it easier for them to do that. There are steps in the lab, but the biggest part of it is your attitude: valuing the process of your receiver taking all the time they need and changing their mind. The more you can do that, the more effective your giving will be.

What encroaches on spaciousness is assuming you know what your partner wants or needs or what would be best for them, or your discomfort with waiting. Or your need for something dramatic to happen or to feel smart, important, or indispensable, your need to be noticed and appreciated, to get turned on, or to see a response you want.

The experience of giving. Getting the response you want may feed the ego, but giving a real gift feeds the heart. The experience of giving is humbling and freeing. Sometimes it's fun as well. Sometimes it's not fun at all, but because it is meaningful to your partner, it becomes meaningful to you. When the direction of the gift is clear, there is a real flow, and the flow feels good to you too. Sometimes the experience of giving engenders gratitude, but the feeling of gratitude doesn't mean you are receiving; it just means you feel gratitude. Go ahead and feel it.

REASONS TO GIVE TOO MUCH

- You think there is something it will get you: safety, self-worth, or connection.
- To reassure yourself you are wanted and useful.
- It's the least awful alternative.
- You don't know how not to.

WHAT WE WANT IN THE GIVING HALF

- We want our gift to be useful and meaningful to the receiver.
- We want to choose when to offer our gifts.
- We want our time and resources to be respected.
- We want to know the truth about what the receiver wants.
- We want to let go of the gift when it leaves our hands.
- Sometimes we want to take action for others; sometimes we want to allow others to take action.
- Sometimes we want our gifts to be recognized and appreciated, and sometimes we want our gifts to be anonymous.
- Sometimes we want to know what the other person wants so we can give them that. Sometimes we want to give a surprise gift.

THE SHADOW OF GIVING

The shadow of giving is giving more than you are happy to give. It's becoming a martyr or doormat and losing yourself. It's using giving to place the other person in the vulnerable place (receiving). They owe you now, and you stay in control. This position of power is manipulation of the worst kind. Or if you are a little ashamed of your eros, you can use "giving" to get your partner going so you now feel safer. It's like saying, "You go first. That'll lessen my shame." You use giving in hope of a reward. This is not a true gift; there's no heart in it.

There is a difference between generosity and trying to please someone where the underlying desire is to make yourself feel better, to keep them around, or some other version of keeping yourself safe. It's tricky because trying to please is seen as normal and good. It's usually some combination of both, which is why it's hard to tell the difference, but they spring from different motives. It often feels different to the receiver and can create underlying doubt and dissatisfaction.

WHEN GIVING IS HARD

When giving is hard, it is usually because we have trouble setting limits. We feel reluctant to give anything at all, fearing we will give too much. We may feel worried or stingy. We may give but resent it, sometimes for decades. Or we strive for control, refusing to give anything at all, to make sure we are in charge. When giving is hard, we have little sense of our usefulness, which leads to despair. It could be hard to give because you are afraid you won't get a turn to receive. What do you need to ask for?

A quirk in both the Receiving and Giving Halves is acquiescence, which is to go along with something reluctantly but without protest. Receiving is based on your desire. If you don't know what that is, you go along with what someone else wants (or you think they want). You acquiesce. Giving is based on your limits. If you don't know what they are, you again go along with what someone else wants and acquiesce. Whether you are setting aside what you want or setting aside responsibility for your limits, it's the same *feeling*. This is why you can't tell which one (giving or receiving) you are doing. You are doing neither. Acquiescence creates a dependable outcome: it dulls desire and creates resentment.

Stuck in Giving. Usually more problematic is being stuck in the Giving Half. There are many reasons: thinking you are supposed to, fear of selfishness, a strategy for love and acceptance, the need to feel empowered and effective, your image as a self-contained person who has it all together, your image as a generous lover, or to justify your existence and ameliorate your self-doubt. Maybe your direct tactile experience is inaccessible (see Waking Up the Hands), so you have to rely on your partner's experience and try to "give" to make that happen. Maybe you avoid receiving because it's emotionally vulnerable. Maybe you equate receiving with being done to and you don't like that.

When you are stuck in giving, everything sounds like a request. Someone says, "You look busy. Would you like to postpone this meeting until tomorrow?" Instead of "Yes, please" or "No, thanks," you say, "Well, we could do that." They were offering you an option, and you hear it as a request and start trying to figure out how you could give that. Take a breath, and listen to the words again. Ask yourself, *Is this an okay-with question or a what-do-I-want question?* If you're not sure, ask them which it is. "Sorry, I'm not clear. Are you asking me what I prefer or what I'm okay with?"

WHEN GIVING IS EASY

When Giving is easy, you know your limits, you say yes and no and negotiate. You are relaxed and generous and don't apologize for having limits. You say your no with kindness and ease. You ask what other people want, don't make assumptions, and give them all the time they need to notice it. When the gift leaves your hands, it leaves your hands. You let them have the experience they have without trying to get something back or get them to respond the way you want them to.

A practitioner I was coaching was stuck in Serving and excruciatingly uncomfortable in Accepting. I said, "You are giving simply to avoid receiving. That's not giving." He asked, "Why do you give?" I thought about that for several days and finally realized: because I can. For that I am thankful.

THE SPIRITUAL DIMENSION OF GIVING

> *A hundred times every day I remind myself that my inner and outer lives are based on the labors of other people, living and dead, and that I must exert myself in order to give in the same measure as I have received and am still receiving.*
>
> —*Albert Einstein*

Giving has an unquestionable role in a spiritual life. In giving, you get to stand in the river and have it run through you. You get to notice our natural connection. In giving we put our desires aside. This shows us the desires we might not want to acknowledge, which sends us right back to receiving. As we learn to truly set them aside, it leads to maturity.

In addition, there are a few themes that show up in Serving and Allowing. We'll talk more about this in those chapters.

SOCIAL IMPLICATIONS

Giving is unquestionable in relation to the world at large. Giving to others underpins the development of civilization. The same principles apply: the ability to set aside what you want starts the process, taking in information about the potential receiver makes it effective, and the ability to say no creates generosity. It varies by Serving or Allowing—we'll come back to those.

This is where we get to ask ourselves how we are taking care of those in need in our communities. Those needing food, money, shelter, and support? Those with disabilities, the homeless, immigrants and asylum seekers, those down on their luck? Those across the globe facing natural disasters and political upheaval, especially due to our own government's messing with them? In giving this kind of support internationally, a relatively small amount of money from us (in the United States) translates to an extraordinary difference to those in serious need. See the online resources.

Altruism means it's completely for them and requires nothing back. It's the same with a gift in the ideal sense. When we need nothing back, the gift is clean and brings both people joy. Do we ever get to 100 percent? Probably not. In real life, we do want to see some effect and want to be appreciated and acknowledged. Part of what makes a community successful is reciprocity and appreciation. It's natural to want something back; I have no argument against that. In the labs, you see how close to 100 percent you can get and what happens when you do. As you experience that, what do you notice about the rest of your life? What do you get clearer on and more generous with?

SUMMARY: THE GIVING HALF

You are in the Giving Half when the other person has requested something, it is within the limits of what you are willing and able to give, and you agree to it. You move from your Want-to list to your Willing-to list.

The Giving Half includes two quadrants:

- **Serve**: Serving combines Doing and Giving; the gift you give is your action.
- **Allow**: Allowing combines Done-to and Giving; the gift you give is access to you.

The agreement creates the dynamic. When the other person says, "Will you…" and you say, "Yes, I will," you create the Serve-Accept dynamic. When the other person says, "May I…" and you say, "Yes, you may," you create the Take-Allow dynamic. Or you can offer, and they say, "Yes, please."

What is the gift? You give your time, your attention, and your willingness to set aside your preference for now.

Giving is optional and by choice. It is based on what you are genuinely willing to give. It can't be taken from you or stolen. The act of choosing brings your heart into it.

The receiver's experience. The receiver's experience belongs to them. You do not create it or control it; you contribute to it. They experience it and use it however they want.

You are doing two things at once. 1) Setting aside your preferences, and 2) keeping responsibility for your limits. Neither one alone is enough.

Limits. The more responsibility you take for your limits, the more generous you become within those limits, and the more joy you feel in it.

The trap. The trap of this half is using your giving to try to get your receiver to respond in the way you want them to (sexual turn-on, gratitude, etc.). This is manipulation.

The art of giving is spaciousness. The art of giving is to create enough spaciousness that it's easier for your receiver to notice what they want and ask for it.

The quality of your giving depends on quality of your receiving. You learn the difference between them; you stop using giving to avoid receiving, to try to get something back that you haven't asked for, or to prove your worthiness or avoid your shame. Your needs are met, so you have something to give.

Shadow. The do-gooder, the doormat, the martyr. Giving yourself away because you don't know how not to. Using "giving" to manipulate or create a power dynamic or debt.

Myths about giving. 1) Giving is more enlightened than receiving. 2) If you give enough, you can make up for not receiving. 3) Giving will make you indispensable. 4) You know what the other person wants or needs. 5) If you give anything, you have to give everything.

RECEIVING, GIVING, AND GENDER

Receiving is an equal opportunity challenger, because no gender is immune from self-doubt. Sex and gender make no difference here. We all need help, support, and enjoyment, but your gender conditioning may tell you what to feel entitled to and what you are supposed to give.

Men often believe that they are supposed to give by doing (Serving), and Taking is especially challenging. Women often believe that they are supposed to give their bodies (Allowing) and find it hard to find the experience of Accepting.

CHAPTER 20

The Taking Quadrant

When I touch you I feel happy inside
It's such a feelin' that, my love, I can't hide.
—John Lennon, Paul McCartney

I grew up with a parent who was violent. I'm fine with being in control
of myself, but I'm afraid to be in control of someone else. I've seen it
misused, so I thought that's what Taking was, and I was afraid of it.
—A student

Your hand rests on their back, and you notice the shape, the hills and valleys. Your hands wander, exploring. You move slower than you thought possible, and your hands come alive. The sensation fills you. At one point, your hands move toward their waist, and you are about to slide down to their hips when you remember what they said when they agreed to give you this: "Yes, from the waist up." You begin your journey back up again, over the hills and valleys. At some point, you remember that this is a gift for you, given to you with a full heart. Your heart aches with gratitude. You are in the Taking Quadrant.

The most important thing to know about Taking is that it is receiving a gift. The gift you are receiving is access. In Taking, you have asked permission to touch someone the way you want, and they have agreed. Taking combines doing and receiving. The action moves from you to them, but the gift moves from them to you.

For almost everyone, the Taking Quadrant is the hardest and the most misunderstood, confusing, and intimidating. The Take-Allow dynamic is the opposite of what feels normal to most people. You are touching for your own enjoyment, and this can be anywhere from mildly elusive to seriously daunting. Taking can challenge who you think you are as a lover and as a person. When Taking is lacking, it tends to be mysterious. You have the sense that something is missing but don't know what it is or where to look for it. You long for an authenticity and freedom you can't name. You don't understand why all your giving is not working or why the spark is missing, or you lack confidence. It's almost always the Taking Quadrant.

Taking is also the quadrant that liberates you. It recovers a fundamental human capacity. You learn to touch another person based on your interest and curiosity without trying to give to them. You come to terms with the impulse to act in your own self-interest, to do what you want to do. You discover that to touch someone, you don't need a technique, don't need to give, and don't need an excuse. What you do need is to recognize that you want something and gain their permission. Once that clicks, it is profoundly liberating. You no longer have to plan, strategize, manipulate, or coerce. Your touch becomes expressive, sensual, spontaneous, and genuine. Taking develops integrity, because you no longer have to pretend you are giving.

The Taking Quadrant is the keystone of the Wheel. Until it clicks, the rest of the Wheel remains confusing or theoretical. If you find yourself struggling to figure out the Wheel or trying to analyze or memorize it, Taking has not clicked for you. When it does, all the rest of it becomes simple and obvious. You say, *Oh! Of course!* Taking brings presence and confidence to your hands, frees up your sense of play and passion, clarifies and cleans up your Serving, gets you out of using touch as a strategy, and generally turns your world upside down. I have come to believe that erotic maturity is not possible without it. The key to developing Taking is learning to become trustworthy that you will not step over your Allower's limits. When you begin to trust yourself, you can relax and receive the gift.

WHAT IT'S NOT

Taking is not stealing, groping, taking advantage of, or taking over. It is not being pushy, demanding, or entitled. It is not doing whatever you want regardless of the other person, nor is it giving in the way you "want to give."

WHAT IT IS

Taking is one half of a dynamic and an inner experience. The Take-Allow dynamic is created by your agreement: You say, "May I…" and they say, "Yes, you may." It is temporary, specific, and within your Allower's limits, which you are respecting. The inner experience is of receiving a gift, and it engenders gratitude.

Taking is a form of receiving, so we're back to two things at once: 1) you put your desires first, and 2) you respect the limits of the Allower and stay within those limits. You are not trying to please them or create any experience for them. They will have their own experience, and the only way they can experience Allowing is if you are in Taking.

Taking is based on the direct route of pleasure—doing because it feels good to you, not because of the effect it has on the other person. This is why Waking Up the Hands (Lesson 1) is necessary before Taking can click.

About the word. The word "taking" has some negative connotations, one of them implying that one is grabbing up everything they can get without caring for anyone else. But the Taking Quadrant has a specific meaning. In this quadrant, you are receiving a gift that is freely given to you with a full heart, and you very much respect the limits of your Allower.

Another way to think of it is this: if I give you some pears from the tree in my yard, I can bring them to you, or I can let you come over and pick them. In Taking, you come over and pick them. The gift is waiting for you; you take the action to collect it. Some other examples of Taking are putting your head in your partner's lap, borrowing your friend's truck, or talking about something that's on your mind and having someone listen.

The challenges of Taking. Taking can be elusive to find the first time, because our habits in touching are often strong and tend to hide it. It can be confusing or emotionally challenging, bringing up shame, grief, and self-doubt.

REVIEW: FINDING TAKING

Detailed steps to find the Taking Quadrant are in Lesson 2. Here is a review.

Though Taking can be experienced with any body part, it's most helpful to find it by using your hands. This is true because of the large number of nerve endings (compared to, say, the elbow) and the fact that the hands are a fairly neutral body part (compared to, say, the lips). I have found that when your hands "get it," you get it.

Finding the Taking Quadrant requires two things to be in place: 1) the ability to take in sensation with the hands and experience it as enjoyable, and 2) permission of the person you are intending to feel. Anything that creates the feeling of working or giving makes it more elusive. This happens in two places: the words you use and the position of your body. If you use words that imply giving ("Would you like me to massage your hand?"), it will be harder to experience receiving. Instead say, "May I feel your hand?" If you lean forward or turn toward your Allower, it tends to reinforce the feeling of giving and working. Instead, lean back, and bring their hand to the center of your lap. The other major factor is moving your hands slowly and allowing them to be curious.

When Taking clicks, you notice that this is a gift for you, and you stop trying to give. There is often an emotional response of tenderheartedness, surprise, shame, guilt, sadness, delight, sensuality, or play. When it clicks, your hands relax. They are no longer tentative or tense. They stop planning, and you begin to follow them. They become sensual, perceptive, and intuitive. When you find Taking, because it is pleasurable, you are no longer interested in going anywhere else.

REVIEW: EXPLORING TAKING

Detailed steps for exploring Taking are in Lab 1. This is a review.

Exploring Taking is a lifelong journey. Once it clicks, it can be slippery. That is, when you include more areas of the body (theirs and yours), it tends to raise the anxiety, and you revert to your default, which is trying to give. It works best to start slow, with short turns in relatively neutral body areas, gain the skills to stay in Taking, and gradually increase what you ask for. It is more useful and interesting to feel a neutral body part and stay in Taking than to try an "exciting" body part and slip out of Taking.

As you gain the skill to ask for your Allower's limits, abide by them, and notice if they are tensing up, you become trustworthy. You stop worrying about harming them and can relax. As your skills increase over time, you are able to stay in Taking in gradually more complex and intense interactions.

As you explore the Taking Quadrant, you discover that the mood can change in an instant: tender, curious, sensual, comforting, silly, sexy, and back again. Over time, you develop confidence in letting your body move in ways that express how you feel, and you use your entire body to play with theirs, rolling and climbing. The need for strategy drops away, so you become creative. This is liberating and satisfying.

THE EXPERIENCE OF TAKING

For a few people, the experience of Taking is natural and easy. For most, it's odd, disorienting even. You have a physical experience that has been absent for decades, and it can be a major revelation. The experience of Taking includes a wide range of moods, but they all have the sense that this is absolutely and unquestionably for you. You stop trying to give, and you receive the gift of being allowed to do what you want. Very often there are feelings of freedom, relief, and gratitude.

There will be times when it's elusive or awkward, and times when the naturalness of it is a relief. There will be moments of playfulness, physicality, and mischievousness, moments of comfort and coming home, perhaps tears. Desires you didn't know you had will come to the surface. You may feel self-conscious or embarrassed. As you develop trust in yourself, you move your body to express what is inside: curiosity, delight, hunger, lust, or tenderness. You wake up your own eroticism and want to reach, feel, wrap around, climb, bite, hump, and grind. That may be a shock or a relief.

What you learn over time. The changes that develop from Taking are hard to imagine until they happen. You may fear that getting good at Taking means you start "taking" everything and become more selfish. What actually happens is that you get good at respecting people's limits.

You develop noticing skills that make you trustworthy. That gives you the ability to cut loose with confidence. You notice where in your life you make assumptions about what is available, and you start to clean those up.

Perhaps the most basic change is that Taking develops the direct route to pleasure and gets you out of the indirect (vicarious) route. This improves the quality of your touch. Your hands relax and become sensual, sensitive, and intuitive. That improves your Serving when it's your turn to do so. Opening the direct route also lets you drop the goal, attend to the present moment, and locate your experience within yourself.

Taking decouples the impulse to do from the need to give. You experience doing that is a natural expression of affection, curiosity, sensuality, and desire. The natural lag time between the impulse to move and the decision to act on it shortens. With less planning and strategizing, physical and erotic play become spontaneous. Taking is the source of confidence. For the seriously geekish among us, it also reveals certain core competencies. See the online notes on these.

THE SECRET TO EASE AND JOY IN TAKING

To find ease and joy in Taking, you have to know you are not going to harm anyone or overstep their limits. To know that, you have to learn how to make an agreement (consent skills) and keep it even if you become excited. That allows you to relax, receive the gift being given to you, and enjoy your Taking.

THE FEELINGS—WHY SO HARD?

Besides the challenging feelings that arise with any form of receiving, Taking is a special case because you are receiving by moving toward what you want. It is a powerful combination. Though there is a range of how deeply you have to go into it before it hits you, at some point you will hit your self-doubt, confusion, shame, guilt, or fear. For some, it's right away.

Others sail into it with ease, but when they reach a certain level of excitement, it's suddenly difficult again. It can be mildly odd or overwhelming.

Sometimes people can articulate it:

"I feel guilty for doing anything for my own pleasure."

"I am afraid of being selfish."

"I feel like I don't deserve this."

"I feel shame that I want this, shame that I want anything."

"I don't trust that the permission I got is real."

"I don't know why, but I feel a huge weight of dread like something bad is going to happen."

"I feel so ashamed. It makes no sense at all." (tears)

"What do you mean it's for me? I don't even know what that *means*."

"This is a remembrance of what my hands have forgotten. There's a sadness there."

I might not have been surprised to hear these when people were excited or turned on; that seems pretty normal for our culture. What did surprise me was that the feelings arose immediately. They showed up with that first experience of feeling their partner's hand or with feeling the object (Lesson 1). This told me that we were looking at fundamental mechanisms. Engage the mechanism *at all,* and you hit the feelings.

Our cultural and personal relationship to sensory reality and pleasure are mixed, complex, and often shame-based. At the root of it, we're not supposed to have pleasure. To some degree, we're not supposed to have bodies. And even if we do have pleasure, it should be an accidental by-product—we're not supposed to take action to create it. This screwed-up belief is patterned into our psyches. Because of the complexities of relationship and sexuality, we may be able to function and find ways around the gaps, but when we slow down, strip away the complexities, and engage the neuro-emotional mechanism at the center of it, we feel discomfort—because there is nothing hiding it. Here are some of those mechanisms.

Sensation as pleasure. Most basic of all is the experience of sensation as pleasure. We all have a comfort level, our pleasure ceiling. *I'm comfortable with this much pleasure but not this much.* The experience of Waking Up the Hands uncovers this relationship, and the Taking Quadrant builds on it.

Taking action toward pleasure. It's one thing to experience pleasure as a result of someone else's activity, if it, you know, just sort of happens to you, but to move toward it is a different thing entirely. It requires excruciating self-acknowledgment. I said in Waking Up the Hands that this is more than a philosophical idea. It's a neurological phenomenon in which the brain areas involved in movement light up at the same time as the areas involved in sensation, and this is not easy for everyone. Then you add a layer of relational complexity—you are not just touching a person, you are *feeling* a person.

Putting yourself first. Almost everyone has mixed feelings about putting themselves first and a varied ability to do so. I can't describe the mountains of shame people feel about this.

The presence of desire. The fact of wanting something, much less verbalizing it, can stir up enough confusion and fear to shut the whole thing down. There's a wide range of how we feel about our desire including that it's okay to have any desire at all or the idea that our desire is automatically harmful to someone else.

Being seen in pleasure. It's hard enough being in pleasure, but to be seen in it, out in the open, is another thing entirely. With Taking, there is nowhere to hide.

Uncovering your lust. Taking is the home of lust—the desire to do something sexual to someone. You'll hit your fear and shame and have to face the sensual, sexual, selfish, primal you. Not only feel it in yourself but possibly be seen in it, reaching, grabbing, humping, moaning, crying, sweating, or slobbering.

You have each of those, and you have the stew that is all of them together. Combine the experience of pleasure with taking action, putting yourself first, and the possibility of sexual arousal. It's hard to imagine any combination that will bring you to shame and self-doubt any faster.

But wait, there's more.

Receiving a gift. There is the fact that you are receiving a gift from someone who cares about you. They have set aside what they might prefer in order to give you want you want. Part of that gift is their body, and part is their acceptance of you as a desiring, sensual, pleasuring being. In case the others have not gotten you yet, that one likely will.

Hitting your passivity. You will hit your passivity head on. Any passive streak you have, and we all have some, will be confronted. You can't hide behind what your partner wants or what your partner is doing, can't wait for something to respond to, can't defer, set aside, or acquiesce. There is no rescue from your discomfort.

Every one of those are things that we need and are central to our sense of connection and sanity, and we have been taught they are wrong. As said elsewhere, combine an innate human need with censure, and there's going to be confusion, anxiety, fascination, and compulsion. Each of those individually is an innate impulse about which we carry confusion, fear, and shame, and then we combine them. It's a wonder any of us can function.

THE EROTIC ELEMENTS OF TAKING

When you do things from your soul,
the river itself moves through you.
Freshness and a deep joy
are the signs of the current.
—Rumi, translated by Coleman Barks

I would never think of rushing you into anything. If something just happened on the spur of the moment, I wouldn't be certain whether I caught you off guard or whether you wanted to, or what. I want to get everything you've got, everything. But when I get it, I want to feel absolutely certain that you want me to have it.
—Claude Brown

Taking affects your experience of eros and sexual activity in many ways: the quality of your touch, the quality of your attention to the present, no longer needing a goal, moving from strategy to expression, and no longer needing a recipe, so each time is new. You are clearer at communicating and accessing your own desire to do.

Take-Allow is what romance novels are full of for good reason. What brings in the erotic element is desire. *I want this person. I want to experience them, I want to touch, feel, smell, taste, explore, and climb all over them.*

When you are in Serving, you rely on the desire of the person receiving. In Taking, you rely on your own desire, and it's not just making room for your desire. *Taking can't happen without it.* If you are unable to access your desire to do, you are unable to access the Taking Quadrant. It is possible to find some erotic charge with Serve-Accept, and it can be a fun way to play with power, but Take-Allow lends itself naturally to erotic charge (or maybe it's just me). This is not to say Take-Allow is automatically erotic. It opens a full range of moods—comforting, nourishing, calming, sensorial, exploratory, curious, silly, the whole gamut.

Why you need it in bed. I can't count the number of couples who have asked me for help recovering their sexual spark. Invariably, Taking is missing. We are taught that the only way to be a good lover is to Serve. Serving is lovely sometimes, but when you set your desires aside *every time*, you will get bored, and boring. Not to mention resentful. If you are going to experience aliveness, you must learn how to take action that expresses how you feel instead of it being a strategy, no matter how right the strategy seems. You have to bring your desires forward. They must animate you. Without them, there is nobody home to play with, and that is frustrating and lonely for your partner and quite often mysterious. What usually happens is that you both know something is missing but have no idea what. It's almost always Taking.

You also need it in bed for a reason we mentioned earlier: the quality of your touch. Touch is not the only factor for great sex, by a long shot, but it's a big one. It is nearly impossible to relax under hands that are tense or tentative. Taking teaches your hands to relax and show up in the present, which invites your partner to show up.

If you are no longer relying on recipes, each time you are together, you notice yourself and what you feel and what you want at this moment. Each time is new; there is no such thing as "the same old thing."

Lust and passion. Taking (not Serving) is the home of lust. It's a natural human capacity; without it, there's no continuation of the species.

Passion is lust plus love (or at least some connection). Everyone seems to want more passion, but in my work with couples, love is rarely missing. Lust is. More accurately, what is missing is knowing how to access and trust the impulse to do. The Taking Quadrant is missing.

In Taking, as self-expression becomes available, lust becomes available. It will naturally show up provided you desire the person (or perhaps even if you don't usually). Taking makes room for it and teaches you how to trust it so you can enjoy it.

When genitals are involved. You can be highly erotic without genital touch, and you can engage the genitals without it being the least bit erotic. For many people, this is pretty much the norm. Nevertheless, a note about if and when you involve the genitals. For almost everyone, if they learn Taking and then begin to include the genitals, the Intensity Factor kicks in, they forget everything they have learned and go right back to technique, trying to get the right result. In Taking, you learn that you are allowed to be curious, to explore and enjoy with no need to go anywhere. This is an extraordinary gift and a profound experience, and it may be erotic, or it may not be.

Erotic maturity. For erotic maturity, you need access to all four quadrants, but there is a kind of erotic maturity found in Taking that is found nowhere else: the maturity of acknowledging what you want to do, taking responsibility for communicating it with respect and care, and bringing your desires forward without shame or excuse. This is the maturity of self-acceptance. In Taking, there is nowhere to hide your desire, no way to pretend it's about giving. There is no way to be passive in any sense of the word. You take full responsibility for yourself and at the same time respect your partner's limits and experience.

The Lover's Touch. The original title of this book was *The Lover's Touch*. Here's why. When there is desire in your hands, it creates a certain tone that is difficult to describe and impossible to fake. It is a tone that is not there in the hands of your massage therapist, only your lover. You want your lover not only to (sometimes) give to you, but you want them to want you, to enjoy touching you, to experience pleasure with your body. You want your lover to be able to access Taking. When your lover's hands discover Taking, they become sensual, intuitive, and attentive to the present. This brings you into the present. Their touch becomes inviting and compelling and invites surrender. The Lover's Touch is the Taking Quadrant. It's what you want to be able to access and what you want your lover to be able to access.

TAKING AND GENDER

I sometimes have people say, "Oh, this is the masculine quadrant!" Not at all. I cannot stress this enough. As I say in chapter 6, assigning a gender to a quadrant is not about the *quadrant*; it reflects your idea of what that gender is. This is why your ideas about your gender may make it harder or easier for you to find Taking.

Men. There is a common idea that Taking is what men are always doing. It's amazing how many men have told me, "I'm not like most men. I actually like to give!" It makes me wonder what they think all those other men are doing. It's also interesting that this comment never arises when they are trying to learn Serving, only when they are trying to learn Taking.

Men are conditioned to think that their role is the active one and that they are supposed to know the right thing to do—at all times! On the other hand, they receive contradictory messages: Men are selfish and disrespectful—don't be that guy!—but to be a "real man," you have to know what you want and get it.

Men are often afraid of this quadrant. They have been taught their lust is dangerous and are afraid it makes them a bad person. Sometimes the slightest dip into Taking can bring up those fears. The shadow of Taking is very dark including groping, perpetrating, assault, and rape. If you don't understand consent, entering the quadrant at all can feel too close to those.

When women complain about their men in bed, they often say that men don't know how to show up and are just going through the motions. What's missing is the Taking Quadrant: learning how to attend to your desire so you stop performing and show up.

Women. Women almost always have an easier time finding Taking than their male partners. Waking Up the Hands tends to click more easily. This is not because women have more nerve endings in their hands but because of gender conditioning around sensation and feelings. It's more culturally acceptable for women to have such things.

Women are conditioned that their role in sex is to be passive as in "She lets him…" The conditioning says that taking action is unfeminine or slutty. Now, in recent decades, women are supposed to learn how to rock his world with hot new techniques. Now they have competing shoulds: They should do nothing, and they should do awesome, hot, cosmic things. Most often, when women discover Taking, they feel like they have been released from prison. Taking is powerfully liberating.

There's no such thing as Taking as a "masculine" or a "feminine" quadrant. Every person has the capacity to enjoy their hands and body, the capacity and desire to take action, and the capacity and desire to express themselves and play.

THE SHADOW OF TAKING

> *I thought I was really good at Taking, but I found out I was good at stealing. I didn't want to ask for what I wanted because it's vulnerable, so I was just sneaking it instead.*
>
> *—A student*

The shadow of the Taking Quadrant is taking action for your own benefit without regard for the effects on other people and other living beings. It's the action element without the gift element. Essentially you are saying *My want is more important than your no*. Again, wiser people than I have developed this. See the online resources.

The shadow of the Taking Quadrant is large, which is part of the reason people are intimidated by it. It is stealing, and there are many ways to steal—groping, bullying, stalking, exploitation, plagiarism, assault, rape, murder, colonization, enslavement, and war. Even the more mundane dynamics of pressuring someone to give in, walking into a room and taking over the conversation, taking up extra spaces on the subway, or sneaking into the front of the line fall under this shadow. On an even larger, institutional scale are the more hidden-in-plain-sight kinds of stealing, like setting up laws and institutions that take advantage of the fact that not everyone can see what you're doing, like polluting the river and transferring the clean-up expenses onto the public. As this book goes to press, there is an upwelling of resistance to racism in the United States and elsewhere, including those laws and institutions that have advantaged White people for hundreds of years, like the homesteading laws which not only stole from the Native inhabitants but disallowed Black people from participating. This is a deep shadow of Taking.

Entitlement. We talked about entitlement in chapter 18. Entitlement is the sense that something already belongs to you. Usually we don't know we feel entitled to something until we don't get what we want, and then we feel incensed or outraged. In our culture, men are trained to believe that women are their source of entertainment, comfort, connection, affirmation, and stress relief, and when a woman says no, they get angry and resort to name calling, threats of violence, and actual assault—a sure sign of entitlement, that they likely were not aware of.

The thread. We talked about this in the Wheel chapter. Imagine standing in the center of the Wheel and looking out toward the edge. If you see the circle of consent, you know that what is inside the circle is a gift, and what is outside is stealing. The difference is clear. If you can't see the circle, if you don't understand consent, you stand at the center and look out, and it all looks the same: assault, rape, and stealing.

It's like a thread that leads through Taking and out into its shadow. When you step into Taking *at all*, you feel that thread; it taps into an impulse that you instinctively know leads to assault. This is one reason people have a hard time learning Taking, especially men who have been taught that their desires are dangerous. They step into Taking, the thread vibrates, and it's terrifying.

The muddy zone. There is a large muddy zone in Taking in which consent is assumed or coerced. It may be seemingly innocuous. You don't ask because you don't know how, so you try it and see if they stop you. *It must be okay; they didn't stop me.* It's a muddy zone because it's not always clear whose "fault" it is, and there is likely to be heated debate about that. And the perpetrator is often not aware that they are doing so.

Maybe you push but just a little: "Oh, come on, it'll be fun!" More commonly, you don't notice that you have an effect. It can be as simple as taking up all the available attention in a conversation, not noticing if others are interested or not. There may be a subtle signal that your partner is not enjoying themselves, and you don't see it, or you ignore it. You don't want to slow down. It may be getting a little more pushy with a scowl or threat, direct or implied. "What do you want me to do, get it elsewhere?"

The shadow of Taking ranges from the muddy zone all the way into the serious shadow: groping, force, rape, a gun to the head, dropping bombs on villages or taking over oil fields. *My want is more important than your no.*

WHEN TAKING IS HARD (OR MISSING)

In bed or in life, you may feel like there is no room for you. You're not able to take up the space your body occupies. It's hard to know what you want or that you want anything at all. The only way to let yourself do anything is to make it about someone else, so you think you are always giving. It may appear that you are generous or easygoing, but what is really happening is that you can't access your own desires. In sex, you feel like you're doing all the work. This may not be terrible, but there is a certain spark you cannot light.

On one extreme is passivity. You have trouble with self-care: eating well and tending to your emotional, financial, and physical needs. You live in fear of doing the wrong thing, so you do nothing at all. You take no action for yourself, assuming that others know what to do or what you want. You have no agency and exercise no choice.

At the other end of that spectrum, you reach out and take everything you can get away with. You are ruthless in business and relationships. You don't notice or don't pay attention to the fact that what you do has an impact on others. If you are unable to occupy the Taking Quadrant, you end up in the shadow of it. This is a matter of degree and applies to all of us. We all have times when we take without integrity in different areas of our lives. For one, it might be with affection and touch. For another, it might be in taking up attention. For another, it might be a corporate decision to use up resources and leave a horrible, toxic mess. Often it's invisible to the person doing it *because they don't know the Taking Quadrant exists.*

Real Taking cracks open the heart. If you are unable to access it, a certain part of the heart goes hungry. You don't know how to meet it, so you steal, grab, use, or manipulate in bed, in relationships, and in business.

WHEN TAKING IS EASY

I really love your peaches, wanna shake your tree.
—Eddie Curtis, Ahmet Ertegun

You might think that getting good at Taking means you get good at grabbing anything and everything. The opposite is true: you get good at respecting others' limits and choices. You are able to trust that what you want is valid and ask for it without being attached to it. You have a beautiful combination of responsibility, desire, clarity, and respect that makes it easy to play with you or do business with you.

In bed, you are sensual, confident, perceptive, playful, and not afraid of yourself. You are able to take initiative and don't always have to wait for someone to start. You are never stuck in a recipe; technique has lost its allure because you are being real.

People who are good at Taking have a healthy practice of self-care. They eat well, take time to rest, and tend to their financial, physical, and emotional needs without taking advantage of others. They are able to recognize when their actions affect others and to check in with them about those effects. They are able to be firm on real needs like health and to bring other interests forward without being attached to them, and they are able to tell the difference.

SPIRITUAL IMPLICATIONS

What you don't understand is that what you are doing is costing someone something. Acknowledge that there is something you want to do, get vulnerable and humble to ask for it, and abide by the answer. Then you feel gratitude for the gift.

—A student

Every spiritual tradition has something to say about desire whether it is reviled, avoided, shunned, or, in some traditions, sought out and explored. Taking is where you come face to face with your desire to do. There is a deep split in our culture that says that spirit is good and body is bad, that sensuality and pleasure are bad. It's obvious in repressive religious systems, but what we may not notice is the effect it has on everyone in the culture.

There is nothing so affirming of physicality as the Taking Quadrant. Learning to find, trust, and value your desire to do and how to follow your impulse reconnects you with the spark of life. Taking is an exquisite opportunity to notice that the split is not true. Active sensuality does not need to become transmuted into something more "worthy." It is already worthy.

It's easy to confuse "spiritual" with passive, but there is nothing spiritual about passivity. Taking is where you learn that.

Integrity. The unexpected quality that develops from Taking is integrity. You acknowledge that there is something you want to do and see how your actions affect others. You stop trying to use giving to get something you are not admitting that you want. Essentially, you stop lying. When you own your desire to touch, you learn to own other desires as well. You start to take responsibility for yourself in a real and profound way. That is integrity, and it creates freedom.

As I said in chapter 18, I have come to see that if there is something you want that involves another person, the only thing to do that has integrity is to ask for it and respect the answer.

SOCIAL IMPLICATIONS

> *(Story told by a fox) With Chikens, we have a Super Fare Deal, which is: they make the egs, we take the egs, they make more egs. And sometimes may even eat a live Chiken, shud that Chiken consent to be eaten by us, threw faling to run away upon are approach. Not Sly at all. Very strat forward.*
>
> —George Saunders

How does Taking show up in our social interactions? There's receiving a clear gift of using your neighbor's truck. There's the muddy zone of taking up space on the subway or taking up all the attention in a room. Where Taking really shines though is in the shadow of it. Our nation is built on the shadow of Taking. I noted earlier how we stole land, labor, and lives and still overthrow democratically elected governments to install dictators so we can have cheap bananas. Essentially, we take what we want. Then we cover it up because we know it's wrong and describe it to sound like we are Serving.

Why we need Taking in the world. It's the integrity we need. When we learn that when we can acknowledge what we want, ask for it, and respect the answer, we stop manipulating and stealing. When we can't acknowledge Taking, we end up in the shadow of it. It's true in bed, in life, and in international politics. We need Taking so we can stop stealing and so that when we Serve, it becomes real and not a cover-up. We need to understand consent and feel it in our bones so stealing and war become impossible.

SUMMARY: THE TAKING QUADRANT

Taking combines Doing and Receiving. When you ask permission to touch someone the way you want to and they agree to allow you to do that, you are in the Taking Quadrant. Taking de-conflates doing and giving.

Take-Allow is created by the agreement. You say, "May I...?" and they say, "Yes, you may." Without an agreement, Take-Allow does not happen.

The most important thing to know about Taking is that it is receiving a gift, freely given, with a full heart. The gift is access. Taking is not stealing, taking away from, or taking advantage of.

As a gift, it is based on what you want and what the Allower is okay with, not the other way around.

The essence of Taking is acting for your own benefit.

You are doing two things at once. 1) Respecting the limits of your Allower, and 2) within those limits, putting your desires first.

To experience Taking, two things must be in place first: 1) the ability to take in sensation with your hands and experience it as enjoyable, and 2) permission of the person you want to touch.

In Taking, you discover that in order to touch someone, you don't need to give. What you do need is their permission.

Shadow. Acting for your own benefit but without consent: stealing, using, perpetrating, assault, exploitation, rape, war.

The spiritual principle of Taking is integrity. You acknowledge that there is something you want to do and stop pretending that all your doing is for someone else.

CHAPTER 21

The Allowing Quadrant

I and I wanna spread the news
That if it feels this good getting used
Oh you just keep on using me until you use me up
Until you use me up.
—Bill Withers

You lie draped over the lap of your partner. Their hands are on your back, exploring, taking in your shapes and textures. You would rather have their hands on your legs, but this is your gift to them, and you give it with a full heart. It's a curious feeling, this kind of surrender, and it's possible because you know you can say "Stop" at any time. Still, it feels so good you almost forget you are giving a gift and begin to feel like you are receiving one. Their hands change, doing some little squeezing thing that doesn't feel so good. It's not bad; it's just not great. But it's not for you and it's within the limits of what you are willing to give, so you go with it. At some point, you remember that this is a gift for them, and your heart opens up with generosity and appreciation for being able to give this gift. You are in the Allowing Quadrant.

When someone asks you for permission to touch you the way they want and you agree to that, you are in Allowing. Allowing combines done-to and giving. The gift you are giving is access to you. In Allowing, the action moves from them to you, but the gift moves from you to them.

While Taking is hard for almost everyone, Allowing is all over the map. It can feel easy and natural, a little tenuous or worrisome, or seriously daunting. That range of comfort depends on the degree of confidence that you have a choice about whether and how you are touched. That confidence is built first on knowing you have a choice and second on having the skill to exercise that choice. That is highly variable, hence the variability of feelings about Allowing.

To the degree you hope someone else takes that responsibility for you, and we all do it to some degree, you will be on guard against what may be coming next or what you may have to confront. To the degree you take responsibility, Allowing can be luxurious, delightful, rich, relaxing, and often pleasurable.

WHAT IT'S NOT

Allowing is giving a gift. It is not giving away something because you don't know how not to, you don't know there are any other options, you assume that's the way it is, or it feels hopeless. It is not putting up with. It is not stuffing yourself down to get through something. It's not enduring, placating, capitulating, acquiescing, or submitting. It's not being passive. Allowing is never about something you believe you *should* be okay with, because, you know, everyone else is okay with that, aren't they?

WHAT IT IS

Allowing is one half of a dynamic in which someone asks you for permission to do something they want to do (that affects you) and you say yes. It is also an inner experience of empowered choice and surrender. The most important thing to understand about Allowing is that it is a gift—not something you should give, but something within the limits of what you are happy to give. When you have the skills to not submit, then you can surrender.

Allowing is a form of giving, so we're back to two things at once: 1) you set aside how you might prefer to be touched, and 2) you stay responsible for your limits. Sometimes the aha is that you can do both at the same time. To experience Allowing, you *must* do both at the same time.

The essence of Allowing is allowing others to take action for their own benefit, even though it affects you, and having a limit to what you are okay with. The heart of Allowing is surrender. Harry Faddis, who invented the Three Minute Game, describes it like this: "We humans have power; it's part of our nature. Because of that, we also have the desire to give it up, to hand it to someone else for a time." Allowing creates a context in which you can.

What it can't do. Allowing cannot substitute for Accepting no matter how enjoyable it is. You need time in both.

The challenges. Allowing combines done-to and giving, so it carries the challenges of both. In the Done-to Half, there is the tendency to think you are supposed to feel good about whatever is done to you. In the Giving Half, there is the tendency to forget to respect your own limits. This makes for a potent combination to make you feel like you're supposed to be okay with anything. You're not. The challenge is to notice what you are genuinely happy to give and to honor that.

LIMITATIONS AND LIMITS

Limitation: Something you are unable to do, a condition of limited ability, a defect or a failing. For example, "He knew his limitations better than he knew his worth."

Limit: What you are willing or not willing to participate in or the extent to which you are willing to give or allow. "I'm willing to give this much but not more," or "Yes, you can explore my legs, up to here," or "No, I'm not okay with that."

The distinction is crucial. If you confuse them, you think that having a limit is a failing or a defect. That is a dangerous idea. You think that you would allow that thing if only you were more enlightened or adventurous, and it sets you up to push yourself to allow more than you are genuinely happy to give.

REVIEW: FINDING ALLOWING

Detailed steps for finding Allowing are in Lesson 2. This is a review.

Like Taking, Allowing can be experienced with any body part, but it is easiest to learn by starting with giving access to some part that feels fairly neutral and not too intimate. For most people, the hands work for that (and forearms, if you like). The hands usually feel a little less intimate than say, the back, legs, or face, though it varies by person and culture.

Your job in Allowing is to tend to your limits. I used to say, "You get to have a limit." What is true is that you do in fact *have* a limit, and it's your job to notice what it is and communicate it. You may not hit it in the lesson because it is already limited, but you do have it. Starting with options to include the rest of the body would be much harder.

Tending to your limits happens in a couple of places. First, when making the agreement, pause and notice whether that is something you can give with a full heart, and be true to that. Then second, when they are feeling your hand, if something is uncomfortable, speak up. "Ouch, please don't bend it that way," or "Wait, I need to move over this way." What makes it a gift is not that you try to make yourself feel good about it. It is that you choose what you are willing to give and what you are not.

It's okay to enjoy it. When Allowing clicks, you notice that you have a limit and are confident that you can speak up as needed. You notice that though you are the one being touched, you are not receiving a gift; you are giving one.

REVIEW: EXPLORING ALLOWING

Detailed steps for exploring Allowing are in Lab 1. This is a review.

What shows up when exploring Allowing is the principle of Adapting Ourselves. You will tend to think you should be okay with anything and try to feel good about it even if you don't. You will discover that instead of trying to change how you feel, you can honestly notice what you are happy to give and what you are not and be true to that, which is usually much harder.

The Intensity Factor will show up. As you get excited or the Taker moves faster, it becomes easier to slip back into your default, which is going along with something and trying to be okay with it. This happens in the agreement making (*I should be okay with that. Why aren't I?*) and in the doing when you slide into enduring and don't value your limits.

Becoming trustworthy is another theme. It sounds lovely to trust your Taker, but you find that you actually need to trust yourself, that you will speak up as needed. As you gain the skill to become trustworthy to yourself, you automatically trust yourself and then relax and enjoy the surprises. To the degree you take responsibility for your limits, you will naturally relax. Like the other quadrants, it's easiest to gain skills if you expand your options gradually. Your trustworthiness increases, and because of that, you naturally become interested in more things.

Ninety percent of the success of your Allowing experience is in making the agreement. When you slow down enough to be true to yourself in setting your limits, the experience of it will follow easily. If the doing part is worrisome or you can't relax, it's because there is some limit you have not yet spoken. Come back to the agreement.

We're back to the questions. The question to ask yourself is not: *Why can't I give this?* It is: *What is it that I can give with a full heart?* Listen to that, no matter how small it seems. There is *something* you're happy to give. What is that something?

THE SECRET TO EASE AND JOY IN ALLOWING

The secret to ease and joy in Allowing is noticing that you have a limit to what you are willing to have done to you and taking full responsibility for it, which means speaking it. Once that is clear, the rest of Allowing falls into place. Within those limits, you become generous, and Allowing is a joy to give.

THE EXPERIENCE OF ALLOWING

There is a kind of affirmation in Allowing. It can confirm what you have felt before but didn't understand (that this dynamic exists). The mood of it will depend largely on the Taking partner. You are following, not leading. There's a huge range: the mood can be meditative, tender, cozy, silly, or sexy. It can be like a couple of kids roughhousing, or it can become lusty and passionate. It often feels very intimate or tenderhearted. Sometimes you are really on your toes; it takes your full attention. At other times (if their hands are moving slowly for a long time), you can enter a gentle trance-like state.

It can be challenging. There will be times when you feel self-conscious, embarrassed, or exposed. Your partner is going to notice your wrinkles, your cellulite, and your hair—where there is too much or not enough. You will finally get the adoration you deserve in spite of all that. Your awareness of how much your lover enjoys your body will give you a new opportunity to appreciate it yourself. You will see yourself with new eyes. The touch itself is often the best ever. It's relaxed and sensual, it's not going anywhere, and there is no goal or mission. It's an easy doorway into the present moment. You find out that you yourself are enough of a gift without having to produce anything.

Allowing is the home of surrender. There's nothing to do, figure out, or micromanage. You get to stop being in charge of what happens. You have a choice about it; you just don't have to orchestrate it. It can get erotic, and you get to ride your partner's desire. You get to be surprised. You get to play with power and surrender. Sometimes just being in the quadrant at all is a turn-on; you can be the star in your own bodice-ripper novel!

What you learn over time. There is a clarity that comes with learning Allowing. When done-to and receive are conflated, being done to is "supposed to" be for you, and you try to make the best of it, but it doesn't feel right. Allowing clarifies that, because in Allowing, it isn't for you. This is often a big relief. You find that you can tell when it's for you and when it's not. You learn to recognize the muddy edge where you are tolerating or enduring. Tolerating becomes annoying and dissatisfying, and giving becomes sweet.

Over time, you gain the skills to speak up for yourself. This lets you become more flexible and generous, both in this context and in life. Because you trust yourself, your limits expand. You experience deeper states of surrender. You may notice that this experience of physical surrender can be a window into mystical states. You get a glimpse of surrender to life, God, or the universe.

THE EROTIC ELEMENTS OF ALLOWING

Being uncovered, seen, admired, wanted, looked at, really closely—I mean really closely. The shame of exposure is overridden only by the glory of it.

—*A student*

The very act of surrender can carry an erotic charge. For many, it is a central theme, and just being in the quadrant at all is a turn-on. It's the land of "Tie me to the bedpost, honey!" Take-Allow is the theme of romance novels, in which the (always) beautiful and voluptuous heroine is ravished (only in the most sensual way, of course), and she finally (gasp!) surrenders.

There is a certain affirmation to being wanted and enjoyed, which can be deliciously slow and sensual or more robust. There is an exquisite state in which the Taker is moving slowly, and it allows you to relax to a greater degree, and you melt open.

GENDER AND ALLOWING

We defined gender in chapter 6. Your experience of Allowing has nothing to do with gender. Still, our conditioning about our genders creates some common themes.

Men. Many men have never felt enjoyed and desired, indeed, don't know they *are* enjoyable or desirable, so Allowing can be a revelation. Men often have discomfort with not being in charge. I imagine this is partly because they are used to doing everything. I think it's also partly because not being in charge means you are vulnerable to new feelings, which is one reason you keep doing-doing-doing. On the other hand, it can be a huge relief to not be in charge. For many men, being dominated and used is a terrific turn-on. Some of the highest paid sex workers are those who guide men (and others) into states of deep surrender.

Women. Almost all women have felt used at some point and have had the experience that their body is for someone else's consumption. One student said, "As I was socialized as a female, the idea of having boundaries is transgressive." At the same time, many feel undesirable because of the ridiculously narrow range of media images of beauty.

Allowing is what women are assumed (and supposed) to be doing. What you "give" in sex is access to your body with the idea that you are supposed to find the biggest satisfaction here. What if you don't? You are not a real woman, not feminine enough? Not surrendering properly? There is a terrible pressure put on women about this, with the result that women get better at ignoring themselves, putting up with what is already unpleasant, and blaming themselves for it. If her partner is a man, it is likely that he is trying to get the technique right and she is trying to make him feel good about himself. Nobody's real desire is there, so there is nothing to surrender *to*. She gives herself, but something is missing, no one knows what, and the blaming goes in all directions.

I was once asked, "Do women like to be ravished?" There's an interesting assumption that all women like the same things, which is ridiculous. It depends on which woman, when, by whom, and how. Some women like it, some don't. Some men do, some don't. Some nonbinary people like it, some don't. Many people like it sometimes and not other times.

Every person has the capacity to experience and enjoy Allowing, just like the other three quadrants, and deserves the opportunity to explore it. Some will be relieved, some will be challenged, and many will be both. For some, it will be an interesting dip, and for others, it will be a major erotic theme. The factor is not sex or gender. It's our inherent predilections, our childhood experiences, the level of confidence that we have a choice about it, and the degree to which we have become trustworthy to ourselves. It's all over the map for every gender.

THE SHADOW OF ALLOWING

The shadow of the Allowing Quadrant is allowing others to act for their own benefit, in ways that affect you, without taking responsibility for setting a limit, or having tried to set a limit but having it transgressed without your consent. It's having things done to you that you did not agree to. It includes being the victim of a crime, like assault, rape, or theft, or the victim of social structures like having to tolerate mistreatment because to object would be dangerous, or having your native lands colonized. In the more personal realm, the shadow also includes our ability to be a doormat—always buffeted by everyone else's desires, putting up with, tolerating, and enduring. You don't know how *not* to go along, you don't know what else to do, and you might not notice it until you've been in it a while.

Another shadow is passivity. Passivity is "too much" Allowing: the inability to take action or make choices or avoiding the risk of making choices. Passivity leads to resentment and despair. When we try to get others to make our choices for us, we set ourselves up to resent the choices they make.

The muddy zone. The Allowing Quadrant has a large muddy zone around it, which is the mirror image to the muddy zone around Taking: not saying no but not saying yes either, or saying yes when you don't mean it, or remaining silent. I'm not talking about situations that are clearly outside consent like coercion, assault, or rape. I'm talking about the muddy area in which you don't notice the choice you have or don't exercise it. The muddy zone is the "Well, sorta, I guess so" zone. It's "Well, I don't have any reason to say no, so I guess I'll say yes." You don't realize that you don't need a reason.

The muddy zone is not a gift, so there is no joy in it. I have never met anyone who has not spent some time in the muddy zone. I certainly have spent time there (a fair bit, actually). What you are learning here is how to recognize it, which is one of the benefits of the Wheel, and starting to recognize it will create some discomfort. It helps to give yourself a little compassion. We have all done this.

There is a long continuum between violent assault, in which you go along to save your life, and messing around in a way that doesn't inspire you. Your partner is moving forward, not noticing that you are not, and things happen. You haven't said no or "Stop" or "Let's do something different" or even "Softer, please." Why? 1) They didn't ask you, 2) they did ask, but you're so in the habit of not rocking the boat that you said yes anyway, or 3) it's too hard to speak up.

If you speak up, if you actually say, "No" or "Stop," you may feel shame, fear, or guilt, so you have to make a choice. You do what makes you feel shame and fear, or you go along with what is boring, unpleasant, uninspiring, or even awful. At least you don't have to feel that fear and shame right now, though you probably will later.

We endure things because it feels safer than confronting them. We lie because it feels safer than the truth. Sometimes it is safer, and sometimes it just feels like it. Sometimes fear of confrontation keeps us hiding all our lives, but it's not sustainable. Eventually we dry up or blow up. Or we endure because we believe the activity is more important than how we feel about it. We believe our feelings don't count and whatever is happening must continue. We ignore ourselves.

Somewhere between the muddy zone and the shadow of Allowing is overwhelm. Our nervous system stores our experiences of having to go along with things that were done to us (Lab 1, in Adapting Ourselves), especially in situations that feel traumatic. When later confronted with anything that feels like pressure, coercion, or violence, we freeze and go along. It's not a matter of *if* we have a freeze point; it's how much and what kind of pressure it takes to reach it. What seems easy to one person seems hopeless to someone else and vice versa.

In some ways, the muddy zone is worse than being outside the circle. It's deadening. It kills desire and passion, it breeds resentment and boredom, and eventually you give up. Many people spend their whole lives here. If you feel resentment, boredom, or annoyance, it's a signal you could be here in the muddy zone. Ask yourself, *What did I not say no to?* or *What did I want that I didn't ask for?*

WHEN ALLOWING IS HARD

> *I couldn't say stop, so I went soft and knew it would be over soon.*
> —*A student*

What makes Allowing hard is not being able to tend to your limits. When Allowing is hard, you have two options: give in or avoid it altogether.

When you give in, you tolerate everything. You feel like you are giving all the time and feel used and victimized by everything and everybody. You don't trust anyone, because you don't trust yourself. You blame others and resent their taking action. You feel like everyone is using you.

The other option is to avoid Allowing by staying in the active quadrants. You try to control everything so that you don't come close to your limits, because you can't hold them, which makes you tense and guarded. We try to control when we are afraid of change.

In a session:

Karl: I want control over my environment.
Me: Why?
Karl: To be safe. I can't be sure I can keep me safe.
Me: What would it take to keep yourself safe?
Karl: Not push the edge by opening up the environment—and having a body guard.
Me: What would they do?
Karl: Stop people from thinking they could touch me.
Me: Thinking it or doing it?
Karl: Doing it. I have so often been touched by people I didn't want to touch me. I need to get over it, I guess.
Me: What else would keep you safe?
Karl: Me telling them not to and if they do, telling them to stop.
Me: In your life you have reached an equilibrium where you have just enough control that you feel safe. Now you want to expand your environment, so you are going to notice where it is you don't feel safe. That is the signal that you can't say no in that situation or fear that you can't. Listen to that fear. It's telling you that you need something. What is it you need?
Karl: The skill of saying no and enforcing it.

Another person said, "I was mad at my partner for always taking up space and doing what they wanted, and I felt used. When I experienced

Allowing, I realized that it's because I was never saying what I wanted or never saying no. It wasn't them at all. It was me."

Allowing may seem like an easy way to go through life with less stress—unless that's your only available mode. Then everyone else has to take your share of initiative and risk. Being stuck in Allowing often reflects a fear of Taking. It can also be used to avoid the risk of making decisions.

WHEN ALLOWING IS EASY

In bed, you stay out of the muddy zone and are genuine and truthful in your permission. You change your mind as needed and don't judge your partner's desire. Because you trust yourself, you are able to melt into it. You have a relaxed flow, and you're generous and in touch with the joy of being desired. You are able to do nothing, to rest. You sometimes find yourself in deep states of surrender and bliss. You have a relaxed freedom to respond and play.

In life, you are comfortable in a wide range of situations. You enjoy surprises and are flexible. You respect others' desires without feeling you have to meet them. You are aware of your limits and don't apologize for them. You stand up to power.

The more trust you have in your skills to take care of yourself, the less interest or need you have to control someone else's behavior. You have a relaxed acceptance for others' interests and desires and are able to step aside and let them choose for themselves.

SPIRITUAL IMPLICATIONS

The ability to choose to not be in charge and to make that choice willingly is at the center of many spiritual traditions. The Baha'i faith talks about "radiant acquiescence" as surrender to a higher wisdom that is not begrudging but gladly and joyfully giving over your life to divine guidance.

In the quadrants, surrender is to a person for a specific time and within specific limits. In a spiritual relationship with God? I don't know. It's not an image I use. I do know this: find surrender in your body by taking full responsibility for yourself, and then decide what it means in the larger picture.

The experience of giving of yourself instead of giving your actions touches on the spiritual. You don't have to produce in order to be of value; your very being is of value. I have seen people have a profound aha moment about this by being in the Allowing Quadrant.

Another way to feel surrender in the body is with a moving meditation in which you let your limbs move and flow like seaweed or a free-form dance in which you let yourself move without a plan or steps. These experiences can feel like Allowing and are often ecstatic; they create an altered state that many people call spiritual.

SOCIAL IMPLICATIONS

The most common way people give up their power is by thinking they don't have any.

—Alice Walker

Once you start to speak, people will yell at you. They will interrupt you, put you down and suggest it's personal. And the world won't end. And the speaking will get easier and easier. And you will find that you have fallen in love with your own vision, which you may never have realized you had ... And at last you'll know with surpassing certainty that only one thing is more frightening than speaking your truth. And that is not speaking.

—Audré Lorde

We need a certain amount of Allowing in our lives—the ability to let people live their own lives without trying to control their choices. On the other hand, the outer line of Allowing is "This far and no farther." This is the line where you stand up to power, where you stop allowing abuse and injustice—in environmental degradation, civil rights, and equality. You speak up for yourself and for those who can't. It's where you say, "Stop. You are not allowed to take advantage of these people."

This is also where the muddy zone and the shadow show up. We assume that things are the way they are and that we can do nothing about it, and this belief is so deep we don't notice our acquiescence.

SUMMARY: THE ALLOWING QUADRANT

Allowing combines Done-to and Giving. When someone asks you for permission to do something they want to do (that affects you) and you say yes, you are in the Allowing Quadrant. Allowing de-conflates Done-to and Receiving.

Take-Allow is created by the agreement. They say, "May I...?" and you say, "Yes, you may." Without an agreement, Allowing does not exist.

Allowing is giving a gift; the gift is access. As is true in all forms of Giving, what you prefer doesn't matter; your limits matter absolutely.

The essence of Allowing is allowing others to take action for their own benefit and setting a limit: "This far and no farther."

You are doing two things at once: 1) setting aside how you might prefer to be touched, and 2) keeping responsibility for yourself and your limits.

Having a choice. To enjoy being touched, you must know you have a choice about whether and how you are touched and gain the skill to exercise that choice. To that degree, Allowing is easy, fun and flexible.

What you discover in Allowing is that you do have a limit to how you are willing to be touched, and the more responsibility you take for that limit, the more joy there is in giving the gift of Allowing.

The social responsibility of Allowing is being able to stand up against abuses of power, both on your own behalf and on behalf of others.

The shadow of Allowing. Tolerating, enduring, putting up with, passivity, the doormat, and the victim.

What Allowing can't do for you. Allowing cannot substitute for Accepting no matter how wonderful it feels or how "tuned in" the Taker.

If Allowing is particularly difficult or intimidating, always start with Accepting instead, so you learn to be completely in charge of how you are touched.

THE TAKE-ALLOW DYNAMIC

The Take-Allow dynamic is rich, fun, sensual, challenging, and liberating. Of the two dynamics, it is the more misunderstood and suspect but still yearned for. It can be confusing and elusive, and rediscovering it is profoundly liberating. The primary factor is the gift. The Allower gives the gift, and the Taker receives it. The gift is access.

Serve-Accept can be found in many situations including massage, medical care, or helping your friend move his piano. Not so with the Take-Allow dynamic. There are few situations where we welcome it. We allow small children to climb on us and stick their fingers in our ears, or we nurse an infant. Other than that, in the case of touch, it's pretty much only between lovers. We instinctively feel this, as it tends to feel intimate. You might recall from Lesson 2: "This feels incredibly intimate, but it's just his hand. How can that be?"

There are some cultural references to Take-Allow, but they are mostly negative: groping, using, or feeling up. There are also references to the erotic power of it—ravishing or being carried away by desire. So we have this dynamic that we recognize intuitively and are both repulsed by and drawn to. What we don't understand is how it works.

(A note about the word "ravish." I have said the quintessential example of the Take-Allow dynamic is ravishing. Until I looked it up in the dictionary. There it says that the archaic use of the word is to seize or carry away, implying rape. Not what we're going for here. The newer use of the word is to desire a passionate consensual interaction. What I am trying to say by "ravish" is the Taker actively and passionately taking their own pleasure. It's "I can't wait to get my hands on you!")

Take-Allow and desire. Serve-Accept is based on the desires of the person being done to; Take-Allow is based on the desires of the person doing. Take-Allow doesn't just make room for the Taker's desire—it can't happen without it. With our lovers, we *want* their desires to show up. Without their desire, something vital is missing.

The many moods of Take-Allow. Not all Take-Allow is erotic or between lovers. Here are some other examples: You are a sculptor and working on a sculpture of a hand. You ask to explore your friend's hand to get a sense of how it's made, and they allow you to do that. You are walking along, have a fright, and reach over to hold your friend's hand for support. You are learning to braid hair and ask your friend if you can practice with theirs. You borrow your friend's truck for some errands, or at their invitation go over and use their hot tub, or pick the pears in their yard. You will find a full range here: curiosity, sensuality, lighthearted, silly, or a childlike sense of wonder and play.

Misunderstood. Here is an example of how Take-Allow is referred to but not understood. Certain writers encourage (heterosexual) men to recover the "manly" take-charge impulse and women to recover the "womanly" surrender impulse, saying that this is what is missing for so many couples. What they are reaching for is the Take-Allow dynamic; they just don't know what it is.

There are a few problems with this. One is they mistakenly think it has to do with gender. They assume that men are this and women are that. Sometimes they are, and sometimes not. This is the way of humans. The other problem is that though it's a nice idea to recover that dynamic, how does one go about it exactly? To recover Taking, you have to access your desire to do, and you have to learn consent skills. The consent skills come first so that you can access your desire and trust it. If you are trying to recover your lust but you don't understand your partner's limits, you are creating a problem!

At the same time, society encourages women to "surrender" more. The problem is that for people who were raised as girls and taught to endure, it's easy to take "surrender" to mean ignore yourself and go along with whatever. If you don't understand the difference between surrender and tolerating, enduring and giving up, you are also creating a problem!

So you end up with one person (usually the man) charging ahead trying to *ravish* but not understanding consent and the other person (usually a woman) going along with something unpleasant and wondering what is wrong with her because she can't "surrender" better.

If you don't know how to Take, you can't fake it. If you don't know how to Allow, you can't enjoy it. This has nothing to do with what gender you are. When you understand consent, Take-Allow becomes clear and liberating. If you don't understand consent, the whole thing is a big confusing, suspicious mess—but still compelling.

Dominance and submission. Take-Allow is a good place to get a peek at playing with dominance and submission. You might find that you like being taken and giving up power for a time or that you like taking charge, having power over your partner for a time. It's a wonderful place to play. The key is in making your agreement. Online I offer some notes on this dynamic. Lots of fun!

CHAPTER 22

The Accepting Quadrant

You have an earthy heart
But your hands are from heaven.
—Pablo Neruda

Asking for help doesn't mean that we are weak or incompetent.
It usually indicates an advanced level of honesty and intelligence.
—Anne Wilson Schaef

You have your head in your partner's lap, and they are scratching your scalp, just as you have asked. You want a little less massage and a little more fingernail, so you ask for that. "Mmm, yes, just right." A shiver runs up your spine, and you let yourself shake. That strikes you as funny, so you laugh, and that makes you realize how safe you feel, and that makes you thankful. You ask them to hold their hands still, and they do that, and you breathe a sigh of relief. For some reason, their hands start moving again, but you're not interested in that. You don't feel like talking, so you reach up and hold their hands still. You worry for a moment that you're being too picky but then remember it's for you and relax about that. After a while, you open your eyes, look into theirs, and say, "Thank you." You are in the Accepting Quadrant.

When you ask someone to do something for you and they agree to do so, you are in the Accepting Quadrant. Accepting combines done-to and receiving. The gift you are receiving is their action. The action moves from them to you, and the gift moves the same direction. It's for you.

Many people call this quadrant "Receiving," but the Taking Quadrant is also a form of receiving, hence giving it another name: Accepting. Calling this quadrant "Receiving" creates problems. When receiving is conflated with done-to and if done-to means tolerate and settle for, Accepting comes to be equated with tolerating and settling for. This is exactly where most people get lost in this quadrant, thinking there is something they are supposed to want or like even if they don't.

The crux of this quadrant is to distinguish between what you're okay with and what you want, and the aha is often that *it is possible* to be touched the way you want, that such a thing exists in the known universe. Combining done-to and receiving can be particularly potent, because receiving is inherently vulnerable, and done-to tends to feel vulnerable. Because of that, this quadrant can bring up deep feelings and take you into experiences that are especially rich and healing.

WHAT IT'S NOT

The Accepting Quadrant is not going along with something that is happening, that someone else seems to want to happen, or even what you think you are supposed to want to happen. It's never about getting a better attitude about whatever you are going along with. It's not about making yourself like something more or making yourself more thankful or appreciative, no matter how generous and sincere your giver. The myth of the "good receiver" is that you appreciate whatever is given to you or done to you, accept it graciously, and don't ask for too much. This myth teaches you to ignore yourself and try to want what you don't want. Accepting is not "letting someone give to you." Neither is it holding someone responsible for getting it right as if it's their job to provide you with pleasure and they are supposed to know how.

It's not a feeling of enjoyment or gratitude. Gratitude is one of the signs of receiving, but we can feel gratitude in any quadrant or no quadrant. It's the same with enjoyment; it's available in any quadrant, so enjoying something and feeling thankful for it does not indicate that you are in one of the Receiving Quadrants. What indicates you are in one of the Receiving Quadrants is your agreement. Did you ask for something, and did the other person agree to it?

WHAT IT IS

The Accepting Quadrant is one half of a common dynamic. It is receiving a particular kind of gift: the action of another. It may be a favor, help with something, or some touch you want. It is a gift of time and attention plus the action. The Serve-Accept dynamic is created by your agreement: You say, "Will you…?" and they say, "Yes, I will."

It is also an inner experience. As a form of receiving, this still applies: sometimes it is the gift itself that satisfies, as when they scratch the exact right place on your back. Other times, it is the fact that they care enough about you to set aside what they prefer that touches your heart and is most meaningful.

Also as a form of receiving, we're back to two things at once: 1) putting yourself first, and 2) respecting the limits of your giver. Neither one alone is enough. Putting yourself first without respecting the limits of your giver is not Accepting; it's stealing or coercing. Respecting the limits of your giver without putting yourself first is, well, nothing. Although we can all be selfish and pushy, in my work with touch and sex, I have found that for most people, putting themselves first is more difficult.

Vulnerable and wonderful. Accepting is inherently vulnerable and wonderful. It's vulnerable because you are exposing your desires, perhaps your body, probably your pleasure. It's wonderful because it's what you want. We're back here again: if it's not wonderful, it's not because you are not receiving well or because you don't like this quadrant. It's because it's not what you want, or it's more of it than you want. When you have what you actually want, enjoying it is automatic.

The word. Like Taking, Accepting has other meanings that can be problematic. The word "accepting" can be used to mean tolerating something unpleasant but inevitable as in "accepting your lot in life" or "accepting" some unwanted touch. I'm not using this meaning. I'm talking about the Accepting Quadrant, which is about receiving what you want.

Accepting is:

"Honey, will you stop by the cleaners on the way home and pick up
my jacket?"…"Sure!" …"Thanks!"

"Oy, my back hurts. Will you walk on it for me?"…"Okay!"…
"Thanks!"

"Hey Grandpa, would you drive me over to Frankie's?"…"Sure!"…
"Thanks!"

"Can you and Fred come over and help me move my piano? Free
beer all around!"…"We can come on Friday; does that work?"…
"Yes, thanks!"

"What an awful day. Would you hold me a while?"…"Yes, I will."…
"Thanks!"

"Slower, honey, yes, right there, don't stop!"…"Thank you. That was
fabulous."

Or you can accept an offer:

"You've had a long day! Would you like a foot rub?"…"Yes, please!"

"The kids tell me you've been sick. I'm bringing soup over"…
"Thank you!"

"Would you like a hand with that?"…"Yes, please!"

The challenges of Accepting. Like Taking, Accepting can be hard to
find because of our habits. Often it takes some real attention to slowing
down and getting clear. Accepting is also challenging because it is inherently vulnerable and tends to bring up feelings we may not be comfortable
with. I have seen, and shed, many tears of relief on the massage table.

REVIEW: FINDING ACCEPTING

Detailed steps for finding Accepting are in Lesson 3. This is a review.

When experimenting with finding Accepting, most people will tend to
go for what sounds acceptable or reasonable or what they don't mind. The
aha of Accepting comes when you slow down enough to notice what it is
you actually want instead of what you think you are supposed to want and
ask for that. The crux is noticing that there is a difference between what you
want and what you don't mind. Once you do that, the rest falls into place.

You cannot learn Accepting by having someone else choose for you, no matter how much you enjoy what they have chosen. To access Accepting, you must make a request. As long as someone else is choosing, you will tend to adapt to it in some way. In finding Accepting, nothing happens until you request it, which also begins the process in you. As you found in Taking, there is often an aha moment when you realize that this is for you and a moment of tenderheartedness, gratitude, or relief.

REVIEW: EXPLORING ACCEPTING

Detailed steps for exploring Accepting are in Lab 2. This is a review.

In the lab, the options expand, so you get to ask for all kinds of things and fine-tune your noticing, trusting, valuing, and communicating. How accurately can you notice what you want? How specifically can you request it? How well can you trust yourself to not settle for "good enough"? The tendency to adapt to what is happening (Adapting Ourselves) will continue to arise, and you will get to ask yourself, *What do I want right now?* Exploring Accepting is coming back to that question again and again.

Another principle that shows up is Follow the Pleasure. Instead of telling the pleasure where you think it should be, follow it where it already is. That applies first when choosing, as you choose what sounds great instead of what you think you should like, and then it applies in the middle of the experience by changing your mind and deciding what to do with feelings that arise.

Another theme is becoming trustworthy to yourself. When you wait until you hear the inner *Hell, yes!* you learn that you can be trusted to not abandon yourself. Based on this trust of yourself, what interests you will naturally expand.

The trap of Accepting is performing your pleasure for the Server, acting like you feel more pleasure than you do. This can be difficult to stop, which is a testament to how deeply it's embedded. As you grow to trust the process, you expand your vision of what it is possible to ask for and how to trust your turn and make good use of it.

The possibilities in this quadrant are profound, nourishing, healing, and enjoyable.

THE SECRET TO EASE AND JOY IN ACCEPTING

The first thing is to slow down so you notice what it is you want instead of what you think you are supposed to want. When it's what you actually want, the enjoying of it is automatic. Then like all forms of receiving, you want to know that you are not taking advantage of anyone. As you develop consent skills, you become trustworthy and then you begin to trust yourself. Then you relax and enjoy the gifts given to you.

THE EXPERIENCE OF ACCEPTING

Accepting is the opportunity to attend to your enjoyment with nothing else to do. It can be tenderhearted with relief, misty eyes, self-acceptance, or gratitude. It can be rowdy, playful, silly, sexy, and sensual. It can be all about you, where you drift off, unaware of your partner, into trance-like states, or it may be very much about your partner and the gift. It may be the dynamic itself that is the richest.

You have the challenges and vulnerabilities of both receiving and done-to, which is a particularly potent combination. It taps into early childhood experiences of being cared for well or poorly. It taps into the spiritual question of worthiness. Your desires and body are revealed, and you are being seen in pleasure. You can't hide behind your partner's body, desires, or arousal. It can bring up unfinished business with your partner. Being the center of loving attention is not always easy, and pleasure may bring up self-doubt (whether you are enough, too much, deserving, selfish, spiritual enough, etc.). There may be moments of guilt, shame, awkwardness, and exposure as well as moments of prolonged arousal and bliss. The emotions can intensify, so you get to the edge of your carrying capacity.

What you learn over time. Accepting teaches you, first of all, that it exists. It is possible to have someone set aside what they want and touch you exactly the way you want. This can be life changing. You learn to notice what you want. It shows you where you have been tolerating and settling for crumbs. You stop settling for whatever you think you are supposed to want and expand your creativity into what it is possible to ask for.

You get better at bringing your attention to your experience. You become able to ask for things that are tenderhearted or erotically edgy. You expand your ability to be with feelings of vulnerability and gratitude. You explore touch that has nothing to do with sex and find that it offers a depth that surprises you. Being seen in pleasure helps you accept your own eroticism and heal your shame. You learn to love your body not for what it looks like (or you fear it does) but for how it feels. You learn to become relaxed and aroused at the same time, and you become intimate with your sensation and pleasure and your emotional response to it.

It teaches you that others are glad to give to you. You get good at asking clearly and without pressure so you can respect the limits of your giver. You learn to appreciate the fact that we need each other. The ease in asking will spread to the rest of your relationships, and you will naturalize asking for what you want. "Honey, will you scratch my back/help me carry these boxes/kiss me right here/hold me?"

THE EROTIC ELEMENTS OF ACCEPTING

One obvious application of the Serve-Accept dynamic is erotic massage. This can be profoundly healing, not to mention fun. One way to play with this is to settle into the sensation and make it all about you, so you "bliss out." Some people fear that this will exclude your partner, but I have found the opposite to be true. Assisting each other to enter profound states of pleasure is very connecting. Another way to play with erotic massage is to keep eye contact and focus on the communication. This plays with another aspect of connection. Either of these tends to make you notice your vulnerability, which can be a profound door to intimacy.

Another way to play with Accepting is as part of a power dynamic, being served by a submissive. How bossy can you get? This could include touch or other acts of service.

Why do you need it in your sex life? So you stop your compulsive giving and discover that you are worthy of pleasure just because you're you. It helps you learn to locate your experience in your own body instead of living vicariously through your partner.

ABOUT THE FEELINGS: WHY IS IT SO HARD?

The Accepting Quadrant shares much with the Taking Quadrant. It's hard!—and it's joyful, liberating, and a big relief. Like the Taking Quadrant, there is a range of how deeply you have to go into it before self-doubt, confusion, shame, guilt, or fear hits you. For some, it's right away. Others sail into it with ease, but when they reach a certain level of excitement or tenderness, it's suddenly difficult. Know that Accepting is inherently vulnerable and challenging, so it's not just you.

There are a whole host of reasons why the feelings here are especially challenging. We have talked about these.

Asking for what you want. This is always risky because you reveal your desires, and that shows you how you feel about your desire, this particular desire, or any desire at all. There's a whole swamp right there! Self-doubt, shame, guilt, or worry about being too much or not enough.

Childhood beliefs. Based on childhood experiences, what does it mean about me that I need help? What, if anything, can be trusted? This is particularly true here when the kind of help we are receiving is tangible and physical. It taps into our earliest body memory of how nourishing, affirming, and necessary that was or how risky, confusing, and shameful that was.

Fear of selfishness. We talked about two meanings of selfish. One is a disregard for others' limits. In Accepting, you know what their limits are and respect them, so this excuse doesn't hold water. What you are afraid of is *feeling* selfish and focusing on your own pleasure instead of theirs. For some people, this fear is nearly debilitating.

Contradicting old feelings. The experience of receiving affirms that we are worthy. This can bring up old feelings of not being worthy.

Having our desires matter can bring up feelings of not having our desires respected.

The pleasure itself. Nothing contradicts self-worthiness fears like pleasure. It matters that we requested pleasure instead of something that just sort of, you know, happened.

The dynamics it creates. In Accepting, you have to acknowledge that you want and enjoy something. In a twisted way, there is the loss of a certain kind of mistaken moral high ground. You are the one who wants or needs something.

We need each other. Ultimately, it is this. In Accepting, we come right up to the fact that we need other human beings. That is a fundamental vulnerability that our lives are built on.

Gratitude. If that is not enough, there is the gratitude. If you feel enough gratitude, the key word being *enough*, you will come to tears. That is the way of it.

So you're not alone in having feelings about the Accepting Quadrant. In spite of all this, we still have a drive to be in Accepting. We know at some level that we need each other, we need attention, and we need time to be helped and served. We crave the opportunity even as we fear it.

ACCEPTING AND GENDER

Receiving the benefit of someone else's action—this is a human need and has nothing to do with gender. Still, there are common themes that show up based on how we have been conditioned about our gender's roles in touch and sex.

Men. Accepting is often harder for men. Mark and his wife saw me to rekindle their spark. At one point, she asked to have him sit on the floor leaning against the wall, and she leaned back against him with his arms around her. They melted into it. He said, "Wow, I could never do what she's doing." I asked, "What do you mean?" He said, "I just wouldn't be comfortable as a man. I'm supposed to be the strong one, the one protecting. I just couldn't do that."

Men often believe they are supposed to do it all and know it all themselves, that it's shameful to be in need. This is part of the way they are subjected to pressures as men and is not true, of course. Everyone needs and deserves help.

In bed, it's often harder to be still and enjoy without feeling guilty, or it's difficult to not feel in control. It's often harder for men to experience pleasure that is not sexual and harder to experience their body as a source of pleasure, so they rely on their partner's excitement (the indirect route). On the other hand, men have the culture of receiving erotic massage from professionals and, when they do, find it's pure heaven.

Women. Women almost never seek out erotic massage from professionals, though that is changing. Why? Many women experience most touch as being for someone else, as giving something up. This is shown by this comment from a woman when asked why she didn't go to a workshop on touch. "Why would I do that? If I wanted to get groped, I'd go to a bar."

Women usually have a harder time finding what it feels like to have it be for them. They will revert to settling for whatever crumbs they can get, settling for the mediocre. Real Accepting—to have something be entirely for them—is often a revelation.

THE SHADOW OF ACCEPTING

The real issue…the same spirit that says you work and toil and earn bread and I'll eat it. No matter in what shape it comes, whether from the mouth of a king who seeks to bestride the people of his own nation and live by the fruit of their labor, or from one race of men as an apology for enslaving another race, it is the same tyrannical principle.
—Abraham Lincoln

The shadow of Accepting is making use of the benefit of the actions of others without awareness or regard for the sacrifices they have made, whether with or without their consent. It is exploitation. We exploited by enslavement in the United States for more than two hundred years. We still have the less obvious kind: slave labor in overseas factories and mines, terrible working conditions at an outrageously low cost to us, set up with international trade agreements that give the local workers little or no choices and supported by pressure on their governments because it gives us advantages. We get the benefit of their labor, but they don't get much choice.

Accepting is a form of receiving, so another shadow is entitlement: thinking that you have a right to the labor of others. As I'm writing this, the coronavirus (COVID-19) is raging, and many people are expected to keep working even though they have no protective gear, no sick pay, and very little choice about whether to keep working—the "essential" workers we all rely on but don't pay fairly.

Some of the more mundane forms of the shadow of Accepting are assuming that others are going to help you or thinking that people who help you are less worthy of your respect: being rude to the barista or assuming the workers mentioned above are always available. As my former husband once said about things getting done around the house, "Those things take care of themselves." I replied, "Uh, no. I take care of them."

How to notice you're in the shadow? Usually we don't notice what we're being given until the other person stops providing it. Then we get incensed. *How dare they?* That is the sign of entitlement.

How to end up in the shadow? By not asking for what you want. Asking makes you notice that you do want something and that the other person has a choice about giving it.

The muddy zone. Like the other quadrants, the muddy zone is those places where we assume willingness that may or may not be there. Or we take advantage of someone who technically could choose but doesn't really have much of a choice, like the workers mentioned above and many other workers around the world.

WHEN ACCEPTING IS HARD

When the Accepting Quadrant is hard, you avoid it—"That's okay. I don't need my turn"—or you revert to Allowing, usually without noticing it.

In bed, you give-give-give and wonder why no one is giving back. You burn out because you are "doing all the work." You get curious about other partners: *Would they be any different?* The problem is not your partner; it's you. You are not getting vulnerable enough to ask, so depth and connection are limited. In life, you don't ask for help and try to do it all yourself. You are chronically disappointed, isolated, and resentful. Are you thinking that everyone needs help but you?

A client had a hard time with Accepting and complained that all his friends were selfish. I said, "If you have a hard time receiving, it's hard to surround yourself with generous people." If you can't accept others' help, the story you create is that they are selfish, which may or may not be true.

If you don't think your partner is good at Accepting, and this is common, the question to ask is, *What do I want and why?* What is it you want to give and why? Maybe there is something you want that you are not asking for. Come back and look at your desires. As I said elsewhere, if there is something you want and it has to do with another person, the only thing to do that has integrity is to ask for it.

WHEN ACCEPTING IS EASY

When Accepting is easy in the Wheel, you take your turn without guilt. You feel well cared for and pleasure-nourished. You have humility and are able to ask for what you like, dive in, and enjoy it. You trust that your partner cares, and you respect their choices. You have a wide range of things you ask for—sometimes nurturing and cozy, sometimes erotic, sometimes sensual, sometimes playful, sometimes exploratory.

It's exactly the same in life. You are able to ask for and accept favors, help, and support with grace and appreciation. You trust that it truly is for you, take it in, and use it however it fits for you. You show appreciation. You don't expect others to read your mind; you take responsibility for communicating. You don't assume or take without asking. You don't pretend to want or like something you don't, though you can choose to be gracious in situations that call for it. When you feel neglected or isolated, you check in with yourself—*What do I need?*—and communicate that. You understand that we all have times we need help, and you have no shame in it. This makes you compassionate about other people needing help and support.

SPIRITUAL IMPLICATIONS

The experience of the Accepting Quadrant speaks to our inherent worthiness. We are receiving this gift not for what we do but for who we are. Accepting gives us a physical experience of this spiritual truth, and the physicality of it makes it hard to miss. The Accepting Quadrant can be a profound shake-up to who you think you are, which is part of why it's so emotionally challenging.

Accepting brings us face to face with the fact that we need each other, are not self-sufficient, and are inherently connected. Accepting is profoundly humbling and at the same time affirming of who we are. Accepting helps us learn to accept ourselves as we are. Receiving attention from an actual person instead of the universe or a deity helps us do that. Gratitude is a spiritual path all its own.

SOCIAL IMPLICATIONS

We are always benefitting from someone else's action but don't usually notice it—the fire station comes to mind as well as the truckers who drive your produce to market, the conservation activist, and the journalist. In the Wheel, what is unique is that it is specifically about you, so it can be intensely personal.

When we learn the Accepting Quadrant, we become respectful of others' limits in what they are willing and happy to do for us, and we become able to take their gifts into our hearts. If we learned to Accept, to take it into our hearts with a tangible physical experience, would we stop stealing and coercing? Would we stop exploiting the labor of other countries? I believe we would.

Why we need Accepting in the world. It is not so much that we need more of it in the world as it is that we need to acknowledge it where it already is.

SUMMARY: THE ACCEPTING QUADRANT

The Accepting Quadrant combines Done-to and Receiving. You are in the Accepting Quadrant when you ask someone to do something for you and they agree. The gift you are receiving is the action of the giver.

This is traditionally called "Receiving." However, Taking is also a form of receiving, so I use the word "Accepting" for this quadrant.

Serve-Accept is created by the agreement. You say, "Will you...?" and they say, "Yes, I will." Without this agreement, Serve-Accept does not happen.

As a gift, it is based on what you want, not what you are okay with or don't mind. The crux of it is being able to distinguish between those two, which generally means learning how to notice what you want.

The essence of Accepting is benefitting from the actions of others.

You are doing two things at once. In Accepting, as in all forms of receiving, you are doing two things at once: 1) putting your desires first, and 2) respecting and abiding by the limits of your giver.

What you discover in Accepting is that it is possible to be touched exactly the way you want.

You cannot learn Accepting by having someone else choose what is going to happen. You must choose. This is often the hardest part but cannot be skipped.

Accepting is inherently enjoyable. If it is not enjoyable, it is not because you are not a "good receiver" or because you don't like this quadrant. It is because it is not what you actually want (or it's more of it than you want).

Responsibilities of Accepting. You may think your responsibility is to appreciate what happens and feel thankful for it. It is not. Your responsibility is to communicate what you want.

Shadow. Free-loader, entitlement, enslavement.

CHAPTER 23

The Serving Quadrant

*When we think about the most precious
things we have—number one, it's our bodies,
number two, it's our time.*
— Dolores Huerta

*We have all been given a gift,
the gift of life. What we do
with our lives is our gift back.*
—Edo

Your hands are on their legs. They're lying on the floor, and you are leaning over and giving them your weight, as they asked. You ask, "How's this pressure?" They say, "A little more, please," so you lean a little more. "Ah, just right, now hold it there." You do exactly that. You have the impulse to move, thinking it would feel nice to them. You almost do that and then remember, *Wait, this is what they asked for,* so you stay there. Later, they ask you to massage their head, so you have both hands intertwined in their hair, and you notice that it feels nice to your hands. At some point, you realize that you are contributing to their enjoyment but not causing it. Your ego sinks a bit, but your heart fills. You are in the Serving Quadrant.

The Serving Quadrant combines doing and giving. When your partner asks you to touch them in the way they want and you agree to do that, you are in the Serving Quadrant. The gift you are giving is your action: the action moves from you to them, and the gift moves the same direction. The key to Serving is not in the doing; it's in finding out what the Accepter wants.

Serving is what most people consider Giving, but because Allowing is also a form of giving, I gave this quadrant its own name. Serving is where many people feel most comfortable and the quadrant everyone seems to want to be better at. Almost everything taught about touch and sex assumes the Serve-Accept dynamic as a starting point.

In Serving, you contribute to their experience, and the experience belongs to them. They get to respond however they do. This makes Serving both satisfying and humbling. If you use it to congratulate yourself on your technique, you are probably not in Serving.

WHAT IT'S NOT

Serving is not magically knowing what to do. It is not doing-doing-doing because you are afraid not to. It's not making something happen that you feel responsible for or that you want to see because it makes you feel good about yourself or turns you on. Nor does it mean being willing to do anything at all; it's not all or nothing. It does not mean giving away responsibility for your limits.

The intention to give does not constitute Serving. What makes it Serving is the agreement—finding out what they want and agreeing to do it.

WHAT IT IS

The Serving Quadrant is one half of a dynamic and an inner experience. The Serve-Accept dynamic is created by your agreement: They say, "Will you…" and you say, "Yes, I will." Or you might offer, "Would you like me to…" and they say, "Yes, please." The agreement is temporary, limited, and specific.

Serving is a form of giving, so we are back to two things at once: 1) setting aside what you prefer, and 2) keeping your responsibility for your limits. The more responsibility you take for your limits, the more ease and generosity you feel. Serving is based on what your Accepter wants, not what you "want to give." The biggest part of Serving is asking what they want and making room for them to be clear. The essence of Serving is acting for the benefit of others.

What Serving can't do for you. No matter how much you enjoy it, Serving cannot substitute for the experience of Taking.

The challenges of Serving. Serving is the most comfortable quadrant for many people. Still, there can be some challenges. You may feel guarded or worried about giving more than you feel good about, or you may feel tentative or unconfident. A common challenge of Serving is not using it to avoid something or to get something you want.

REVIEW: FINDING SERVING

Detailed steps for finding Serving are in Lesson 3. This is a review.

Finding Serving the first time is usually straightforward. Unlike Taking, most people at least have an idea of what Serving is. Serving can be done using any body part, but starting with the hands is most natural, and that's what we used in the lesson.

A common mistake is getting started before finding out what your receiver wants or adding things they have not asked for. To find the Serving Quadrant, you have to ask what your Accepter wants and wait for the answer. Once that is clear, the doing part follows easily. Then, if you are willing and able, you do that and nothing else.

REVIEW: EXPLORING SERVING

Detailed steps for exploring Serving are in Lab 2. This is a review.

You may think that Serving is about developing ever fancier strokes and techniques. Not at all. Serving is about making room for your receiver to notice what they want and request it and making it safe enough for them to speak up and change their mind. This is the art of Serving, which I call spaciousness.

Creating spaciousness means slowing down and doing nothing until they ask, not making up new stuff (no matter how brilliant you think it is), not letting them defer to you, and conveying by your demeanor that you are not rushed and they have all the time in the world to notice, ponder, question, and change their mind. As you get better at spaciousness, you will find that your receiver will begin to trust that you care what they want. They will care themselves and ask for more things. Your repertoire will expand together.

The trap in Serving is trying to get the response that you want to see like their pleasure or their turn-on. When you do that, you focus on what works and lose sight of the person. This is unfair to your receiver, brings tension into your touch, and tends to make them perform for you. This is not giving; it's using your receiver for your own ego or entertainment.

THE SECRET TO EASE AND JOY IN SERVING

First, respect your own limits. The more you tend to your limits, the more freedom and joy you have in giving. Like Allowing, it's limits first, then the joy. Second, set aside any idea of what they should want and how they should respond to what you do. This lets you stop trying to make something happen and frees you up to enjoy what *is* happening.

THE EXPERIENCE OF SERVING

Serving often feels more familiar than Taking. For many people, it's the only quadrant that feels comfortable. You may feel relieved when you finally are able to give something real. You feel valued and useful. When you find out what is meaningful, useful, and pleasurable to them, it becomes meaningful (and often pleasurable) to you too. Serving is humbling. You notice that though you do not cause their experience, you contribute to it, and that satisfies your heart. When you can experience that, instead of hanging on results, it's a relief.

In Serving, you are following, not leading, so the mood will depend on the Accepter. It can feel meditative, sensual, silly, raucous, or erotic. You may melt into the bliss of the moment; you may get tired, distracted, or bored. You may get turned on. It can be focused on the connection between you, or your Accepter can focus on their own sensations, settling into a trance-like state. You may feel well used, grateful, or honored to have the chance to contribute.

What you learn over time. As you get better at finding out what they want and tending your limits, and cleaner about not wanting anything back, Serving becomes easier. You become more flexible and generous, and your Serving becomes deeply satisfying for both of you. You will most likely become interested in expanding your repertoire too, which you can do with instructional videos and books, which is fine to do—*after* you get really good at finding out what the person in front of you wants.

THE KEY TO SERVING IS TAKING

I used to say learning Taking improves the quality of your Serving. I have come to see that learning Taking is what makes Serving possible. Here's why.

Taking opens the inflow. When you switch your attention from the outflow (trying to give) to the inflow (noticing your sensation), your hands relax. It's immediate and automatic. Your Allowing partner probably noticed this in the lesson. If that's all you learn from the Taking Quadrant, you are miles ahead.

The second effect of opening the inflow is that you are better able to notice changes in the state of your partner. You notice their skin temperature and muscle tone, whether they are relaxing under your hands or have become tense. As you become better at noticing with your hands, you expand to noticing their words, facial expression, and tone of voice. The feeling is that your hands become intuitive, but what is actually happening is that you are taking in more information. Though you may not consciously notice it, it's in there. This ability to notice your partner is crucial in Serving.

Another effect of opening the inflow is that your need to touch is met, so you are full and have something to give. Your hands are not hungry.

Taking teaches you that you are welcome here, as you are, without having to get the stroke right. What a relief. This, too, lets your hands relax. It is extremely difficult to relax under a pair of hands that is tense or tentative. Hands that are relaxed and know they are welcome tend to move more slowly, which almost always feels better to the person being touched. They tend to make full contact, drape, curve, and wrap. They are not predictable, repetitive or rhythmic, or on a mission. This makes a world of difference to the person you are touching.

When your hands relax, become attentive, and feel welcome, they develop what is called presence. Presence means you are right here, right now, with all your attention. So the skills are not in the hands. The skills are in communication. Presence is in the hands.

Taking teaches you the difference between the two quadrants. Only when you can tell the difference between Taking and Serving can you *do* either one. Learning to feel the difference almost always requires learning to Take.

In the Taking Quadrant, you learn to put your desires first, and until you can put them first, you can't put them last, because it's not clear what they *are*. Taking teaches you what they are and gives them a home so you don't have to pretend they're not there. As long as you pretend your desires are not there, they will sneak into your Serving. Only when you can access the Taking Quadrant can you take the Taking out of your giving.

Perhaps more importantly, when you discover the joy of Taking, you stop trying to avoid it. You stop using Serving to avoid Taking. This is a profound switch. You stop pretending you are Serving when what you really want is to get your hands on someone. You stop using Serving to try to get safety, validation, appreciation, or entertainment. You stop using Serving to meet your need to touch, justify your existence, or get the response you want. When your Serving becomes clean and clear, it becomes actual Serving. As one friend says, "If you can't Take, I can't trust your Serving."

About Taking and Serving at the same time. Sometimes people ask, "Can't you do Taking and Serving at the same time?" The answer is no. In Taking, you put your desires first, and in Serving, you set your desires aside. You can't put your desires first and also set them aside at the same time.

Some folks then ask, "Yeah, but suppose we both want it?" For example, they want a back rub, and you want to give them a back rub. Lucky you! However, at some point, they want your hand to move this way, and you want your hand to move this other way. Whose desire wins out? When asking this question, what you are most likely trying to do is avoid the vulnerability of fully entering the Taking Quadrant.

Sometimes people wonder if experiencing pleasure in their hands means they are Taking. Taking doesn't mean "taking in pleasure with your hands" (though that happens). Taking means you have asked for permission to touch the way you want, and your Allower has agreed to give you that. As said elsewhere, pleasure is available in any quadrant and is not the indicator of which quadrant you are in. What determines the quadrant you are in is your agreement. Who is it for? Again, you can't put your desires first and set them aside at the same time.

THE EROTIC ELEMENTS OF SERVING

One erotic element is being of service. This can be played with as a power dynamic in which you are at the beck and call of your Accepter. For many people, just being in the quadrant is a turn-on. Your service may or may not include sexual touch. It may include other services like cleaning the house, polishing their boots, or doing errands dressed in your leopard skin tights. It can be letting someone lean back on you while they self-pleasure or witnessing them. It can be soft and nurturing like holding someone gently or wiping their tears, which can be erotic in its own way.

Another element is erotic massage. Erotic massage can be loads of fun to give. Besides the pleasure of it in your own hands, there is riding the wave of your partner's pleasure and knowing you contributed to their enjoyment in a meaningful way. If this is new territory, start with an agreement to bring eros into your massage and do so without genitals. What does erotic mean and how can you welcome it? Then when and if your Accepter would like to include the genitals, start with the notes online, with relatively shorter sessions so you can try out how it feels before diving into a full two hours.

SERVING AND GENDER

Again, these themes are not inherent to gender. They show up based on how we are conditioned.

Men. Men usually think they are Serving and often feel stuck here partly because that's their assumed role in sex but also because they don't know where else to be. It protects them from the more vulnerable quadrants, Accepting and Taking.

For a man, it's often harder to experience your own body (your full body, not just your genitals). When that is the case, all you have left is to do the stroke so you get the right response. This is the trap of Serving and is sadly extremely common in men. It has to do with centuries of acculturation that teaches you not to feel too much. It's well understood by physiologists that body sensation is tied to feeling states (emotions). In some ways, body sensation is what emotions *are*. When you are trained that it's dangerous to feel, you learn to not notice yourself. Adding the training to get the job done, without asking for directions or help, makes the trap almost inevitable. But not quite. Learn the Taking Quadrant. Serving then becomes clear and satisfying for everyone involved.

Women. Women are not immune to the trap. We tend to be trained to be passive in sex. What a loss for everyone! In my generation and before, if you actually *do* anything, you're suspect. "Where'd you learn to do that?!"

Because of that, women are often unconfident but are supposed to try new tricks, you know, to keep your man coming back for more. Now we have double pressure. Don't do too much, but do fancy stuff. That's where the trap comes in. Do the fancier stuff so you get a fancier response. Cosmic volcanoes—that sort of thing. Learn the Taking Quadrant, so your Serving becomes real and full of heart.

THE SHADOW OF SERVING

The shadow of the Serving Quadrant is taking action for the benefit of others, without taking responsibility for setting a limit, or having tried to set a limit but having it transgressed due to coercion, pressure, force, or lack of reasonable alternative. The shadow of Serving is the mirror to the shadow of Accepting. We talked there about exploitation and entitlement. In the shadow of Serving you may have little or no choice about the work you do or the conditions in which you do it. The quintessential shadow of the Serve-Accept dynamic is enslavement.

In the more personal realm, the shadow of Serving is the martyr who gives everything. Or like a good country-western song, you can use Serving for all the wrong reasons:

- To avoid the Receiving Half
- To avoid the Done-to Half
- Because you can't Take
- To prove your worth and what a good lover you are
- To justify your existence
- To get the response you want to see
- To keep your partner around or so they will let you do more
- To keep the power
- To take the moral high ground
- To protect your image as the giver

Another shadow of Serving is giving unsolicited advice or trying to help someone without finding out what they need because you don't ask them, assuming you know better than they do. That is the rescue industry—groups hell-bent on "rescuing" other groups but who don't bother to ask them what would actually be helpful. This is currently happening to sex workers. See the notes online.

There is one place where the shadow of Serving overlaps the shadow of Taking. It's hard to tell which it is. This is when you are doing something that you presumably believe is the right thing to do, or that you are hoping others see as the right thing for you to do, but in actuality has a negative impact on the person you are trying to "help", like our country's covert support for dictators to protect our business interests. Or police departments attacking peaceful demonstrators or armed militias preventing people from voting. Presumably someone believes they are doing the right thing. Or do they? I don't know.

On the other hand, you may feel stuck here. Serving feels the least vulnerable, you don't know what else to do, or you don't know how to ask for anything. And sometimes when we want to "give," what we really want is for them to like what we want to do.

The muddy zone. Like every quadrant, Serving has a muddy zone when you are not quite willing but haven't said no. This creates resentment and is where many people spend most of their time. The more consciously you make your choice, the more heart will be in it for you.

WHEN SERVING IS HARD

When Serving is hard, it shows up in a couple of main ways. On the one hand, you might forget you have limits and lose yourself in give-give-give. You are depleted and burned out and wonder why nobody else gives as much as you do. You feel like everyone wants something from you and resent them for it. Or it might show up the other way. You may feel worried and stingy and unable to give anything at all. You fear you will give too much, so you can't afford to give anything or the gates open and out it all goes. Both overgiving and worrying arise from the same thing—having difficulty with respecting your limits.

Don't feel appreciated? It's likely your partner doesn't know you are giving because you didn't make an agreement or didn't ask them what they wanted. They may be giving something you are not noticing. Or you may feel unappreciated because you're in the results trap.

WHEN SERVING IS EASY

When Serving is easy, you are comfortable having limits and communicating them. You don't apologize for them. You respect other people's desires and don't feel guilty if you can't meet them. You are relaxed, generous, and flexible, and because you trust yourself to say no, you can easily experiment with new things. You find out what they want before jumping in. When you notice that you invested your hopes in how it would turn out, you forgive yourself, ask yourself what you wanted, and decide if it's something you can ask for when it's your turn.

Because you have experienced Accepting, you know how vulnerable it is, have compassion for it, and don't feel superior for being the giver. You enjoy sometimes giving things anonymously, needing nothing in return. You can tell the difference between helping and compulsively "rescuing."

SPIRITUAL IMPLICATIONS

Everyone has been made for some particular work, and the desire for that work has been put in every heart.

—*Rumi*

Just as every spiritual tradition has something to say about desire, every tradition has something to say about service. Serving the community can be a spiritual practice in itself, and many groups follow this path. Serving develops generosity and humility and is an expression of love. Giving by doing can be an experience of letting the generosity of life flow through you, opening your heart to the other. There is something spiritual, too, about taking responsibility for your desires so that you can set them aside to Serve.

SOCIAL IMPLICATIONS

It's a human need to have some effect on others. Without it, we despair. We want our effect to be beneficial, to contribute to the joy and well-being of those we care about. The need to have an effect could be part of why we fall into the trap of trying to get a response.

Is it Serving if you get paid for it? Yes. Is it a gift if you are taking turns? Yes. During that turn, you are fully in Serving. Your agreement makes the difference. Are you offering it as a gift and expect nothing in return? Are you offering an exchange in which you expect something back? Either way is fine. We need both. Just be clear which it is in your offer.

Why we need Serving in the world. We need it in the word so that we help each other. As friends and neighbors and for the community at large. There are many ways to contribute to our community: serving as a volunteer firefighter or at the community kitchen, running email campaigns, writing checks to beneficial organizations, or bringing your sick neighbor a pot of chicken soup.

SUMMARY: THE SERVING QUADRANT

Serving combines Doing and Giving. You are Serving when someone asks you to do something for them and you say yes. The gift you are giving is your action.

Traditionally called "Giving," but Allowing is also a form of giving, so I call this quadrant Serving.

Serve-Accept is created by the agreement. They say, "Will you...?" and you say, "Yes, I will."

As a gift, it is based on what your receiver wants and you are willing to give—not the other way around.

You are doing two things at once. 1) Setting aside what you prefer (which includes both what you might enjoy doing and how you hope they respond), and 2) keeping responsibility for your limits.

What you discover in Serving is that you do not cause their enjoyment. You contribute to it, and the experience belongs to them.

The trap of Serving is doing something to try to get the response you hope to see.

The art of effective Serving is creating spaciousness for your Accepter to notice what they want and to change their mind.

What Serving can't do for you: Substitute for Taking.

Taking is the key to Serving. It improves the quality of your touch. It shows you the difference between Taking and Serving, so you are not using Serving as a way to avoid the vulnerability of Taking.

The shadow of Serving. The do-gooder (helping someone whether they want it or not), the martyr, and enslavement.

THE SERVE-ACCEPT DYNAMIC

In the Serve-Accept dynamic, the action moves one direction, and the gift moves the same direction. It's the massage, medical care, holding a child to give comfort, pulling a thorn from your dog's paw, or stopping on the road to help a stranded driver.

Almost all teaching about touch assumes this dynamic, including most sex therapy, which often includes getting the "receiver" to learn how to like what is being done to them. As you now know, this is backwards. I believe this confusion arises from conflating Done-to with Receive, which implies that if you are being done to, it's assumed it's for you. You'll also notice that most popular media is about this dynamic, in particular about getting a response. "Drive your man wild!" "Give her six orgasms tonight!" "Make her squirt!" (Did they ask her if she *wants* to squirt?)

This is a powerful dynamic. It allows the Accepter to dive into their own vulnerable experience, with support, in a way that is not possible otherwise. For example, the erotic massage in all its glorious, healing, enlightening, and transforming variations. It allows the Server to be of support, which tends to be humbling and affirming at the same time.

PART 4

Social and Spiritual Implications

CHAPTER 24

Domain, Boundaries, and Limits

M y friend runs a wolf sanctuary, taking in orphans or those born in captivity that have lost their homes. What a place to learn about human nature! Wolves are both familial and territorial. They know their home and defend its borders. My friend's acreage is large but not unlimited, each pair or small pack has its own domain, and many of them share the opposite sides of a chain-link fence. She tells me that they are peaceful with their neighbors, all of whom they can see and smell. Proximity is not a problem—as long as the fence is up. If the fence came down, holy havoc would ensue. Even though each family would have just as much space as before, they would defend it against each other, fang to fang. Not a scene I would care to witness.

This got me to thinking about boundaries and domain. "Boundary" has so many meanings it's easy to misunderstand. When you say boundary, do you mean something you don't want to do at the moment? Do you mean privacy, your right to choose, or some other aspect of what's yours? A more useful idea may be domain. For the wolves, the fence is their boundary; the space enclosed by it is their domain.

In our personal domain live those things we have a right to and those things we are responsible for, and they are the same things. I have a right to enjoy, use, develop, explore, and claim certain things as my own. I have responsibility for those same things—to respect, nourish, and tend to them. They go together. No one can take them away, and I cannot give them away.

With that, let's look at a few distinctions. These are the ways I use these words. They are certainly not the only way to use them. I give them to you here to clarify the distinctions between them.

Domain. Domain is what we have a right to and a responsibility for such as our bodies, desires, and feelings. What is in our domain does not change. We are always responsible for it.

What is included in my domain? My body and my inner experience: desires, feelings, pleasure, pain, fear, the whole gamut. I have a right to experience them, and I have a responsibility for them; I don't get to blame them on someone else. I have the right to say no, and I have the responsibility to say no. I can't blame anyone for not reading my mind (though I have certainly tried more than once).

The more we take responsibility for our domain, the more freedom we have. Perhaps more important is that when we own what is in our own domain, we respect what is in others'. It follows naturally and automatically.

Boundary. With this understanding, we can define boundaries. As I'm using the word here, I mean the edge of your domain. Your boundary is what delineates what is inside your domain from what is not. It's the fence around your domain.

Limit. A limit is a choice about activity. It is what you are willing to participate in and what you are not. A limit is your no. You have some limits you will not do at all, for anyone, ever, and other things you are available for depending on who it is, what the situation is, or how tired you are. You might set a limit today and change it tomorrow or five minutes from now. Limits change, and this is a good thing. For example, I am happy hugging almost anyone most of the time—except when I'm not. My boundary hasn't changed (owning my body), but my limit has (when to hug).

The stronger your sense of domain, the more responsibility you take for your limits, and then your limits can become flexible. Flexible means the ability to respond to change and still take responsibility for yourself. That lets you enjoy any situation, because you know you are able to choose and communicate. This is not the same as being a pushover. Recall the thought experiment about entering a room in which you can't say no (chapter 19). The ability to say no allows you to enter the room.

Edge. Edge is another word that sometimes gets used in this context. I think of an edge as what is unfamiliar or a stretch, or you may be uncertain whether you want it. Something can feel edgy, meaning it brings some discomfort. You know it will stretch your zone of familiarity and confidence. With an edge, you get to choose what to do with it, and it is your right and responsibility (domain) to do so.

The essence of respect is taking my own domain to heart and allowing you to do the same. The primary language of respect is consent. When a person owns their domain and respects the other's, they are naturally more careful about consent. The converse is also true: if you are not using consent, question your respect. (Or it could be that you feel respect but don't yet have the skills to express it.) What we owe people is accurate, relevant information and respect of their domain—that's it.

MESSING WITH OUR DOMAINS

There are a few ways we can mess with our domains. One is to take something that belongs in our domain and try to move it into someone else's—such as our desires. We try to get someone else to want what we are reluctant to admit that we want. A classic example of this is wanting to reach over and touch someone but framing it as an offer (Serving), trying to get them to want us to touch them. The crux of integrity is owning our desires.

Another is to reach over into someone else's domain and try to change something that belongs to them. We try to get them to feel the way we want them to feel. One way we do that is the trap in Serving. We want someone to have the experience we want them to have. How arrogant! We are saying, "What you are feeling is not good enough for me. I want you to feel this other thing." In reality, their experience is in their domain.

Another way to mess with our domain is to allow someone to reach over into our domain and take something that is our responsibility or right—telling us what we should want, what we should feel, or what we should be okay with and going along with that. It's often caused by not saying no.

The primary job of a boundary is to keep things out that don't belong in. The appropriate response when you feel a breach is anger. Wolves are great examples; step into their domain, and they bare their teeth. We have a natural and crucial ability to draw the line. We might start with a polite "No, thanks," and if the other person doesn't abide by our limit, we escalate until they do. It's also possible to feel you've had a breach even if no one intended to do so. If you can't say no, it feels like everyone is stealing from you, but they may not be. You have given away your responsibility, but it feels like they have stolen it.

What if someone wants to give us a responsibility that belongs to them? They don't want to ask for what they want and want us to guess correctly what it is. It is easy to get hooked into this, because we have some idea of what they might like. We might want to get started, or we might be trying to save them the discomfort of asking. This is common in professional touch sessions, in which the provider is likely to think they know what's best.

So their feelings are in their domain, but we can reach into their domain and try to make them feel what we want them to feel. Our responsibility for our desires and limits is in our domain, but we can try to slide it over into theirs by not setting a limit and hoping they guess it or by not asking for what we want, or aaack—it's a mess! This is entanglement. It's exhausting. This has also been described as codependence (taking responsibility for making you feel a certain way). It's a trap stickier than a tar pit, which may be why I am passionate about this. I spent enough years there to last me a lifetime.

Ultimately, the only choice you can make is about yourself. You don't get to choose what your partner should want or what they should or shouldn't ask for. You get to choose whether or not to participate and how. If you find yourself grumbling about what someone else is asking for, get out of their domain and back to yours.

What about caring and kindness? Of course we influence and affect each other in pleasant and unpleasant ways, in ways we are aware of and ways we are not. Thank goodness! This does not negate the idea of domain. The more responsible you are for your own state, the more acceptance, generosity, and compassion you have for others'.

DOMAIN IN RELATIONSHIP

In relationship, the role of domain is that you get to want whatever you want. That's in your domain. It's your right and your responsibility. In my domain is whether or not I am interested in participating.

Autonomy and connection. Each is an inherent need. Many of us fear that they are opposites. *If I have too much autonomy, I will lose connection, because people won't stick around, but if I have too much connection, I'll lose myself.* Sound familiar? It's been said that relationship is learning to be with myself and be with you at the same time. A healthy sense of domain makes this possible. In the example of the can't-say-no room, your ability to say no means you are responsible for your domain. It's what allows you to be in the same room. Autonomy makes intimacy possible.

No boundaries? There is a fallacy that if we love enough, we need no boundaries. This could be an example of different meanings of the word "boundaries." It could be that you use boundaries for what I call limits, and of course we are interested in doing more things with our lovers than with others. Or it could be that you're using "boundaries" to mean a resistance to emotional vulnerability, as in "putting up boundaries" to say you don't reveal much of yourself. It could be that with love and trust, this relaxes.

Here's another use of the word "boundaries" that may have to do with love. There are times when we engage certain brain processes that create a sense of oneness. The areas of the brain that create distinctions quiet down, and the areas that create a sense of oneness light up. It feels wonderful and tends to be bonding. Entering these brain states, which often happens with love, can feel like you're losing your boundaries. You feel like you're merging. In chapter 15, we talked about this in relation to separating receiving and giving.

None of these negate your domain. They're just different uses of the word "boundaries." Giving up responsibility for yourself can't work in the long run, and each person needs their own domain no matter how deep the love.

This awareness of what's ours and what isn't is a developmental milestone in a child's growth and depends on body experience to develop it. It is the hallmark of maturity in relationship and the sign of integrity in business and politics. It could be considered the primary spiritual lesson for life in a physical body. If we were clouds, we would not have this question.

Respect and kindness. We cannot have kindness without respect. We can have sentimentality but not kindness. With kindness, you are not responsible for others, but you care, and you can make it easier. You invite or offer, and they get to choose what to do with it. I grew up thinking that kindness meant never hurting anyone's feelings and keeping everybody comfortable and happy. Since I was a nice Southern girl in the 1950s, that applied especially to men. My place was to do everything I could to "make him happy," including, apparently, taking away his right to be unhappy! It turns out that the most respectful and generous thing I can do for you is to respect myself and my choices and to be truthful.

Responsibility and freedom. When you take back into your domain what belongs there and give back to their domain what belongs there, it creates freedom. It's what enables us to be generous and kind to each other. I stop trying to get you to want something I am afraid to admit that I want, and I stop trying to get you to feel the way I want you to feel. I acknowledge that there is something that I want, communicate that, and respect your answer. To that degree I become free.

What am I not asking for? When I feel resentful, I have learned to ask myself, *What am I not asking for?* or *What did I not say no to that I wanted to say no to?* Essentially, *What am I trying to move from my domain over into theirs?* The cure for resentment is rarely easy, but it requires taking full responsibility for your domain.

EACH QUADRANT OFFERS WAYS TO EXPLORE DOMAIN

Serving: In your domain is your responsibility for self-care and limits. In their domain is knowing what they want and how they respond.

Accepting: In your domain is communicating what you want, experiencing your pleasure, and responding however you do, as well as changing your mind or stopping. In their domain is the responsibility for their comfort and their limits, and you respect that.

Taking: In your domain is your desire to touch and the responsibility to acknowledge it. In their domain is their limits, and you respect that. Also in their domain is their comfort, and because you care, you support them.

Allowing: In your domain is your limits, to own them and to communicate them. Their desires and experience are in their domain.

CHAPTER 25

Desire

Desire is a horse that wants to take you on a journey to spirit.
—Malidoma Somé

One of the things in our domain is our desires. My mother was in her fifties when we kids were home from college and talking about going out to eat. I asked her, "What would you like, Mom?" She said, "Well honey, I don't know. No one has ever asked me what I wanted." Knowing her family background, that statement was probably true. No one had asked her, and she had long since forgotten how to know.

I have asked hundreds of people how they would like to be touched and noticed a huge range of responses to being asked—relief, gratitude, confusion, or embarrassment. Some feel put on the spot as if they are supposed to produce something. Some feel lost, as if they don't know what the question means, or suspicious of why someone would want to give them anything. Some deflect by saying, "Anything you want." Common, of course, is "I don't know." All these reflect a relationship to our own desire. We fear our desire, crave it, deny it, shame ourselves for it, or try to hide it. We're worried about not having enough desire or having the wrong kind, or we have forgotten how to know what it is. We walk right over it or ignore it. It's nothing but trouble. The whole thing is mysterious. What is it?

Many people think of "desire" as sexual desire, but I use the word broadly here. It's whatever you want or prefer. A hug, a walk in the woods, a cup of tea. A better situation at work, social justice for wage earners, protecting the coral reefs, or as quoted in the introduction, "less dioxin in every mother's breast milk." Desires are your Want-to list. Desire is essential, an innate part of who we are. Our lives depend on it. It points to what has meaning and value for us.

Your desire and choice is a sacred trust. You are the only one who can carry it. If you don't listen, no one can. Hoping someone will guess correctly and get it right is a self-imposed jail sentence. The only option is to go along with someone else's or what you *think* is someone else's, which may or may not be accurate. The outcome, whether immediate or eventual, is resentment. Your desire dries up, and you forget how to know. As I said elsewhere, resentment is a sign to ask *What did I want that I didn't ask for?*

Marshall Rosenberg, of Nonviolent Communication, says that our real needs are inherent to being human and are common to every person. We need food, water, and shelter, of course, but also respect, autonomy, rest, meaningful work, creative outlet, sexual expression, connection with others, touch, and many more. Based on these needs, we come up with strategies for how to meet them. To the degree we don't understand the real need, the strategy can be ineffective, rigid, or distorted. The actual need is likely to be more vulnerable. For example, we may need affirmation, but the only strategy we have for that is sex, which may or may not meet the actual need. When you get good at noticing the underlying need, you're able to be flexible about how to meet it. "I'd like this, but if that's not available, this other could meet it for now." Desire is an arrow pointing to the real self, and it always points to a real need. Look underneath.

WHY WE DISTRUST IT

I sometimes ask people in a workshop, "Who here heard this from their parents: 'Gee, Suzie, I can't give you that thing you want, but you sure do a great job of wanting it. I'm so proud of you!'" I have yet to have anyone raise their hand. Most of us learn from an early age to distrust our wants or that they are shameful or make us weak or vulnerable. I talked about this in chapter 18. We learn that what we want doesn't count or is not the right thing to want. We spend so long not listening to ourselves that eventually we forget *how* to want—more accurately, how to notice, trust, and value what we want.

It's risky; there's no way around that. We risk disappointment and possibly ridicule. It feels safer to not let desire show, but when we don't acknowledge what we want, some part of us has to shut down. We give up and forget it's in our domain. We try to put it in our partner's domain and try to get them to want what we are afraid to want.

FOUR FALLACIES ABOUT SEXUAL DESIRE

Having no desire means you are being generous. Not true. Of course, there are situations in which your preferences are mild or the other person's desires are clear and strong enough that you don't mind setting yours aside. Generosity means setting aside your desires willingly and with a full heart. Being completely unconnected to your own desires, because you don't remember how to have them, is not generosity.

Knowing what you want precludes spontaneity (or you have to know every detail of what you want ahead of time). Not true at all! Surprise and spontaneity are wants just like anything else. You might at times want to be surprised. You might say, "I want to experiment, and I'm not sure what I will like," "I want to be your plaything for a while," or "I'm not sure what I want, but I am sure what I don't want." That is a fine starting place.

There is such a thing as no desire. This is based on the idea that unless you desire (some particular version of) sex (as you have known it so far), you don't desire anything. There is such a thing as not desiring sex, but there is no such thing as no desire. There is something you want or at least prefer. Your job is to slow down enough to notice what that is. Widen your options of what is okay to want. Maybe a foot rub. Maybe to be read to. Maybe help with the laundry. There is something you want—what is it? Start there.

You could read that paragraph and still think I mean those things are preludes to get you warmed up for sex. No—I mean that that is what you want, and that counts as something you want.

Fake it till you make it. This is the worst advice I have ever heard. This assumes that you should want sex, and if you don't, the cure for it is starting the activity, and you'll get turned on enough to complete that activity.

Still, there is something that works about this strategy. What is it? If you stimulate the reproductive organs enough, they will eventually engage and create the physiological conditions needed to complete whatever sex act you're going for. It sometimes works, but this is not your pleasure system. It's your reproductive physiology kicking in. If earlier in life or the relationship your reproductive system is strong, your biological urges will override your low standards, and you won't notice how mediocre the sex is. When the reproductive system slows down and you don't have those strong impulses, you are left with the opportunity for pleasure, but if the whole thing wasn't that pleasurable to begin with, why bother?

What to do instead? We're back here again: there is *something* you want. What is that something? As I have said elsewhere, the question is not: *Why don't I want this?* It's: *What is it I do want?*

HOW TO RECONNECT WITH YOUR DESIRE

Desire is like a spring whose source is deep in the earth. Its nature is to rise up to the surface. You can't demand that it show up, but you can make room for it. You can build a fence around the spring so you don't trample it. You protect it from your judgments, your hurry to get through discomfort, or your habit to ignore it and get going—then it naturally bubbles up.

That's what the practice of the labs does. Your partner asks what you want, and you wait until you know. You commit to waiting for the inner *Hell yes!* These seconds or minutes can be uncomfortable, but there is no substitute. It takes time for the message to arrive in your awareness, but the amount of time is finite. It will arrive. If you get started before you hear the *Hell yes!* you deepen the habit of ignoring yourself.

We're back to the magic four: notice, trust, value, and communicate, noticing what bubbles up to your awareness and trusting that the incoming information is accurate. The thing itself may not be what you ultimately choose, but trust the need that is under it (the need for connection, affirmation, comfort, expression, etc.). Valuing it means knowing that it matters, not dismissing it, and then communicating it. To ask for it, you have to know that such a thing exists and have the confidence you won't be ridiculed for wanting it.

It's gradual. You learn that it works, you learn to trust yourself, and you learn to trust the process. As that expands, you think of more and different things to ask for. It's always a push-pull of what we want in our heart of hearts versus how much of that we want to be vulnerable enough to receive. The practice of the labs narrows that gap.

What you desire is a feeling. What you are asking for is what you think or hope will create that feeling. Sometimes you intuit the action, but you're not sure what feeling is calling. When you get it, the feeling is right there. "I have no idea why I want this, but put your hand right here on my face…oh my, I had no idea I felt that way!" Other times, you know the feeling you want (safe, connected, loved, desired, aroused) but don't know how to get there. Or the feeling calls from deep down, but if you don't understand it or trust it, the idea of how to get there can be off base. If you feel desperate, the need is real, but the strategy is likely off. Ask yourself, *What feeling do I want, and what will help me feel that?*

As noted in the labs, you cannot ask for a feeling to be given to you ("Make me feel special"). You can only ask for an action ("Listen to me, hug me, hold me," etc.). The example I gave was that what makes one person feel special is tender holding while what makes someone else feel special is whips and chains.

WHEN YOU WANT YOUR PARTNER TO HAVE MORE DESIRE

This is common, and the dilemma is natural. We want our lovers to want us and to want to play in the ways we like to play. This is something of a paradox. Your partner's desire lives in their domain, not yours. If you truly want your partner to own their desire, you have to accept that their desire will be different from your own. There is only one way to awaken it: make room for it. If you want a guarantee, you're not open to their desire, only your own. I have seen this countless times. One partner wants the other person to have more desire but moves ahead anyway and doesn't know how to slow down or make room. To make room for your partner's desire, get comfortable doing nothing. If you are in a hurry, look at your own discomfort, and deal with it.

For some couples, slowing down is enough, and being asked what they want helps. More often the pattern is so well established that it takes a serious shift of structure to learn how to make enough room. The practice of the labs does this. The key is to claim your own desire so you are not trying to get your partner to want what you are afraid to want and make room for theirs to be different than your own. The more you understand and value your own desire and take it back into your domain, the more you understand that their desire is in their domain. The more room you make, the easier it is for them to learn, but it is ultimately their journey, not yours.

CHAPTER 26

Consent

There's no "Get out of consent free" card.
—Nadine Thornhill

*It's more fun to talk with someone who doesn't use long, difficult words
but rather short, easy words like "What about lunch?"*
—Winnie the Pooh

'd like to redefine consent. The dictionary describes consent as agreeing to do something or allow someone else to do something. By consenting, you agree to something someone else wants: "I consent to X." If you say "give consent" or "get consent," this is what you're talking about. I'd like to expand the definition and think of consent as being an agreement that two or more people come up with together. You don't give consent, you arrive at consent—together. Really, a better word is agreement, but it's too late to change the title to *The Wheel of Agreement*.

There is an excellent body of work these days about enthusiastic consent, ongoing consent, and implied consent and a growing and important discussion of the role of an imbalance of power in any interaction. Much of the conversation is about touch. The field is rich, and I expect it will continue to get richer. The contribution that the Wheel of Consent makes to this conversation is not that consent is a good thing. You already knew that. The contribution of the Wheel of Consent is that there are two factors to an agreement: what may or may not happen and who it's for (and that those factors combine in four ways). As you have seen, the who it's for factor is significant.

People often confuse consent with permission. When there is something you want to do that affects someone else, permission is what you need. It starts with "May I…?" and is the Take-Allow dynamic. But what about "Will you scratch my back?" Now you are asking someone else to do something, and permission doesn't fit. (I don't know of a word that describes only the Serve-Accept dynamic the way "permission" describes only the Take-Allow dynamic.)

When you explore the quadrants, it simplifies the interactions so that other things become visible. For example, you notice where you have a hard time asking for what you want or setting limits. It brings to light the difference between Want-to and Willing-to, between doing something for yourself and doing something for the other person, and more. Because of all that, my understanding of consent has become both broader and more specific.

A school teacher described consent for kids, "If the other person is not enjoying it, you have to stop." For adults it's the same but with the added layer of who it's for. If you go through this process for a while, you will have better consent skills than most people. If someone is not clear about whether they want something or are doing it for you, you stay there and gently, without shaming them, guide the conversation so that you both can be clearer about it, and you don't start what you're doing until you have that. To be a Jedi Master of consent doesn't mean you guess correctly. It means you don't stop conversing until you are both clear, and you do that with grace, generosity, and kindness.

Based on working with the Wheel of Consent, I have come to see consent skills as:

- Noticing what you want, asking for it, and abiding by the answer
- Noticing the difference between what you want and what you are willing to give and communicating that
- Finding out what the other person wants and what the other person is okay with and distinguishing between those two
- Abiding by your agreement even when things move quickly or get exciting
- Being able to abide by someone's no or limits

- Being able to change your mind and make room for the other person to change theirs.

REQUESTS, OFFERS, AND INVITATIONS

Oh, I get it! No more guessing!

— *A student*

Here are a couple of distinctions that the quadrants brought to the front and many folks have found useful: the difference between requests, offers, and invitations.

A request. A request is for something you would like to receive: some help, a gift, a favor, or touch or affection. It is based on your desire. Either you want to do something, or you want someone else to do something. There are two ways to make a request: "May I…?" (or "Can I…?" or "Would you mind if I…?") and "Will you…?" (or "Could you…?" or "Would you…?"). Examples of requests:

"Will you please pass the salt?"
"Can you pick me up at the airport?"
"May I play with your hair?"
"Less pressure, please, and slower. Slower still…Ahhh."

An offer. An offer is for the other person, based on what you think they might want or need and that you are willing to give. It is based on your willingness to meet another's desire. An offer is about being available for what they want, and it requires that you are open to at least some range of what might be asked for.

There are many ways to make an offer. "Would you like…?" or "What would you like?" or "What would be most helpful right now?" or any number of other variations. It might be showing up on the doorstep of your sick neighbor with a pot of chicken soup. Examples of offers:

"Would you like me to pick you up at the airport?"
"Would you like a foot rub?"
"How would you like to touch me for the next five minutes?"
"What would be helpful for you?"

Making an offer is a time-honored strategy for avoiding the vulnerability of making a request. For example, if you want to touch, but you've been socialized that it is not appropriate to touch for your own pleasure (which most of us have), or it feels too vulnerable, you might find yourself offering "Would you like a back massage?" rather than asking for what you actually want, which is "May I feel your back?" Making an offer may sound nicer, but it's confusing for both of you.

If it is you who wants it, even if you like to think of it as giving, it is still your desire and belongs in a request. As you get clearer in your requests, your offers can be trusted. If the intended receiver declines your offer, see how you feel about that. If it's a true offer, it matters not. If you are disappointed, resentful, or indignant, it's a signal that it was something you wanted, not an actual offer.

An invitation. When you make a request, you put your desires forward, and you hope the other is willing to set their desires aside. But sometimes you don't want them to put their desires aside. You want something but only if they want it too. This is an invitation. "I'd like this. Would you like this too?"

Some examples:
- Request: "Will you hold me?"
- Offer: "Would you like to be held?"
- Invitation: "I feel like a cuddle, do you?"

- Request: "I'm going to a party and would like some support. Will you come with me?"
- Offer: "I'm going to a party, and there will be somebody there you have been wanting to meet. Would you like me to get you in?"
- Invitation: "I'm going to a party. Would you like to come with me?"
- Not so clear: "Hey, how about that party next week?"

Negotiation. Negotiation can be a scary word until you learn how useful and effective it is. Some of the examples in the labs were of negotiation. Examples of negotiation:

"Yes, only up to here."

"No, but I could do this other thing. Would that work for you?"

"Oh wow, that sounds interesting, but I don't think I'm up for it. How about we do this first and then come back to that?"

"I'm not sure. Can you tell me more about what you have in mind?…Oh, I didn't realize that's what you meant. Sure!"

WHY IT MATTERS

Deciding between a request and an offer makes you get clear about what you want and take responsibility for it. You stop trying to slide your desires over into the other person's domain while they aren't looking.

Being clear about what you mean creates freedom for others to respond accurately and with generosity—and can change the answer. I have no interest in a documentary on race car drivers. If you offer it to me, I will say, "No, thanks." But if one of them is your daughter and it means a lot to you to have me join you for the premiere, the answer is "Yes, I will. I'll be glad to." If you offer, I am going to have one response. If you request, you may get a different response. If I hear an invitation, I am going to ask you about your interests, and I'll say more about mine.

Sometimes we hear everything as a request. Back to the party example: "Hey, how about that party next week?" You might have meant this as an invitation, but I might hear it as a request. That's going to change my answer. Or maybe you meant it as a request, but I heard it as an offer. Or maybe you just use language differently. With a friend of mine for whom English is not native, when I say, "Let's…," I mean an invitation. To her, it's a command. Oops!

EXAMPLE: A TRIP TO VICTORIA

We had been living together for a few months when one morning my partner said, "How about a weekend in Victoria?" (Victoria is a beautiful ferry ride from Seattle.) I heard it as a request: "I'd like us to go to Victoria for the weekend. Would that be agreeable to you?"

I was raised a nice Southern girl, so my supreme mission in life was to not be disagreeable. (That has changed.) Because I was not particularly excited about Victoria, I gave a noncommittal answer: "Oh, they have that British hotel that serves high tea." Was that a yes or a no? Who knows? A few weeks and several hundred dollars later, we were having high tea at the Empress Hotel. A little later, we were strolling down the tourist-y streets, window shopping. I mentioned that I was glad to be with him but that it wasn't so important to me that we go places where it takes money. I'm happy camped at the beach, and in fact, I prefer the beach.

"But wait," he said, "We're here because you wanted to be here." I said, "No, we're here because *you* wanted to be here."

It turned out that neither of us really wanted to be there, and neither of us liked window shopping. He thought he had made an offer, but I had heard it as a request. He heard my non-statement about high tea as an acceptance or even a request. Looking back, I wonder why we didn't laugh at ourselves. Maybe we did. I recall feeling foolish and resentful that we hadn't figured out what we were trying to say. We didn't have the words for it then, but I had been aware that this was a dynamic I wanted to change, and here it was right in my face.

Now when someone makes an offer, request, or invitation and I'm not sure which one it is, I ask. "Thanks. Is that something you are wanting, or are you asking if I want it?" or "I'm not interested for myself, but I'm glad to if it means a lot to you. Will you tell me more?"

CHAPTER 27

Spiritual Implications

Enlightenment has something to do with understanding the constant and inescapable nature of your own vulnerability.
—David Whyte

I'm not sure what the word "spiritual" means any more. Like many people, I thought of spiritual as something to do with the "not physical" or maybe the "beyond physical." Or maybe something about a sense of awe and oneness or altered states. Along my journey of exploring eros, I noticed that the more physical the experience, the more spiritual it felt. The more I was able to attend to my sensation, the more it took me places I was not expecting and the more connection and self-awareness it engendered. I have come to see spirituality as being inherent in the physical. It's what will show up if you are really in the body. A friend once said, "You think having an out-of-body experience is radical? Try having an in-the-body experience!"

Then along came the quadrants, and I learned to take responsibility for myself. These days spiritual has come to mean living a life of integrity and compassion. I don't care if you feel like you are "in the flow" (and I had one "spiritual teacher" define spirituality as that!), if you can meditate for hours on end, or if you can achieve all manner of altered states. Does it make you more responsive to people in need? Does it make you more responsible for yourself? That's all I want to know.

What does the Wheel of Consent have to do with a spiritual path? Not much really. It's just a model. The experiences you have while exploring it, though, can be profoundly life altering. Some of it has to do with the experience of the quadrants, but much of it has to do with the primacy of physical experience.

The senses as a doorway to the present. Many paths and practices talk about being in the present moment. Sometimes they specify a process for that but not always. Attending to your sensation is one way to do that. We played with this with Waking Up the Hands.

The senses as a doorway to awareness. A natural outgrowth of becoming more aware of the senses is that the more you notice your body sensations, the more aware you are of your emotions. They are essentially the same. Sensation and body awareness become a doorway to self-awareness.

A physical experience of the intangible. Desire, worthiness, surrender, power, generosity, gratitude, humility—you can talk about them all you want, but the physical experience of each of them at their most basic is what changes you. In the quadrants, you find things within yourself you would never find otherwise.

Pleasure as a guide and healer. Pleasure changes your physiology and thus your sense of connection to others, which is what we call "heart." I have learned that when I follow the pleasure instead of trying to use it to get somewhere I think I want to go, it takes me wherever it does and often surprises me. It breaks my heart open.

Desire. Every spiritual tradition deals with desire in some way. This practice tackles it head-on. You come to see the beauty and power of desire as a tool for creating and to understand the value and role of desire in your own life. At the very least you come to take responsibility for your own pleasure, and as said elsewhere, this develops integrity.

Healing the split. We live in a culture that splits "physical" and "spiritual." In this split, spiritual equals good, worthy, and elevated, and physical equals trouble. This is a false dichotomy and the source of untold heartache and shame. The practice of the quadrants, because it is physical and pleasurable, can be a road to healing this split. It was for me.

A radical act. This process is a radical act in the sense that it challenges the roots of who we think we are. More than that, it runs counter to thousands of years of cultural and religious conditioning about the basis of our relationships and how we think the world works. The practice described here develops a solid familiarity with your own body signals and natural inclinations, and out of that a functioning and trustworthy inner guidance system can grow.

SACRED SEXUALITY AND TANTRA

What's this got to do with sacred sexuality and tantra, because, you know, aren't those spiritual? "Sacred" means we deem something worthy of a kind of special attention. In our shame-based culture that splits body and spirit, we end up with sexuality feeling shameful. Just saying "Nah, sex is good!" is not enough. We need to pull it all the way back to the other side of the split. It's not shameful, it's sacred! Calling sexuality sacred allows you to reframe it and give it your full attention and regard. It lets you explore things you otherwise would not. This is an important step for many; it was for me for some years.

Another modern movement, which is impossible to define, is tantra. In the largest sense, tantra says the body is not the baggage; the body is the ticket. Traditional tantra is a centuries-old system of discipline and meditation. In some lineages of modern tantra, the focus is on these disciplines. In other lineages, especially in the West, it's mostly used to increase feelings of sexual connection between partners, which is mainly ways to slow down and pay attention. Sometimes it includes emotional and communication tools. There is nothing unique about most of these methods; they're just good tools (many of them from the 1960s Human Potential Movement), but giving them a form lets people take them seriously and actually do them. Sometimes tantra is marketed as a way to learn esoteric, exotic, ancient, magical sexual secrets—which are mainly about slowing down and paying attention.

A while back, I was teaching a tantra teacher about the quadrants, and we had a private session in which she discovered the Taking Quadrant. It clicked. She said, "That was the most tantric experience I have ever had, and you never mentioned the word tantra."

One problem with sacred sexuality and tantra is that we adopt a new "specialness" about sex that ends up reinforcing the original dichotomy.

The only sex that is worthy is "sacred sex" as if ordinary, worldly sex is somehow less-than. This is a big mistake. It becomes another way to reinforce the split we started with. I have come to feel that either everything is sacred or nothing is sacred.

IN THE QUADRANTS

We talked about the spiritual aspects of each quadrant in those chapters. Here is a quick review.

Receiving (both Accepting and Taking) teaches us that we humans need each other, that we are not self-sufficient. It tends to crack our hearts open and teaches us we are worthy as we are.

Giving (both Serving and Allowing) teaches us how to set aside what we want, which is part of maturity. It tends to be both humbling and affirming.

The Taking Quadrant teaches us to take responsibility for what we want to do, and that leads to integrity.

The Allowing Quadrant teaches us to take responsibility for our limits, teaches us that we ourselves can be the gift, and gives us a taste of surrender.

The Accepting Quadrant gives us a physical experience of our own worthiness and engenders gratitude.

The Serving Quadrant teaches us generosity, how to take action for the benefit of others, and to respect their choices about how they use our gifts.

CHAPTER 28

Social Implications

*With 50% of the world's wealth but only 6.3% of its population,
we cannot fail to be the object of envy and resentment. Our real
task is to devise a pattern of relationships which will permit us to
maintain this position of disparity. To do so we will have to dispense
with all sentimentality and day dreamings. We should cease to talk
about vague and unreal objectives such as human rights, raising
of the living standards and democratization. We are going to
have to deal in straight power concepts. The less we are then
hampered by idealistic slogans, the better.*
—George Kennan, 1948 Cold War strategist

*If we want to heal the planet, we have to heal ourselves.
That's the bitch of it.*
—Teri Ciacchi

*There is no flag large enough to cover the shame
of killing innocent people.*
—Howard Zinn

For some people, the Wheel of Consent is of most interest in thinking about intimacy and sexuality, for some it's mostly about other relationships, and for some it really starts to shine in wider social contexts. I fall into the latter group.

The Wheel was born in my practice of coaching people around sexuality, but it was clear from the start that it applied to other interactions as well. To be clear, not every interaction falls into the quadrants, nor does it need to. Interactions in the real world are far more complex than feeling each other's hands. Still, the quadrants can shed some light on these other dynamics.

I stood at the window in my new apartment, looking out over the city, pondering. It was the apartment I had moved into when I ended the relationship with my lover. I was still pondering, over a year later, what had happened one night and why I could not make myself be okay with it. It seemed like I *should* be able to, but I could not.

It had happened like this. One night he was in Serve and I was in Accept, though we didn't have those words then. We were having a wonderful time. I felt particularly vulnerable but chose to receive the gift, which was a tender moment and took some courage. Later, we talked. It came out if he could get me turned on first, he wouldn't feel shame about his own arousal. I felt like I had been punched in the gut. I had agreed to receive what I thought was a gift, but it turned out to be something else. My job, apparently, was to take the risk so he wouldn't have to, like the snowplow in front of a train to clear the way. He later said that no, that was not what he meant. He meant that he didn't want to go charging ahead and leave me trying to catch up. That seemed like it *should* be a better reason, but try as I might, I could not make myself feel any better about it. I did try.

I struggled with it. Why couldn't I make myself be okay with his reason? I did believe him. What was wrong with me? Standing at the window a year and a half after the incident, it hit me: It was not that *his* reason was not a good enough reason—it was that *no reason* is a good enough reason. No reason is a good enough reason to do something to someone they did not agree to.

It was a "holy shit" moment. *No wonder.* Then the next thing hit: That, right there—doing things to people without their agreement—is the basis of our civilization. It is what our nation was built on. We (Europeans) stole the land, decimated the people living on it, and enriched ourselves on the backs of another people we enslaved. Today we send our military to prop up petty dictators because it gives us access to oil, or ridiculously cheap labor to make our garments. Or bananas, for God's sake.

That day when I stood at the window and realized that it wasn't that some reasons for doing things without consent were good enough and other reasons were not—it's that there is no reason that is good enough—changed me. It was no longer a theory; I knew it in my bones. No reason is good enough. None. If we understood this principle to the core of our being, what would we have to change in our lives?

I don't think any of us wants to hurt our lovers or family. None of us wants to hurt people halfway around the world either, but it's all so abstract. Then the experience becomes tangible, in our own bodies, and something of a different magnitude happens. That is one of the doors that opens along this path. It may not be a door that's particularly fun, but I wouldn't trade it for anything.

Many people say to me, "Hey, this applies to more than touch, doesn't it?" It does, but I have noticed that when you experience the quadrants through touch, they sink in. They change you, and those changes carry over into your other relationships. In the practice, you start noticing how hard it is to trust what you want, and then you notice how hard that is in other areas of your life. In the practice, you notice how hard it is to set limits, and then you notice how you don't do that in other areas. In the practice, you notice how hard it is for you to take action for your own benefit, and then you notice where you do that in ways that are not with consent.

Perhaps the most far-reaching impact of the practice is getting very clear on what you want and taking responsibility for it in the simplest and most tangible way. That enables you to notice that other people are setting aside their preferences for you, and that teaches you to respect their limits. You stop stealing. That right there would change the world.

Another impact is understanding your Willing-to, where you are setting aside what you want in favor of what someone else wants. As we learn we have limits, we learn "This far and no farther." We learn to stand up for ourselves and others. We stop going along with the usual social expectations that allow entire groups of people to be mistreated. We stand against racism, sexism, and unfair conditions for workers. We stand up for the earth. In other words, as we experience the quadrants, we find that their shadows become visible and loathsome.

The question is not simple. I own a cell phone, so I participate in the economic system in which children in another continent extract the tiny bits of minerals that go in it. I buy food at the supermarket, so I contribute to the system in which oil is shipped around the world so that my food can be shipped across the continent so that I can eat strawberries in the Pacific Northwest in the middle of winter. I fly across the country to teach a workshop in an airplane that burns fossil fuel. These are not simple choices—the world we live in is complex—but they do make me look at my desires and question what things I am given freely and what things I take without consent, no matter how far away or complex the systems I am part of.

With this practice, you come to see that consent must be the basis of civilization. You have a "standing at the window" moment, you get it in your bones, and you cannot ignore it anymore.

CHAPTER 29

Conclusion

You cannot get through a single day without having an impact on the world around you. What you do makes a difference, and you have to decide what kind of difference you want to make.
—Jane Goodall

When I began experimenting with asking my clients two questions—"How do you want to touch me?" and "How do you want me to touch you?"—I never could have imagined those two questions would open so many windows into the human experience. Neither could I have imagined the possibilities to relate with clarity, generosity, gratitude, and integrity.

In writing this book, my intention was to share with you the simplicity of this practice and invite you into a profound inquiry into receiving and giving. What I found through my own exploration, and I hope you have found through yours, is that this practice goes well beyond a game of touch. It is a profound inquiry into who you are as a person—friend, lover, parent, colleague, citizen, and human. It exposes how you do life in relation to others. As the Zen saying goes, "How you do one thing is how you do everything."

The knowledge and insights that come from this practice are secondary to the experience. It's the experience that changes you. In order to access the experience, I guided you through laying the groundwork for the practice and then showed you how to experience the quadrants; this was followed by an in-depth explanation of the model of the Wheel and finally a discussion of some of the ways this applies beyond touch to the world around us. When we gain the skill to notice our experience, that's when we become empowered to make other choices.

What have you discovered about yourself in the process of exploring this practice? What have you noticed about your capacity to receive? Your capacity to give? Your ability to ask for what you want? Your ability to say no and set a limit? What's easy for you, and what's hard for you? How do you see these patterns playing out in different areas of your life?

I invite you to continue practicing and continue asking yourself these questions. It's a lifelong journey. It's the experience that illuminates our blind spots, where we get lost, where we tilt into the shadows because we don't know any better. When we start to see the shadows in our personal life, we will start to see the shadows in society. Our systems and structures are built on shadows—often the shadows of the Receiving Half of the Wheel (Taking and Accepting). These are the shadows of entitlement and exploitation, based on greed, privilege, oppression, and expecting more. We have learned that the easiest way to take is by force or coercion. For good or ill, this is what has propelled society forward. And it comes at a high cost to the health and well-being of people and the planet.

How do we clean up these behaviors? We learn how to be in the quadrants. This means asking for what we want and waiting for a clear yes. This means speaking up for what we don't want or are not willing to give, feeling comfortable with our no. This starts in our personal relationships and extends to every form of human relating.

It means slowing down to notice—do we need this new phone? Jacket? Oil well? What do we need to adapt—as individuals, as a society—to sustain the greater whole? Our desire for ever more convenience, our desire for bananas all winter?

This is where this book ends and the next chapter of humanity begins.

CHAPTER 30

More About My Work

I want to say a little more about my work and make a statement in support of sex workers. Much of what I shared in this book has come from my time with the hundreds of students, clients, and fellow explorers I have had the honor of teaching, guiding, and being guided by. Some of that has been nonsexual, and some of it has included sexual arousal, on purpose.

I am a sex worker. Whatever image that conjures in your mind is incomplete. Sex work includes a very wide range of ways to serve, guide, support, teach, and entertain people. It ranges from erotic dancers to medically sanctioned surrogate partners who work with a therapist and client in a three-way support team to give the client experiences they need to progress in their healing. It includes people who teach a modern version of an ancient spiritual practice called tantra, which includes learning how to breathe, move, and meditate to increase personal awareness. The part for which it is famous includes sexuality and eroticism.

Sex work includes the euphemism "escort," which mainly refers to sexual activity but often includes listening, comforting, counseling, coaching, and teaching. Sex work includes phone sex operators, writers, actors and actresses, and sex party hosts. It includes sensual, erotic, and tantric massage. If you work in some way or other with human sexual arousal, you do sex work.

I believe in sex work—because I have experienced how useful, beneficial, nourishing, and life changing it can be to have someone who knows more than you do, has more emotional slack than you do, and has compassion for you, to guide and support you in an experience that is new, challenging, enlightening, empowering, relaxing, or just plain fun for you. This is what I (and, these days, most of my friends) have been doing for some years and of course what many before us have done for centuries.

I guide people through experiences that help them learn about themselves. Learn how to notice their sensations, feelings, and impulses. Learn how to notice what they want and to trust that, value it, and communicate it. Learn how to notice their limits and to trust them, value them, and communicate them. Learn how to respect the limits of others. Learn how to experience pleasure that is not about sex, pleasure that is about sex, and how to tell the difference. Learn how to move, breathe, touch, feel, express, play, and enjoy—sometimes sexually and sometimes not.

Most of my sessions are clothed; some are not or partially so. Many sessions, though certainly not all, invite and support sexual arousal if that is where people need support. More often, and more fundamental than that, is helping people learn how to "show up"—how to bring their attention to the present, how to relax in their bodies, and enjoy anything at all.

I love my work. In a society in which the erotic is vilified, deeply misunderstood, and pitifully narrowly defined, it takes a particular kind of courage (or recklessness) to do this. It is a calling, and I am thankful to have had the opportunity to pursue it. I am aware that I enjoy a certain amount of privilege in my work, being able to work in my studio and not on the street, and being financially stable enough to decline to accept clients who feel unsafe to me. Not every sex worker has these options. Nor does every domestic worker, barista, farm worker or factory worker. Or office worker.

In a society in which there is so much confusion, longing, fear, and shame about sex, one must be mindful of how one describes their work. I have at times called myself a sex coach, intimacy coach, sacred intimate, erotic educator, erotic guide, sensual companion, sacred whore, and among friends, just plain whore—said with love, tenderness, and pride for the extraordinary presence and generosity it requires.

My hope is that this understanding, and outing myself, can contribute in some small way toward the movement to decriminalize sex work. That is a topic for another day—except this: as long as we are two (or more) consenting and mentally competent adults, what we do is none of your f**king business. And attempting to legislate your particular fear of sexuality onto others is an affront to my sovereignty. Yeah, that's a different book.

So yes, I have had my hands on many, many people. I have seen and held people, both literally and emotionally, in tender, vulnerable, challenging, and sometimes sexy experiences. I have seen them learn how to stop pushing themselves and start honoring their inner no and the profound relief and freedom that allows. I have seen people baffled, intimidated, confused, and brought to tears of relief by being asked what they wanted. I have seen them collapse in relief at being supported to listen to themselves instead of going along with the program, whatever they believe that program is. I have seen their faces light up with discovery, joy, freedom, and empowerment.

In the last ten years or so, I have been coaching and mentoring other professionals, both sexuality professionals and non-sex professionals, and this is where my heart is these days. I love my work, and this book has grown out of it. I hope you found it useful and fun.

THE AUTHORS

DR. BETTY MARTIN

Dr. Betty Martin has had her hands on people professionally for over 40 years, first as a Chiropractor and upon retiring from that practice, as a certified Surrogate Partner and Somatic Sex Educator. Her explorations in somatic-based therapy and practices informed her creation of the Wheel of Consent.

Betty developed the training "Like a Pro: The Wheel of Consent for Professionals" to support practitioners to create empowered agreements in their client sessions. Originally developed to teach consent skills to sex workers and touch providers, the training is now attended by somatic therapists, sexuality educators, medical and health care workers, activists, and the spectrum of touch-based professional providers. It starts with touch and expands into all forms of human relating. www.bettymartin.org

ROBYN DALZEN

Robyn Dalzen has been training, traveling and teaching with Betty since 2014, and her insightful collaboration on the book helped get it across the finish line.

Robyn has a BA in Anthropology and an MA in Sustainable International Development, working for 15 years in the non-profit environmental sector. She is certified as a Transformational Leadership Coach and a Tension & Trauma Releasing Exercise (TRE®) provider. Robyn has been teaching the Wheel of Consent around the world since 2016, helping people discover how to have safer, deeper, and clearer interactions and to fully respect and honor those with whom they interact. www.robyndalzen.com

THE SCHOOL OF CONSENT

The School of Consent offers workshops and trainings in the Wheel of Consent. Both Betty and Robyn are co-founders of the School, which is where you can find their events and many other resources on the Wheel of Consent. www.schoolofconsent.org

Book website: www.wheelofconsentbook.com

SOURCES

Allende, Isabel. *The Infinite Plan: A Novel.* New York: Harper Perennial, 2010.

Artemesia. Facebook post, 2018.

Baczynski, Marcia. *The Naked Truth About Desire Smuggling.* https://www. askingforwhatyouwant.com/desire-smuggler/

Blanton, Brad. *Radical Honesty: How to Transform Your Life by Telling the Truth.* Stanley, VA: Sparrowhawk Publications, 2005.

Brown, Claude. *Manchild in the Promised Land.* New York: Touchstone, 2011.

Brown, Stuart. *Play is More Than Just Fun,* TED talk, https://www.ted.com/ talks/stuart_brown_play_is_more_than_just_fun

Ciacchi, Teri. Personal conversation, 2018.

Cumming, Alan. *My Father's Son: A Memoir.* New York: Dey Street Books, 2015.

Curtis, Eddie and Ahmet Ertegun. "Lovey Dovey." https://en.wikipedia. org/wiki/Lovey_Dovey.

Edo. Quoted at https://www.goodreads.com/quotes/1019030-we-ve-all-been-given-a-gift-the-gift-of-life.

Einstein, Albert. *Ideas and Opinions,* based on *Mein Weltbild.* Edited by Carl Seelig. New York: Bonanza Books, 1954.

Faddis, Harry. Personal conversation, 2018.

Feynman, Richard. *Surely You're Joking, Mr. Feynman! Adventures of a Curious Character.* New York: W. W. Norton & Company, 2018

Franti, Michael & Spearhead. *Hey World (Don't Give Up Version).* Quoted at https://www.azlyrics.com/lyrics/michaelfrantispearhead/heyworld-dontgiveupversion.html.

Goodall, Jane. Quoted at https://www.goodreads.com/author/quotes/18163.Jane_Goodall.

Grace, Amrita. *Reclaiming Aphrodite: The Journey to Sexual Wholeness.* Author's Republic Audiobook: 2018.

Hancock, Justin. BBC radio interview, Sept. 10, 2018. https://www.bbc.co.uk/programmes/b0bj79fq.

Hanh, Thich Nhat. *Teachings on Love.* Berkeley, CA: Parallax Press, 1997.

Huerta, Dolores. https://www.pbs.org/independentlens/films/dolores-huerta.

Hyde, Lewis. *The Gift: Creativity and the Artist in the Modern World.* New York: Vintage Books, 2007.

Jensen, Derrick. Interview at https://www.democracynow.org/2010/11/26/author_and_activist_derrick_jensen_the.

Jung, C. G. *Collected Works of C. G. Jung, Volume 16, The Practice of Psychotherapy.* Princeton, NJ: Princeton University Press, 2014.

Kennan, George. Quoted by Noam Chomsky in *Turning the Tide: US Intervention in Central America and the Struggle for Peace.* London: Pluto Press, 1987, p. 48.

Lennon, John and Paul McCartney. https://en.wikipedia.org/wiki/I_Want_to_Hold_Your_Hand.

Lincoln, Abraham. Quoted at https://www.goodreads.com/quotes/602394-it-is-the-eternal-struggle-between-these-two-principles.

Lorde, Audre. *The Cancer Journals: Special Edition.* San Francisco: Aunt Lute Books, 2006.

Milne, A. A. *Winnie-the-Pooh.* New York: Dutton Books for Young Readers, 1988.

Morrow, Susan Brind. *The Names of Things.* East Rutherford, NJ: Riverhead Hardcover, 1997.

Neruda, Pablo. *The Poetry of Pablo Neruda.* Edited by Ilan Stavans. New York: Farrar, Straus and Giroux, 2005.

Oliver, Mary. Quoted at https://www.goodreads.com/quotes/62038-instructions-for-living-a-life-pay-attention-be-astonished-tell.

Parker, Dorothy. Quoted at https://www.goodreads.com/quotes/8211285-the-cure-for-boredom-is-curiosity-there-is-no-cure.

Rosenburg, Marshall. *Nonviolent Communication: A Language of Life: Life-Changing Tools for Healthy Relationships.* Encinitas, CA: PuddleDancer Press, 2015.

Rumi, Jalal al-Din. Quoted at https://www.goodreads.com/quotes/7368103-wear-gratitude-like-a-cloak-and-it-will-feed-every.

Rumi, Jalal al-Din. Quoted at https://www.goodreads.com/quotes/405812-everyone-has-been-made-for-some-particular-work-and-the.

Rumi, Jalal al-Din. *The Essential Rumi, New Expanded Edition.* Translated by Coleman Barks. New York: HarperOne, 2004.

Rushdie, Salman. *The Satanic Verses: A Novel.* New York: Random House Trade Paperbacks, 2008.

Saunders, George. *Fox 8: A Story.* New York: Random House, 2018.

Schaef, Anne Wilson. Quoted at https://www.goodreads.com/quotes/8668090-asking-for-help-does-not-mean-that-we-are-weak.

Segal, Lore Groszmann. "The Ice Worm" in *Harper's Magazine,* 2011. https://harpers.org/archive/2011/05/the-ice-worm.

Somé, Malidoma Patrice. See https://malidoma.com.

Thornhill, Nadine. YouTube video. See https://www.nadinethornhill.com.

Trombone Shorty. http://www.songlyrics.com/trombone-shorty/do-to-me-lyrics.

Walker, Alice. Quoted in *The Best Liberal Quotes Ever: Why the Left Is Right,* edited by William P. Martin. Naperville, IL: Sourcebooks, 2004.

Whyte, David. Interview with Tami Simon, syndicated from soundstrue. com, July 07, 2014. http://www.dailygood.org/story/699/david-whyte-on-being-at-the-frontier-of-your-identity.

Withers, Bill. "Use Me." https://en.wikipedia.org/wiki/Use_Me_(Bill_With-ers_song).

Withers, Bill. "Lean on Me." https://en.wikipedia.org/wiki/Lean_on_Me_ (song).

Zinn, Howard. *Passionate Declarations: Essays of War and Justice.* New York: Harper Perennial, 2003.

INDEX

A

D

Made in United States
North Haven, CT
14 August 2023

40296325R00232